What people are saying about

HALF-LIFE/DIE ALREADY

"The comedy in *half-life / die already* is more than self-deprecating; it's painfully, ruthlessly honest. Mark has laid out his inner thoughts on the autopsy table for all of us to laugh at, as well as relate to. Not that I laugh when I'm standing at an autopsy table … but Mark probably would."

—CORY EDWARDS, WRITER AND DIRECTOR OF THE HIT MOVIE *HOODWINKED*

"The next time you hear someone say that Christian books aren't honest or don't deal with real life, grab a copy of *half-life / die already* and smack him with it."

—PATTON DODD, SENIOR EDITOR FOR BELIEFNET, AUTHOR OF *MY FAITH SO FAR*

"Mark is one of the most creative writers out there today. His ability to re-create the way readers navigate life truths is unmatched. I found myself laughing out loud throughout *half-life / die already*, and then quickly realized the journey Mark was taking me on. If you're ready for a fresh new writing style, you won't be disappointed by this incredible work of comedy coupled with real-life moral lessons."

—ANDY BRANER, PRESIDENT OF KANAKUK COLORADO,
AUTHOR OF *LOVE THIS! DUPLICATE THIS!*

HALF-LIFE / DIE ALREADY

MARK STEELE

HALF-LIFE / DIE ALREADY

HOW I DIED & LIVED TO TELL ABOUT IT

David C Cook®

transforming lives together

HALF-LIFE / DIE ALREADY
Published by David C. Cook
4050 Lee Vance View
Colorado Springs, CO 80918 U.S.A.

David C. Cook Distribution Canada
55 Woodslee Avenue, Paris, Ontario, Canada N3L 3E5

David C. Cook U.K., Kingsway Communications
Eastbourne, East Sussex BN23 6NT, England

David C. Cook and the graphic circle C logo
are registered trademarks of Cook Communications Ministries.

The Web site addresses recommended throughout this book are offered as a resource to
you. These Web sites are not intended in any way to be or imply an endorsement on the
part of David C. Cook, nor do we vouch for their content.

Scripture quotations are taken from *THE MESSAGE*. Copyright © by Eugene
H. Peterson 1993, 1994, 1995, 1996, 2000, 2001, 2002. Used by Permission of
NavPress Publishing Group. Scripture quotations marked NLT are taken from
the *Holy Bible, New Living Translation,* copyright 1996. Used by Permission of
Tyndale House Publishers, Inc., Wheaton, Illinois 60189. All rights reserved.

The lyrics on page 31 are from the song "Step by Step" by Rich Mullins
from the album *Songs II* from Provident-Integrity Distribution.

LCCN 2007942527
ISBN 978-0-7814-4552-8

© 2008 Mark Steele

The Team: Andrea Christian, Jaci Schneider, and Karen Athen
Cover Design: The DesignWorks Group, Jason Gabbert
Cover Photo: © iStock
Interior Design: The DesignWorks Group
Exhibit Illustrations: Eric Lee

Printed in the United States of America
First Edition 2008

1 2 3 4 5 6 7 8 9 10

012608

To Kaysie

My better half.

ACKNOWLEDGMENTS

Last time around, I thanked everyone who had played a significant role in my personal history. That was when I thought I might only write one book in my lifetime. Now that I am on a roll, I think I'll keep the acknowledgments restricted to the key players in this particular narrative alone.

Kaysie—one book could never do our journey justice. I cannot imagine life or faith or the present and future road without you. You are my muse, my conscience, and my Huckleberry all rolled into one gorgeous package. I love you forever.

Morgan, Jackson, and Charlie—I hope that someday when you walk down your own hard road, you will see that your imperfect parents did so with honesty, a passion for Jesus, and an overflowing love for you.

Roger, Susan, Kathy, and the Believers Church Staff—thank you for your willingness to create an environment that allows us to walk through the toughest stuff arm-in-arm with those who want us to come out the other side healed. Your love is the very picture of Jesus.

Matt, Mike, and Jason—thank you for shoving me into the straight and narrow. I couldn't beg for better friends.

Eric Lee—thank you for the amazing illustrations throughout the book (exhibits A–N). They exude wit and painfulness and I do believe you are a creative genius.

The Steeles, the Dodds, and the Steelehouse team—thank you for your undying love and support.

To all those who went through the marriage intensive with Kaysie and I—thank you for your intense vulnerability, kindness, and acceptance at the single-most pivotal window in our lives and marriage. You made all the difference.

And Zachary—thanks for helping with that pile of leaves.

mark steele

(Exhibit A)

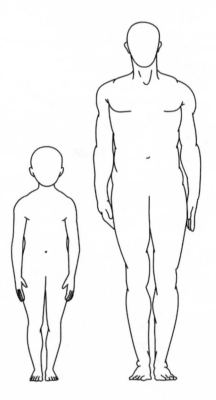

EVERYTHING DIES

Most authors have writer's block.

I, on the other hand, have writer's neighborhood.

I rarely have moments where I am stuck without words. On the contrary, I tend to have far too many to juggle into sense. I get lost within the nooks and crannies of all the different paths between where I currently stand and where I want to go. This, of course, makes sense in my writing because it is also true of my life. The roads are plentiful and seemingly open to my own interpretation. However, the moment I avoid a dark alley in favor of a wide sunny street, that is the moment a meteor fells a redwood into my path creating a startling new detour. My life, therefore, has often been circular: I face the same issues and frustrations over and over. I take a left turn and end up in the roundabout deceiving myself with perpetual movement while I am, in fact, just as stuck as if I were standing still.

To this end, entire sections of my life have cycled around and around to a frustrating conclusion that looked suspiciously identical to the first chapter. Days and weeks and months of intended change fueled by pain and effort fast-forward to an end of the calendar year defined with zero growth. The question begs: What is it going to take for me to transform? I don't truly comprehend what this transformation should look like, but I do know that I should not come out of the cocoon as a caterpillar.

Everything dies. And to be honest, everything should. Well, everything except the battery in my Toyota Highlander. Certainly I have experienced pain when someone or something dear to me died before I felt ready. But most of the pain in my life has come from things I kept on life support long after I should have let them go. This is the problem in question. Not timely death, but rather, playing dead.

In the world of roadkill, there is a creature called the possum (or opossum if you're Irish) that daily masters the defense mechanism called "playing dead." Certainly you've seen photos. The possum has the ability to let its body instantly go limp with its tongue hanging out like a slug and its eyes skewed cross near the top of its lids. I believe it even emits a smell—of course, it's possible that all possums smell like death to begin with. To all observers, this insinuates that the possum now belongs in a Hefty bag. This keeps enemies away.

I, for one, am grateful that this has not caught on with human beings. Funerals are tragic enough without the individual in the casket hopping to his feet fifteen minutes into the ceremony and yelling to the back of the room, "Is the tax guy gone yet?"

The possum, however, will take this position the moment an enemy or a Volvo crosses its path—and it tends to work quite efficiently. This is because possums believe the failed concept that if you can convince the world that you're too beaten to live, the beatings of the world will stop.

And I had lived much of my life that exact same way.

I had lost my edge and, at times, my footing.

The myriad of hardships that had walloped my wife and I had tempted us into a regular routine of rolling over, eyes glazed, hoping the antagonists would beat something else that moved more frisky. And so I faced my next crisis, my next decision, and continued to find myself right back where I started.

My life, as stated, is circular.

⊙ ⊙ ◉

Why can't my life come equipped with a GPS system like NeverLost, a talking navigator with the insight to interfere with my choices? A clear, calm voice of a woman that gently nudges me (accompanied by colorful maps) into the exact unforeseen turns on my path toward a perfect resting place. Of course, my optimum NeverLost would need some improvements over the model currently on the market. Something about having an audible voice in my car causes me to relax a little too much, to assume I don't really need to pay attention to my way because someone else is currently doing so. To this end, when the NeverLost lady (who, for brevity's sake, I will call Gwen) states "next turn in 2.9 miles," my mind begins to wander, wondering why she didn't just round the total up to three miles and deciding that Gwen must consider herself too good for that sort of thing. How dare she talk down to me and what does she know about math (this digresses for a few moments) until finally, she declares: "You missed your turn; recalculating journey" in that same over-enunciating hooked-on-phonics voice that has a hint of flipping me the finger. She KNOWS it ticks me off. Don't even go there, Gwen.

Oh, the recalculation of the journey. How I know this process well. It isn't pleasant, the recalculation: the doubling-back and revisiting what was not really all that welcome a visit in the first place. And yet, I (and more than likely you) consistently end up in places I thought I was through with, repeating behavior and frustrations that indicate zero growth has taken place in my life.

This never ceases to perplex me because I WANT to do right. I desire to make correct choices. I made a decision a long time ago to follow Jesus Christ with the entirety of my life. That decision was a joyous moment, but the thirty-something years of follow-through have been less than stellar. There are daily deterrents that attempt to shove me off the side of the road—a myriad of billboard-size distractions that would like nothing more than for me to take an early exit. So, while God continues to say, "Wait, Mark. The Grand Canyon is just over the next bend," I find myself saying, "Maybe, but just four hundred yards off this highway I can visit the world's largest exotic llama farm."

Perhaps if my NeverLost took a terse attitude in her approach to my direction, I would find myself on a shorter path through the subdivision. If I created the next version (say Gwen 2.0), I would give her a reeeeal voice. Not that Gwen 1.0 doesn't sound feminine enough. She simply doesn't have the essence of humanity that I need. She doesn't warn me five times before the turn with a shrill of RIGHTHERE RIGHTHERE RIGHTHEEEERE because I am distracted.

This is what I crave. Direction, yes. But direction that is much more direct. Direction that commits and cares how, when, and why I take the turn. With attitude and exclamation points. Multiple exclamation points and perhaps delivered in all-capital letters. Direction that assumes my intentions to find the right path are noble. Still, chances are good that I won't be paying attention when the right turn cometh. I have a heart after the things of God, but that heart is shrouded in the body fat of my personal distractions. So instead of straightforward, the path circles and circles. Never progressing. Not even halfway.

Ah, halfway: the rest stop that would allow one to reflect on the lessons learned from the climb upward before cascading life's assumed easier downhill half. Somehow, society has labeled this scenic exit the "midlife crisis," but so very few of us reach this point having actually journeyed midway. In effect, most of us reach this point facing the same dilemmas as when we started, the only difference being the number of chins.

Perhaps I shouldn't be measuring the half-point of my life by time at all, but rather by progress. Maybe I'm not searching for midlife. Maybe what I'm grasping at is my half-life: the apex of my experience where learning turns to application and the circular path finally gives way to the straight and narrow. But this sort of seminal moment cannot arrive serendipitously. There has to be intention. An exact defining moment or action.

A death.

Up to this point, my life has been separated into two portions: the first lasting thirty-seven years and the latter having started—oh, let's say last Tuesday. The first of the two portions revolved around a definition of serving Christ where I did my best to become the right person. The predicament at hand was that I was referring to my own definition of what a "right person" should mean. If I could somehow become happy, fulfilled, esteemed, effective, financially stable, popular, at peace, etcetera, then I must be in God's perfect plan. It was a euphoria-based faith that few would admit to, but most embrace. I convinced myself these desires were selfless because (I reckoned), if I could become this type of person, I would be superhuman for God's purposes. I would earn the right to be myself.

Myself.

Someone I have always intended to someday become.

◉ ◉ ◉

It seemed impossible as a young boy living in Roswell, Georgia, to earn my way in life, but my friends and I made our best attempt by establishing criteria for adulthood. Okay, maybe adulthood is not the most accurate term. What we were actually aspiring to become was, well, ninjas. We developed a point system, and if the sum total of a single individual ever skyrocketed high enough, that individual would attain NMS (ninja master status) with all rights and benefits therein. As the following chart indicates, it was an extremely complicated point system:

jumping off someone's roof	10 points
jumping off someone's roof you don't know	25 points
jumping off someone's roof blind-folded	40 points
waking an angry cat	5 points
allowing someone to throw sharp objects at you	100 points

doing yardwork for the pointmaster	120 points
experimenting with electricity	15 points
accepting a dare to drink an unknown substance	50 points
wrestling other children to "the pain"	3 points
learning to juggle	40 points
memorizing "99 Luftballoons" by Nena	30 points
surrendering all monies	95 points

This was my first foray into attempting to deserve my way in life. The pursuit of ninja points seemed innocent enough, but eventually built a monster that needed to outwit, outplay, and outlast in order to become. I was no longer Mark. I was *Mark Steele*.

To this day, my efforts to become more than the sum of my parts—or at least to seem like I am more than the sum—has stolen much. This will change in the second portion of my life. The second portion is far more profound.

Also, far more painful.

Why? Because I am suddenly sensing variations in the circular cycle. Nuances, yes, but nuances that I just know are going to change everything. A life of twists and turns one would normally reserve for an old towel being rung out by a Russian woman just before she snaps someone with it in the shower.

I know these twists and turns well.

Because I frequent the fair.

The Tulsa State Fair, to be exact. An event organized by people so brilliant, they believe Tulsa to be a state. I have never comprehended why the fair is called thus, as the word *fair* has multiple definitions, and none of them describes what goes on under the carnival tents in midtown. This citywide bacchanalia of livestock competitions, '80s rock anthems, and barely legal thrill rides draws my friends and me on a yearly basis because we are convinced that they ship in people from other planets to attend. I mean, we know at least a thousand people in this town, but come October of every year, they are evidently body-snatched and replaced with slightly pudgier versions who stopped listening to the radio once Whitesnake peaked. They wear cut-off T-shirts. They sport mullets. Of course, it could be the fair itself that transforms the inhabitants of my community. After all, for a few nights each autumn, we convince ourselves to consume objects called "fatballs."

This is the renaissance aspect of the fair.

Where other cultures pride themselves on the arts and sciences, we in Oklahoma look forward to discovering new objects to deep-fry. This year, we deep-fried Oreos. The year before that, it was Twinkies and Snickers bars. Five years back, we deep-fried charcoal. Next year: cotton swabs. Yum. Each bite actually eliminates eight months from your life span. I have now stopped eating the treats and instead, insert them directly into my aorta. This skips the middleman. Are you beginning to see how this circular living works?

Though I don't like my life patterns to rotate, I do enjoy spinning round and round on the occasional midway ride. One year in particular, my friend Matt and I took our families on a ride called The Scrambler. The apparatus itself has the appearance of a spider that doesn't have the energy to lift its torso off the floor. Each arm holds four cars that spin on that arm's axis while the four arms spin around the body. If you are the sort to work out the mental math, you would realize what Matt and I realized: that if we sat in different cars attached to adjacent arms, the simultaneous spinning would allow us to pass one another multiple times throughout the course of the ride. Discovering this led us to a natural conclusion: an internal dare. Each time our cars passed, we would fake a high-five.

Not the apex of wisdom in my life.

I strapped myself, my wife Kaysie, and our daughter Morgan into one car while Matt did the same with his wife and son. Once we were buckled in, we tested our plan. We discovered that though we could almost touch, we were not close enough to one another to merit actual contact. This was a good thing. A best-case scenario. For now, we would be able to freak out our wives without any actual danger. We would spin around and around the same paths and patterns throughout the entirety of the ride, reaching toward one another without any real risk as our children fell into hysterics.

But, we did not count on the variations.

Somewhere within the mathematical formulas that involve trajectory and speed, the pain-free distance between Matt and I was bridged.

SLAAAAAM!

My arm batted against Matt's and then my knuckles bounced off of the side of our Scrambler pod at the speed of a thrill ride. The pain. Deep, pulsating knuckle-to-elbow pain. I could have gnawed my arm off at the shoulder just to eliminate the pain. The sky grew black and the last thing I remembered was a sign reading "keep arms and legs inside vehicle at all times." I decided that I loathed that sign and that whoever painted it deserved to be deep-fried. I moaned, partially incoherent, while residing in that subtle place where agony and self-loathing intermingle. On fire. My arm was tangibly on fire. Had I glanced down to discover it being consumed by field mice, I would not have been entirely surprised.

Our children were no longer laughing.

Our wives, on the other hand …

Matt and I lip-synched a series of grave profanities in time with the Scorpions song blaring from the speakers of the tilt-a-whirl DJ on the ride adjacent to us while clutching what was left of our appendages. I looked down and realized that my arm was no longer the color of human skin. It was now beet red and bore an exact replica of the outline of Matt's hand somewhere around the bicep I would have if I were not infatuated with cake.

All because of the variations. We had reached out the same length, each turn, over and over again without allowing for the possibility of actual contact. The nuances changed everything.

So, the question arises of whether or not I am willing to welcome the variations to my circular existence. The variations will bring the beginnings of change—but only with the guarantee of intrigue, danger, and oh yes, great pain.

I suppose this is what has kept me stagnant for so long. I didn't want to face the pain. I preferred the illusion of safety. I desired a world where my loved ones and myself could become everything we needed to become but without risk.

Answers without arguments.

Lessons without scars.

Character without failures.

Love without work.

I didn't want to live my path to my final destination. I only wanted to insinuate my way there. Monorail my path. That way, if my perception of the destination was incorrect, I could always save face without having taken actual footsteps.

Safe.

I thought it was my mission. To land there. Keep my wife there. My children.

Safe.

It was the enemy of growth.

(Exhibit B)

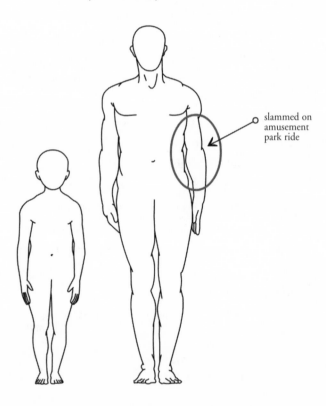

slammed on
amusement
park ride

The irony is that I never thought I was playing it safe. I had convinced myself that I was a man of tremendous faith because on what could only be called a roller coaster of a life, I consistently raised my hands.

Certainly you empathize with this action. To trust the thrill ride so deeply that, even when your stomach is sinking, you keep those hands aimed straight for heaven. You may will them down in your mind. You may scream all the while. But, by sheer resolve (and because others are watching) you keep them up. This was me. Always reaching. A tangible expression of faith in the coaster-maker, proving that I couldn't possibly be as frightened as the wet spot on my pants indicated.

But it never dawned on me that faith is not tested on the hill of the thrill ride.

It is not tested on the dips or the loops.

Faith is tested when the coaster disappears into the dark tunnel.

And, just like you, regardless of how many times I have ridden a particular theme-park attraction. No matter how often the tunnel opening has proven not to lop off human hands, I cannot help myself. I see the opening. I see the darkness. And something in my heart tells me …

Not this time.

I bend.

My arms retract.

Do I really think for one moment that the maker of the roller coaster has never measured the length of a human arm? Do I believe that a reputable theme park would allow someone to pay a ticket price just to have their digits severed? Are there human remains scattered near the tunnel opening? No. I can trust the coaster-maker to make the tunnel the perfect combination of proven and scary in order to build my faith for the next time I ride. And yet, in my own life, I hesitate to trust when I approach the darkness. I believe that God knows me. I believe that He knows that tunnel. But I am not fully convinced that He knows me inside that tunnel.

The real truth is,

> I don't know me inside that tunnel.

Which comes as a surprise, because I have always believed myself to be a person of great preparation. I make momentous attempts to think through every scenario and then steady my skills, my mind, and my heart so that nothing can catch me off guard. Perhaps that is the real issue—that I want all of my preparation to be fail-safe. I want the nuances and variations, but I do not want those variations to sucker punch me.

But, the truth is, when I least expect it, the road itself is going to change.

◉ ◎ ◉

A year and a half of my life—the eighteen months you and I are about to share—I came to the firsthand understanding that my circular experience could not be broken without the road changing underneath me. I learned that though change is painful, avoiding it had secured my state of stuck. It was the very reason I had not yet reached the apex of my half-life.

One year would make the difference.

It would not be pleasant. But, it would break the circle.

This book is the story of the variations and the pain they brought.

The story of my dark tunnel.

The year I stopped being safe.

My half-life.

Everything dies.

This is the year that I did.

And it all begins—and ends—with my hero.

ONE LOVE OF THE DOG

Without a care in the world.

These are words that describe me as I enjoy the June sun, leaning into a particularly warm square foot of my yard. I have crosswords in hand; the smell of donuts is nearby. My wife, Kaysie, is convincing a stranger to purchase a ten-year-old alarm clock sitting on a table in our driveway. It is early summer 2005, and I am basking. Basking in the warmth of the weather, basking in the thought that the most soul-sucking parts of this God-forsaken garage sale are almost over. Basking in the thought that my dog is resting peacefully at my feet. Basking in the sheer joy of it all—of life, of this moment.

In three hours, all of that is going to change.

But, for the time being, I suckle a Krispy Kreme while Hero (the dog) licks my ankle. I have no earthly idea why the ankle. This is just the sort of thing that dogs choose to do. Their love is gross. Especially hers. Most people assume Hero is a he because of the Die-Hard-esque name that insinuates she has just given a smaller dog CPR. And because she is big and dark. But Hero is a she. Still, people try to argue otherwise.

ME:	*She.*
THEM:	What? You mean he.
ME:	*Hero is not a he. Hero is a she.*
THEM:	But heroes are he's.
ME:	*Shakespeare freaking invented the name Hero and it was for a she.*
THEM:	Your dog's named after Shakespeare?

ME:	*No. No. No. That would be a sissy thing to do. My dog is named after one of Shakespeare's imaginary women.*
THEM:	I thought all the women in Shakespeare were played by men.
ME:	*Yes. All of them except my dog.*

Seven hours ago I was rousing myself from the eighty-seven minutes of slumber a husband gets the evening prior to a garage sale. Now, I am witnessing a subculture of Midwest Americana that I did not know existed—the morning-dwellers who hunt mercilessly for dime-priced tchotchkes no human has ever or will ever find use for.

✓ Used batteries.
✓ Books that have clearly fallen into the toilet.
✓ Remote controls that don't come with anything to control.
✓ A headless Barbie.
✓ One chopstick.

They purchase these items in Sam's Club quantities. I believe we have sold three hundred coat hangers. And at least eighty-seven of them had the little white cardboard tube at the bottom broken in half. I am having difficulty deciding which is more troubling: the fact that someone would need three hundred additional coat hangers, or the evidence that my clothing is hefty enough to damage eighty-seven of them permanently.

I am not a fan of garage sales because I do not want to purchase, or even browse through, anything that an unknown person has manhandled in the privacy of their home. This is because people are bizarre and they tend to use items with designated purposes for undesignated purposes. That butterfly net may have captured a rabid hamster. That suit may have been soiled in front of the President. And yet, strangers are snapping up bathing suits, bed sheets, old mattresses, a plunger, and what could very well be the most personal item of all.

Mix-tapes.

I spent many years courting Kaysie with my uncanny mix-tape abilities. My music awareness is widespread, and my collection is vast. I spend an unhealthy amount of thought considering not just what songs I want to include, but what song would sound both perfect and unexpected before and after that song. I have made her mix-tapes that covered the gamut from declaring my love to celebrating a road trip. From chilling out on a snowy day to anticipating morning sickness. It's practically my love language. When Wilco and Beck are preceded by Lizz Wright and followed by the *Love Boat* theme it somehow makes a day practically perfect in every way.

One of my favorite mixes ever was from 1994 (the year we were married). The track list went like this:

SIDE ONE
1. "My Sharona" (The Knack)
2. "Brother" (Toad the Wet Sprocket)
3. "Cantaloop-Flip Fantasia" (US3)
4. "The Brady Bunch" (Greg soundbite)
5. "Evenflow" (Pearl Jam)
6. "Get Ready 4 This" (Jock Jams)
7. "Crazy" (Seal)
8. "Tempted" (Squeeze)
9. "Got No Shame" (Brother Cane)
10. "Maniac" (Michael Sembello)
11. "Sweetest Thing" (U2)
12. "Return to Innocence" (Enigma)

SIDE TWO
1. "Seven Days" (Sting)
2. "Throw the R Away" (The Proclaimers)
3. "This Time" (Bryan Adams)
4. "Linger" (The Cranberries)
5. "Happy Happy Joy Joy" (Ren & Stimpy)
6. "Under My Skin" (Frank Sinatra and Bono)
7. "Mr. Jones" (Counting Crows)
8. "Locked Out" (Crowded House)
9. "Every Little Thing She Does Is Magic" (The Police)
10. "Thief of Your Heart" (Sinead O'Connor)
11. "Little Miss Can't Be Wrong" (Spin Doctors)
12. "The-Evening-Wore-On" (speech from *Harvey*)
13. "Your Love" (The Outfield)

Kaysie loved that tape. Every minute of it was constructed with care and love and knowledge that the tape-mixer knew the listener inside and out.

Just like life should be.

And, unless I'm mistaken, we just sold that tape to the fellow walking away with our old headboard.

Wow. Hero is really going to town on my ankle. Perhaps it's lunch. I cannot complain. I mean, I could. And I do. I do complain about the dog. I don't know why. She adores me and lives only to comfort me. As a matter of fact, I expect that her life would be quite meaningless without the constant need to coddle me. She has the loyalty of a concubine and absolutely no respect for personal space. Her joy comes only from providing me joy. And I don't even have to return the favor.

I like this.

Hero did not begin life as my dog. She originally belonged to my brother-in-law who had trained Hero, a beautiful black labrador/rottweiler mix, from a puppy—running her up Colorado mountain trails, keeping her in shape and refining her into a regal specimen of dogness. When he moved his family to a smaller space in Boston, Hero was passed on to my household, and as I was the only one in the house willing to handle and dispose of feces, my brother-in-law's Hero became mine.

Certainly her affection for me is reciprocated, but this is not challenging because Hero has become quite old. When she first joined our household, I ran her and walked her and threw the tennis ball back and forth, but time passed and she can no longer move as quickly as me. This truly redefines slow. My brother-in-law owned Hero in the days she sprinted up hills while I own her in the days she licks whatever is closest.

So, right this moment—the sun, the breeze, the dog, I feel complete.

Well, only partially complete.

For a while now, something has been missing. Or, rather, something feels unsettled. I cannot wrap my mind around things. I cannot absorb. I almost reach an epiphany but then lose what I was trying to grasp. It's a strange place to be.

Lately I have felt my love becoming lazy. I am quick to make someone laugh or offer an encouraging word, but it never crosses my mind to do something that actually requires effort—to grieve alongside them, or help move their furniture.

My love has become a sort of form letter: the same words and motions for everyone regardless of what they might, in fact, need. I have become junk mail.

These flaws are, of course, not evident to me at the moments they should be. I want to be a good person. Most of the time, I dupe myself into believing that I actually am a good person. I long to lead others to Christ, but MAN, if I don't have a dickens of a time following through with all those good intentions when it comes down to actually doing right. Goodness constantly argues with myselfness and myselfness always rips goodness a new one. So, instead, I spew all of my flaws and inconsistencies on paper. Lucky you. I'm actually quite charming in person.

It begins to rain. This is a problem as hordes of clothing, books, and furniture are strewn about the driveway and yard unprotected. You would think I would have noticed the storm clouds coming as I am a planner. And yet, sometimes (often) the dark clouds roll in and cover my sunshine while I am otherwise preoccupied with that spaghetti smudge on my collar.

We scurry to cover what we can, shoving most of it back into the garage. It is clear that the call has been made. God has canceled our garage sale, which makes sense. He doesn't have a use for that remote control either.

◉ ◉ ◉

There is a reference in the Bible to "the least of these." Jesus tells us that what we do to those we consider least important in our lives is actually extremely important because it is as if we are doing those things to Jesus. This turns the whole idea of status on its head and is very stressful to people like myself. It took me a while to realize that this rule also applies to moments in our lives. The moments that we sometimes deem insignificant are often extremely significant. A seemingly trivial occurrence might just become the apex of our half-life.

This is definitely true of my life. For instance, I deem it extremely insignificant when Kaysie wants the boxes of clothes put back into our attic. But, in the light of this story, it was extremely significant.

I do not want to return the clothing to the attic.

I have prearranged multiple excuses to keep me from having to do so. But Kaysie wants the clothes separated and stored and in the attic. This stems from the fact that Kaysie wants events maximized while I want them finished. I am fueled by knowing that something is over while she is energized by things potentially never ending.

It is hot and I am tired, but that doesn't matter. There is future money to be made by re-storing, rediscovering, rearranging, repricing, and re-garage-selling these items that we just finished storing, discovering, arranging, pricing, and garage-selling. I do my best to argue this point. But I lose.

ME:	*You want me to what?*
KAYSIE:	Simply put those back in the attic.
ME:	*You say "simply" as if you're asking me to move a Q-tip. Are we staring at the same twelve boxes?*
KAYSIE:	I know it's a lot of work but I was up until 2:37 this morning pricing three hundred coat hangers individually, so the least you can do is carry them up one flight of stairs.
ME:	*I was up until 2:37 watching you price coat hangers while I paper-cut my finger on that box of Ho Hos.*
KAYSIE:	Please just do this.
ME:	*OR I could simply throw them in the van and dump them at the Salvation Army. Then there would be less lifting and more salvations.*
KAYSIE:	You're going to need salvation if you don't put these boxes in the attic.
ME:	*I think I just had a come-to-Jesus moment.*

So, I will box all of the items back up and carry them upstairs into the sauna of our attic. Even though I have a headache. Even though I am angry because my mix-tape has been sold to a stranger. And even though I have soreness in my back and fingers.

Because I am a husband. And because I love my wife.

◉ ◎ ◉

Kaysie and I met in the middle of one of those warehouse churches that looks as though it is desperately trying to avoid the appearance of a church. You'd be less surprised to discover a sale on a twelve-pack of salsa in the aisles than you would be to find a hymnal. It was ten o'clock at night and she was finishing up music practice. I had just driven twelve hours in for a job and I was laying down on a row of seats (not pews—that would look like a church, wouldn't it?). My hair was as long as it has ever been—down to the small of my back, which in my case was never exceptionally small. I was worn and certainly grumpy and somehow at that moment introduced to her.

She was not impressed.

In my defense, it would not have been plausible to impress her. It was late, I smelled of Mazda, and I looked like Billy Ray Cyrus collapsing of exhaustion at the end of the official Achy Breaky dance. She reminds me of this even now, almost twelve years later as if to say "see how much you impressed me eventually," or perhaps to say "you almost didn't get me," or possibly "you still smell like that now."

It wasn't until we met the second time that things heated up.

And by "heated up," I mean that she was not impressed the second time either.

I returned to her church several months later to lead a group of junior high students on a mission trip only to discover—lo and behold—that I had been paired up with Kaysie to colead. It doesn't take a Rorschach test to discover that the only thing I enjoy less than coleading is coleading with a stranger, so I was all business and very little personality. By the time we loaded the bus for the all-night drive across the border, Kaysie was not my biggest fan.

This was a problem for me because in the Midwest I was an actor and a stand-up comedian and I had what a desperate person might call fans. Not real ones. Just frightening ones. The sort of individuals that flailed towards me at the mall in a sprint, skin-folds flapping like Old Glory. But their love was easy. In a crowded store, they might call my name out, which would please me because people who were not crazy might hear this and decide that they wanted to be my fans also. I highly recommend fans: tons of attention without any genuine knowing. And the adoration will continue even if you never see the individual again. No risk on your part—just tons of ego-stroking. You might even get your ankle licked.

So, it was difficult for me that Kaysie did not choose to be my fan. What had gotten into her? Didn't she know all the important things I had done with my life—especially the jokes? Didn't she know there were dozens of (potentially two) other girls who would kill for a date with the guy they thought I was, however incorrect the assumption? I was certainly put out. Kaysie had been assigned as my coleader, which meant that she should be, on some level, asking for my autograph. But NO.

We arrived in Mexico after an exhausting all-night drive (these were becoming de facto in my life), but despite hunger and heavy eyelids, we decided to have a worship service in my favorite room on the planet.

The room is located at Hogar de Niños Emmanuel, an orphanage at the top of one of the tallest hills in Ciudad Juarez, Mexico. The church built a meeting room at the highest corner of the building, two of its walls' windows facing the city of El Paso and the mountains. The room is always surrounded with the clang and clatter of the orphan children, laughing and living their days toward an unknown something. And, in the dark of night, you can look out those windows and see the lonely lights of two nations blending together. The intersection of sorrow and hope. It is a powerful place. And, whenever I have taken groups there, God meets us in that room.

Then again, maybe He is always there just waiting for us to come meet Him.

We turned down the lights and due to a lack of both an instrument and talent to play an instrument, worshipped with only our voices. I would love to say that the worship was anointed, but that would be avoiding the fact that few in the room knew the actual lyrics to the songs. This encouraged an awkward combination of humming and mumbling with an occasional whispered, "yes Lord" to cover where one perhaps knew most of a chorus, but was missing a word. I, on the other hand, simply mouthed the names of farm produce. But, either way, it was the opposite of bombast: still and quiet. We sang song after song until, finally, a moment of silence.

Heavy silence. Like something was about to happen.

I, being the resident moron, decided to break the silence with a song. Couldn't tell you why. Maybe I felt led by God. Maybe I felt the silence was awkward. Maybe just a bad taco. But nonetheless, I began: voice only, with one of my favorite refrains.

> Oh God, You are my God, and I will ever praise You
> I will seek You in the morning, and I will learn to walk in Your ways

And as I sang, Kaysie heard an audible voice speak to her.

You first must understand that we are not those freaky-deaky "the spirit summoned a leopard and put him under my shirt so I must ROAR" sort of followers of Christ. Kaysie and I have seen so much and been disillusioned by so many people (including ourselves) in our walk toward Christ, that we are very hesitant to jump to the conclusion that the voice in one's head is God. But this was unmistakable. It was the furthest thing from her mind. She was simply standing there silently loving God. And He dropped the bomb.

You can't live without this man.

Wowzers. Me likey when He gets detailed. Tears start pouring down Kaysie's face and I assume I have kept her awake too long against her will. She begins to wrestle through these thoughts with God as I send the group to bed. Kaysie remains silent. And we head off to our respective floors until morning.

The sun rises early on that high hill, but we rise ahead of it, beginning our first day of rebuilding portions of the orphanage with a time of prayer. We converge in the same great room and now look out over the horizon to see how these two cities intermingle in the daytime.

I am tired. The room is silent. I have my coffee. I am staring out the window at an ice cream truck selling propane to the tune of a musical horn playing "La Cucaracha." I sip my java and mouth something indiscernible that I hope by sheer will becomes a prayer for someone. And then suddenly.

The voice.

You can't live without this woman.

This concerns me as all the women in the room are twelve years old. But I instantly know *Who* is speaking—and who He is speaking of. I freak out. I remain silent. I say nothing.

This marked our relationship for years. A deep knowing. A certainty that we were for one another. As a matter of fact, as the Juarez Legend of the Steeles grew, we reveled in others' fascination with us—their joy that our discovery of one another was so effortless, so pain-free. The world deemed us made-for-each-other and to this day, I know that we were.

But neither of us realized how long it would take to truly understand one another. We loved others' ideas of our perfection so much and for so long that it did not dawn on us that there was a great deal of work to be done. Perhaps the façade of perfection was actually enabling us to dodge our issues.

I, of course, was willing to dodge. Because I needed a fan. I wanted someone who believed she was created for me and that our union was some miraculous intervention of the Almighty. Something that epic would mean that I was special and that she was lucky. I would be validated, and our union would be a symbol of happiness for those poor slobs who make up the rest of the world.

I wanted to be better than them.

And that was the real problem: Our love was not as much rooted in a willingness to work through whatever hardships may come in the future as much as it was a goal to never have any hardships at all. We wanted our love to be safe. And so we took the ease of discovering our love as a sign that all future days would be as equally orchestrated to perfection as the first one.

Our love, our affection, our story, was envied. And I never realized how deeply I reveled in all of it. For the longest time, people had been fans of my comedy. Now they were fans of my romance. It was like a good fantasy book they could curl up with, daydreaming about how their life might potentially become something similar (but paling in comparison).

So, we played it up. The perfect proposal. The perfect wedding. The perfect couple. And then, real life began.

Of course there is nothing wrong with real life. That is, unless you have already decided it would never happen to you.

Don't get me wrong. I adore my wife and I always have. But, something inside me thought marriage would be like the love of the dog.

⦿ ⊙ ◉

Hero hates this part of every evening when I close her inside the garage for the night, putting her away like Lincoln Logs to the closet. She wants to be near me, lying close enough to my feet to feel my warmth. But I don't allow her to have those moments very often. Normally I don't put her in the garage until late when it is a bit cooler, but tonight, I have to finish putting these boxes of clothes in the attic. I am attempting to finish out my duties for the day before I fulfill this last task because I am exhausted. And not just because I didn't sleep much last night.

I find myself waking constantly these days—three or four times throughout the night. I have done this for years, but lately it is beginning to affect the way I see things. I get very little sleep, and I am finding myself stressed, impatient, short-tempered. This is not like me.

For instance, right now. I'm so tired, I'm practically furious. I could just spit that, after everything I've done today, I still have to heave these boxes that are evidently filled with cannonballs into storage. I could paint myself a little more attractive but it would not be accurate. I am really steamed. I am in one of those "how dare the world expect so much of me" states. Ugh. I lift the next-to-last box of clothes. At least forty pounds. What the heck is in here? The cast of *Maude?* I turn to grab the other box, but my friend Matt has already chosen to assist.

Sheesh. Why does he do this? Matt is one of those jolly "let me get that for you" leprechaun people. He is always ALWAYS eager to help. I would say this impresses me, but before there is esteem, there is first nausea. Matt is so quick to be like Jesus and it ticks me off because I am NEVER quick to be like Jesus. It is real EFFORT for me. We're talking prepare-for-several-days-and-write-reminders-on-my-knuckles effort. And then, after I do the thing I didn't want to do that I felt Jesus wanted me to do, THEN I feel guilty. As if the only reason I did it was to meet some unspoken criteria or perhaps seem more like Matt. I cannot fathom that selflessness can also be effortlessness because, before I give a dollar to the guy panhandling for food, I first make certain I have enough left over for the new Fountains of Wayne CD.

And once again, Matt has chosen to help me. He's been helping me all day. He unloaded the heaviest boxes from the attic this morning. He helped set up all the tables and price all the tchotchkes. He's more than likely done more than I have, but that doesn't stop me from being hacked that I have the heavier of the two boxes. Sure, Matt has a bad back, but I had a bad back in COLLEGE—a nerve pinched in between a slip disc in my vertebrae, causing me to walk with one leg a few inches shorter than the other for eighteen months. I would bobble back-and-forth, short-then-tall. I looked like Katie Couric holding hands with one of the Nephilim.

The truth is: I do NOT want to put this box away. But, alas, these are my own clothes. My own responsibility. My own weight to carry.

So, I open the attic door and heave the forty pounds up, blocking my sight as I work my way into the dry heat.

Hero begins howling from the garage. She does this often. I have always assumed it was a call-and-response to an ambulance siren or perhaps dogs far away indiscernible to the human ear. Dogs can do that, right? Don't they have a secret spy-hearing capability? It seems I read somewhere that if you whistle high enough, it will cause all the canines in your neighborhood to ram their heads repeatedly into the nearest Dumpster.

In retrospect, I believe it is possible that her cries were loneliness. She lay there each night in the dark, in solitude, on a pillow that smelled of diesel fuel as we lay inside spooning under crisp cool sheets. She was relegated to a virtual prison for ten hours each evening, and yet, the moment we opened that door in the morning, there she was—forgiving and ready to begin fresh—well, fresh except for her breath, which always smells of a tuna melt sandwich, though I don't believe she's ever actually eaten one.

Her love is in every way unconditional. Hero loves every single aspect of me and if for some reason on a particular day I smell especially rancid, it only causes her to sniff all the more. Not only does Hero love me just as I am, she actually nuzzles just as close to the dirty me.

And I love her too, but not in the same way.

Because I can't really love myself like she does.

It just seems like too much work.

So, the howling continues night after night, and where Hero yearns for one of us to say "I hear you. I am coming," instead we yell from our bedcovers, "Shut up, you stupid dog!"

She had begun digging holes in the backyard out of boredom, searching for a way under the fence. And we found ourselves fantasizing about at least one night without the constant howling, the trenches in the yard, the slobber on my ankle.

We began to daydream of a life without the dog.

⊙ ⊙ ⊙

That trip to Mexico held some hidden doubt.

Kaysie and I had not spoken of it, but there were moments when we questioned whether the voice we heard was, indeed, God. We were each in a unique place. We were wedged between the moment God spoke and the moment we would take action. Caught between revelation and obedience. This was an interesting predicament, because we had each spent the previous three years praying for exactly such a window.

We were the type who needed proof. Exact names. Clarification.

NeverLost.

And when God granted it, it scared the fool out of us.

This is important to dwell on, because it begins a pattern:

We ask God to be specific.

He is specific.

Because He is so specific, we assume it could not possibly be Him.

What does this mean? It could only mean one thing: that our prayer lives were rooted in requesting what we thought we were supposed to be asking for, even though we never really felt like we deserved to receive it. It was a wake-up call to how guilt-ridden we each were. In between the epiphany and the obedience, we expected there to be an additional moment.

The explanation.

We had always expected the big revelation by God Almighty to make perfect sense. We expected resolution before we had to act upon our life trajectory. And now, in the quiet drylands of Juarez, we were left with a dangling participle of an instruction.

We had requested God to be clear, but we never expected the clarity to be so foggy.

We wanted safe, but reality seemed daring.

As I drove back across the Mexico border, I knew that my out still existed. Neither of us had verbalized our God moment to the other. I had not hurt anyone yet. I could still walk away. The path towards her was filled with the unknown. Difficulties and negotiations. But the path away from her held only the loss that

I had not yet gained. I knew that I could keep my emotions safe forever—not even by saying *no*—simply by saying nothing.

But, I had sensed what could be.

I sensed, even then, how God could become revelatory to each of us through the other. I saw our future children. I could taste the half-century of ups and downs, hurts and miracles, being the greatest wound and the greatest joy the other would ever experience. It was daunting. It was not safe.

But it was full.

And so, in a rare moment of clarity, I pulled Kaysie to me and whispered into her ear.

Don't be afraid of this.

And even then, we both knew that we were going to embrace the many wonderful things that our life would entail—even though there would be plenty of reason to be very very afraid.

⊙ ⊙ ◉

I snap back into reality. My mind has been wandering. What was I doing? Oh yes. The heat. The box of overweight Oompa-Loompas. The attic.

I begin to tightrope my way across the two-by-four that bridges the path from the attic entrance to the makeshift plywood floor we have installed for additional storage. I feel myself inches away from being through with this hellish day.

A creak.

My left foot slips.

I throw my right foot down to balance myself.

I feel myself falling. I think to brace myself with my arms, but they are wrapped around this large box.

My stomach dips.

A blur.

An explosion.

And suddenly, nothing but white light.

When I come around, I am sopping wet from head to toe. My body is wrapped around something. Little spikes—no, nails, exposed nails—are pricking me. It takes me a moment to determine what I am seeing.

My bedroom.

Only it is suddenly pink.

And I am hovering above it.

Before I have the chance to assume I am having an out-of-body experience, I realize that I am holding on for dear life to a crossbeam in the ceiling. I have free-fallen and crashed through. There is fiberglass strewn about the floor of the bedroom below me as my feet dangle just shy of the ceiling fan. I hear a voice.

Are you all right?

I turn slightly. It is my wife. She stands next to Matt, who has both hands cupped over his mouth aghast, as if he has just observed the neutering of a pet.

And then, I attempt to move.

It suddenly becomes clear to me what has taken place.

My foot slipped off to the left of the two-by-four I was standing on.

My other foot slipped off to the right.

I free-fell and blew out the ceiling with my feet.

Other than my legs, nothing else fell through the roof.

Because I was stopped.

My hands were not free to catch my fall, so something else had to stop me.

Another body part.

A pair of body parts.

And with the full force of my own 215 pounds, plus the forty of the box I was carrying, I crashed downward onto the crossbeam, literally slamming every inch of my being against …

My precious.

As I attempt to uncoil my appendages from the protruding nails sticking out of the crossbeam, I began to fully feel the ache.

Is *ache* the right word?

Have you ever crushed an egg?

Well, imagine that you're the egg.

Only set the egg on fire.

And then hit it repeatedly with a baseball bat.

I was literally dripping with cold sweat. The pulsing intensity of pain was unbearable. The pain that would mark the next year of my life. And as I lay there, damaged and broken and counting how many ninja points this stunt would probably be worth, only one thought ran through my mind.

Now I don't have to put this stupid box away.

(Exhibit C)

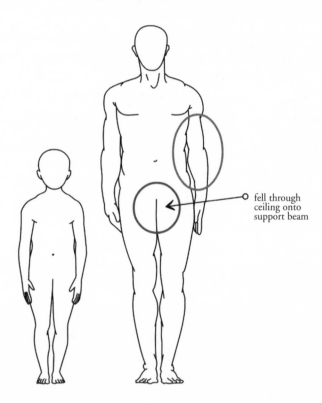

fell through
ceiling onto
support beam

SIX DECISIONS THAT MATTERED

decision #1:

OFFENDED / TEACHABLE

There have been too many important decisions to count in my life —

but six are instrumental to this story.

The first of which was the transition from offended to teachable. My assumption had been that this would be an evolution—something that would grow in me over time without much effort on my part. This was, of course, ridiculous, because offended is easy and teachable is a state of being about as attainable as invisibility. I had assumed I was already teachable because I was sometimes teachable, but of course, this also means that I was at other times offended. This is not a decision. This is a state of stuck. I had always hoped that in every instance where I experienced tension between these two states

oppositions would eventually

merge into one really

awesome whole.

no dice.

It became evident that change would not come until I began deep introspection in every aspect of my life. The first aspect: When things did not go my way, how did I respond to disappointment? More often than not, by holding on to the offense. So funny. I have hurt so many people in so many ways and, because I understand what I intended, I think the wounded should leap tall buildings to forgive me. But when the hurt is done to me, I think the wounder should pay. I don't actually say this, because that would be un-Christian. I instead imagine lengthy conversations that are awkward for them and rewarding for me and when I am finished with the imagination, I have less hair and a pit of acid in my stomach. In certain seasons, I have carried unforgiveness, and it has tangled and soured in my stomach like spilled milk in a shag rug. Many ask me: Why do people keep hurting me? But I think this is the wrong question. Maybe when wounded, we should ask,

what am I refusing to learn?

TWO DEAD OF WINTER

JANUARY 16

Enter Charlie. My third-born and my second son.

Charlie is about to turn five, and he reeks of awesomeness. As I lay in my cold, dark January-morning bedroom, I am reminded that he was born right here in this bed—a few inches from where I lay right now. Kaysie had been on bed-rest because of a bout with pneumonia at the beginning of her ninth month that left her constantly coughing. Suddenly, one night in the dead of winter, her fits launched her into labor.

And, pop. Charlie was born.

Okay, the pop took thirty-two hours.

Charlie is named after my maternal grandfather, Charles, who died when I was in high school. It was the first death in my life that authentically rattled me—confused me. My grandfather had always seemed so young in his old age. His suffering had gone on for some time, and I just assumed he would pull out of it. Then, the same afternoon I expected to climb into the car and hear he was doing better, I instead heard that I would never see him again.

My grandfather was the first to tell me I was a writer before I had written a single word. And now, Charlie, as tiny as he is, continues to be that sort of inspiration in my life. He is filled with joy. It is virtually impossible to drag him down. This is because, regardless of where Charlie may be at the moment, he is always able to make himself at home. Laughter and camaraderie follow Charlie like mice to a piper, and I am grateful that for some reason, I have been given the opportunity to be his father.

Charlie is adventurous, which can be frustrating to a boy whose backyard is fenced. It should be no surprise then that he has developed quite a kinship with

Hero, the other prisoner of the family. He spends a great deal of time with her, most often in dialogue. I'm not kidding. Actual conversation. More than likely regarding the wide-open spaces they are both missing. Kaysie or I will look out the back window and will see Hero, laying in the sunshine while Charlie sits on her back, discussing the day and dumping a cup of dirt on her head.

I don't fully understand why Charlie feels the need to dump dirt on the dog's head, but she doesn't seem to mind. As a matter of fact, she seems to fully understand. She will lay there, panting with this breathless sort of smile, insinuating that she has discovered her best friend in this boy smothering her with earth. Of course, to you or I, dumping dirt on someone else's body would be insulting. But this is Charlie's love language. He lives for the cold, damp, filthy layer just below the epidermis of grass. When we check on him in the backyard, if he is not dumping dirt on a living creature, he is either eating the dirt or rolling around in it naked.

Charlie spends a lot of time naked.

We try. We really do. But he has disrobing down to a science. That kid can get every item of clothing off his body before you hear the zipper. He understands he has to be stealth, because it's the only way he can get away with running through the living room au naturale during our group Bible studies. It's truly embarrassing. We'll be talking about Ezekiel and suddenly BAM! Naked child, right there next to the appetizers. He'd be an awesome Navy SEAL if they ever go nudist.

And everyone loves Charlie.

That's just the way it is. Some people are born with it, and Charlie is the king. He always gets the laugh or at least the smile. Me? I can't theorize plot points on *Lost* without friends audibly rolling their eyes, but Charlie could yell "come wipe me" from the top of the stairs and people would send him fruit baskets.

It's all because of the joy. Unbridled, passionate, fervent joy. He embraces the ridiculous. He skips instead of running. He makes me kiss his face in fourteen different places before we finish saying good night. He is in every way wonderful.

But, right now, there is a problem.

Charlie is currently at that age where he loves to run at his father in head-butting stance. He is also at that height where the top of his skull is just below my belt buckle. We'll call it the perfect storm. This would be bad enough without the fact that I am still reeling in pain from the damage suffered six months ago when I fell through that roof.

And there it is.

I lay in bed in the cold and stare up at the rectangle of drywall that has been inserted where so much epic sorrow came to pass. Just glancing at it, I feel a phantom bamboo chute of agony pulse up my leg.

I have not gone to the doctor concerning this. Because I am a moron. Also, because I am a dad and to be honest, I get thumped in my dadhood so often by my children that I can't imagine being inspected down there of my own free will.

Plus, I am afraid.

I mean, this is my manhood we're talking about. If there was trouble down there—well, it would affect an awful lot of things that I would prefer not to think about.

And as we all know, if it has not been diagnosed, it is not actually happening. So instead, I limp a lot.

A few days after the ceiling debacle, I thought perhaps I was fine. There had been some lingering pain, but really more numbness than anything as if the member in question had been removed entirely. But then, a few days later, I was driving and realized that a mosquito had gotten caught inside my car. I swatted at it hard in a downward motion and realized my mistake only after the unfortunate trajectory had been established. I attempted to stop my arm, but the velocity of my hand was unwavering. I tried to pull it back, but the tiniest tippy-tip of my hand made contact.

Thub.

You know when Frodo puts on the ring and all of the world gets sucked toward that eye made of lava as hooded undead kings scream like banshees?

Yeah. Just like that.

I practically drove into the median.

Not since Men at Work released their third album have so many disappointing things happened down under.

But six months have passed, and I have done a fine job of ignoring the warning signs. The ceiling has remained irreparable, and most days I wonder if I am. The current state of the ceiling is no one's fault in particular. Multiple friends rallied to fill the chasm (the Mark-shaped hole) the very same evening the accident occurred, but we kept running into roadblocks. Matt, his wife Molly, and Kaysie took up the slack first as I was curled up into the fetal position on the bed with an icepack muttering something about a happy place. Well, Matt took up the slack for the first forty-five minutes until he sliced into an artery in his hand while attempting to shape the drywall to fit with a retractable blade. A fountain of blood later, there was more to clean than fiberglass. So, my best friend Jason showed up.

I think best friends are important. It's a concept that most leave behind in junior high, but for me, there is value in deciding that someone has the right to open a can, to know your junk and hold you responsible for it. I never had a best friend growing up. I always had my brothers' best friends. I was a default friend. A second best. This was fine when all I needed was someone to compete against on the Tron arcade game on Friday nights, but it didn't do much for my level of honesty and accountability.

I understand now, as an adult, that I desperately need to be known. Otherwise it is virtually impossible to walk out faith with integrity. We all need to be significant to a few someone elses. We need to be priceless and indispensable. Jason is that individual in my life. He and his wife, Sarah, consistently help push Kaysie and I closer to God. And as I have aged, I have found myself less and less willing to know or be known by anyone else. It's too much work. I have to say that I am fortunate. I have Kaysie to open up to, but when what I need to process would be unfair for her to help me wade through, I go to Jason.

I am not surprised that he showed up tonight. I am not surprised that he took up the slack while Matt sat next to me bleeding like a Monty Python sketch. But, none of us have ever fixed a ceiling before, so we took it as far as we could and what remained is now staring me in the face.

◉ ◯ ◙

Charlie is awake now. I nodded off again and when I awoke, he was laying on top of me.

It's Monday. January 16. One of those dreary, bitter rainy days when you simply cannot believe the weekend happened already. They say it may snow. People assume I am a snow person because I get so excited at the first snow, but let's be clear: This does not make me a snow person, it makes me a first-snow person, as in a pre-Christmas-snow person. I would love for it to practically blizzard from November first to New Year's, but come January 2, I'm ready for the pool to open. I love *thematic* snow, but in my mind all precipitation needs a quantifier. I like rain if it's "sit-at-home-with-a-book rain." In other words, all meteorology should be required to fall in line with my moods. But today is not one of those days.

Charlie turns to me.

> CHARLIE: Daddy, can I feed Hewo?
> (Charlie hasn't learned his r's yet.)
> ME: *Sure. Go feed Hero.*
> CHARLIE: Can I give Hewo hew watew?
> ME: *No, I'll give Hero her water.*

Charlie gets up to go feed the dog. He doesn't roll off the bed like adults have learned to do; rather, he stands on my nether regions and vaults off them like Kerri Strug sticking the end of a routine.

I've been concerned about Hero. She has been sleeping inside because of the cold, but she hasn't been eating very much, just drinking. We've tried moistening her food, but she just doesn't seem interested. She's getting up there in years. Thirteen. They say that's ninety-one to you and me, and I've always wondered who the first guy was to do that math. I hope I get to chew as many tennis balls when I'm that age. Listening to Charlie feed her brings a dichotomy of emotions: warmth because I hear her wagging tail thumping against the floor as Charlie communicates how much he adores her, and stress, because I also hear a mountain of dog food spilling all over the linoleum.

Ergh.

This is one of those moments where I feel the frustration rise up and I sense myself wanting to get angry. It's ridiculous, and I don't know why the anger is there. I've never struggled with anger before. Not even when drivers cut me off. They'll flip the finger while I smile like I've been cast in a Mentos advertisement. I've always been such a jolly individual. VERY jolly. The sort of attitude that Santa Claus and Kelly Ripa's lovechild might have.

But, lately, I've felt the blood randomly boiling. I've never flown off the handle at my wife, but just a few months ago, we were at a group party playing one of those games involving colored dice. A random toss did not go my way, and you would have thought I was Jack Nicholson in *The Shining*. Disturbing even for me. I've never had a lot of rage. I've even found that things that rile others don't tend to get me going all that much. And that's what is so bizarre about the recent anger: The bile rises over the most inconsequential things. It's as if anger is seizing me for anger's sake.

And I have no earthly idea why.

I'll probably need to look into that fairly soon.

As I climb into the shower, Charlie is continuing his canine conversation.

What did you do to your watew, Hewo? Stank!

This is Charlie's new word.

Stank.

He invented it and utilizes it in places an older individual might reserve for a casual obscenity.

He doesn't even know what an obscenity is and yet he has invented a temporary replacement. And then, I hear Kaysie.

When do you think we might fix that ceiling?

And there goes the bile again. Because I know that "when" really means "why not already" and "we" really means "you."

It is a fair question, of course, because it has been six months and the ceiling looks horrible. An atrocity of décor. I would prefer for her to ask me a different way, but she has already asked me a different way seventeen times in as many weeks and I still haven't done it. I don't know why I haven't done it.

I don't feel particularly capable of fixing the ceiling. I don't really know where I would start. But I want her approval. So, instead, I fix something else around the house where I am confident I will succeed. I believe this should bring me accolades, but she never asked me to fix *that*. She asked me to fix *this* and *this* is not fixed. So while she is busy pointing to *this*, I am busy pointing to *that*.

And the bile rises.

So, our house is currently a series of broken things that I have been asked over and over to fix mixed with areas I have upgraded that were not previously a problem.

I've never really known what to do with broken things. Something over time fooled me into believing that to touch something broken without all the answers would leave it worse than I found it. That I am simply not qualified enough to attempt to mend anything. It has developed a state inside of me where I stare at the leg that has been lopped off and reply, "It's just a flesh wound."

I'm not certain how this developed, but I have a deep need to be just fine—to not rock the boat or disagree. To convince myself that all despair is fleeting and that all gaping wounds are mere scratches. Band-Aids for bullet holes. Not for others, of course. If I see that someone is hurting, I will comfort, I will do my best to console, to counsel, to encourage.

But not for myself.

I feel that this is wrong and I desperately do not want to pass it on to my children, but I haven't the foggiest idea how to address the problem. I do, however, see the cracks.

In my ceiling.

My body.

My marriage.

My faith.

And I put on another Band-Aid.

As I shower, I sneeze up wood chunks.

This coming Saturday is the Cub Scout Pinewood Derby: the yearly competition where all the Scout Dads carve blocks of wood into tiny automobiles and ooze lava out of their nostrils while cheering on their sons' victories. I have spent most of the weekend attempting to fashion rectangles of termite-food into champion racers. It isn't exactly working. I'm like Gepetto without the fairy. I assumed this event would be a charming little January diversion. I had no idea the only way to place would be to engage in massive quantum physics. To see some of the fathers put winning entries together, you would think it had been their doctoral thesis. Where did they learn this? Did I miss a retreat? This is the sort of father-son event I longed for when our children were born. However, I am neither mechanical nor crafty so my miniature automotive creations tend to drag a little in the race. They don't win anything. And everybody wins something. If you don't win one of the ribbons for first through twelfth place, there are always the awards for "most creative," "most colorful," "clearly built by a child," "remained intact," "smells slightly like wood," and "well, it was a nice thought."

We win none of these.

But that doesn't keep me from making my best effort. Jackson wanted his car to look like a rocket with a little man seated in the cockpit. I tried to explain that this would slow the device down. He stated that he did not care. I retorted that the whole point was to win the race so that he would be happy and other children would want to exchange their fathers for me. This did not seem to matter to him, though I'm certain it will matter more come Saturday when the same family that won last year walks away with eight ribbons and a signing bonus with NASCAR.

Morgan and Jackson are awake now. I know this because Morgan, my eight-year-old, is singing at the top of her lungs in the living room and Jackson, my six-year-old, is verbalizing his every thought while following me around:

> Guess what Dad you know what you know what you know what I figured out level seventeen on my game my video game that I'm going to invent from my movie my movie that I'm going to make when I'm grown up and I work for you and you die and I get your office the Everythingman movie about the superhero who can do everything except he gets weak when he's around electricity and his enemy is made of electricity and it's just like cool movies only Everythingman's got a Bible verse on his shirt and level seventeen is a BOSS level and the BOSS' name is "Dark" and Everythingman beats the BOSS and it's all in a volcano can you believe that guess what.

The story then loops back to its beginning and continues infinitely like a snake swallowing its own butt. Jackson is truly imaginative, and I know this because it is rare that I am able to pull him out of his imagination. I love this about him. After all, he is the spitting image of his old man in this regard. I mean, yes, I could do without his continual excitement over seizing my office when I'm dead, but other than that, I am flattered that he wants to pursue the same creative profession. I'm certain he won't change his mind. After all, he is six. The career path heavy-lifting is clearly complete.

Morgan, on the other hand, has a new career path every seven minutes. Right now, she is determined to be a country singer. Last night: a gymnast. By lunch: a missionary. There may be a way to maximize all three into the same occupation, and if there is, Morgan would love to star in the reality series.

Honey?

Kaysie is calling me. Normally, she would be asking me if I would like for her to make me something for lunch. She is a bit of a superwoman this way. On top of all the other details she needs to take care of each morning as a home school mom, she continues to take care of my details as well. However, today her tone does not seem to be suggesting soup or a sandwich. It sounds like something is wrong.

Honey? There's something the matter with Hero's water.

I make my way into the garage to see what all the commotion is about. My wife and three children are standing over the dog bowl. Hero, on the other hand, is laying peacefully beside it.

The water is red.

We circle around it and stare.

Red.

Red water.

Which means, either the ten plagues are making a comeback, or something is desperately wrong with my dog.

———————————

One year from now, I will be momentarily hopeless.

I will be reeling from the chain of events that began a year prior.

Yet, I won't be able to pinpoint an exact moment, an apex or half-life where it all turned around.

I will make great attempts to find this moment in question, but it will be futile because, to be honest, the moment doesn't really matter all that much.

I will believe that it matters a great deal because I will reach a point of despair where my life path seems irreversible—where I will be unable to drudge through the black cloud and see any chance of change.

But, that is because the change on the other side of the ice storm looks unlike anything I have seen before.

For a moment, however, it will seem like the very end.

And in many ways, it will be.

The clock begins now.

The real sign that something is wrong with Hero comes when I make my best attempt to load her into my SUV. Normally, the moment I open the door, she leaps inside before I can stop her. But this time, she cannot muster the strength to pull her body weight up into the vehicle. I try to grab her, two legs at-a-time (she is not a small canine), loading her front, then back. Not only is this ineffectual, but I now have to explain to my neighbor why I was holding up the back legs of my pet while her front half clung to the car. As I grip her entire torso, she yelps in pain. I am assuming that the bleeding from her mouth is some sort of gum disease, but find this inexplicable as we just took her to the dog dentist a few weeks back and he said nothing about any major damage. If her teeth are hurting, it would certainly explain why she has not been eating much the past few days.

Finally, Hero is in the car. She sits in the backseat, happy to be along for the ride. I roll the back window down halfway so that she can eat the breeze. She loves this. As the wind comes whipping at her face, she tastes at it with her mouth as if she enjoys the sensation so much that she just has to take a bite. Either that, or she's catching bugs.

I arrive at the veterinarian and explain what we have discovered. She agrees that it is more than likely gum damage that they didn't catch when they last cleaned her teeth because she may have cut her gums on a bone or chew toy. She is, after all, getting up there in years.

Ninety-one, I remind her.

Yes, she concurs.

This seven-years-to-one ratio thing has really caught on.

I drop her off as one would the kids at the pool, and I make my journey to work.

As I get my computer bag out, I see that there are droplets of blood all over the back seat of the car. I try very hard for this not to exasperate me. I tell myself that her suffering is far more important than my anal-retentiveness. I also tell myself that her suffering could have just as easily dripped on newspaper instead of my upholstery. I am internally spazzing. I scrub for a good fifteen minutes before I finally get inside the office (an hour late due to all of the dog business) and start actual work.

My business resides in a four-story red brick locale on the periphery of downtown Tulsa, across the street from the park where the city launches its annual Fourth of July fireworks. This provides an excellent view out of my office, which is windowed on three of the four walls. I face out toward the window to write, just like I did in my bedroom growing up, only back then, it was a manual typewriter and I gazed at a greenbelt. One of two walls displays a myriad of music and books from which I gain inspiration; the other features a collage of artwork from my children intermingled with design elements from projects past, present, and hopefully future. I am often asked what I do, and this is a complicated question. The obvious answer is that I create media for all sorts of reasons, but the real answer is that I am searching for meaning through the things that make me tick. As is true for anyone, I have very specific talents. I daily throw these talents at opportunities, hoping that at some point one or a few will stick to my heart. I don't really know what satisfaction is supposed to feel like, but I'm told that I must feel it. People say things like:

It must feel very satisfying to have accomplished that.

To which my answer is:

Sure.

Many projects I have worked on over the years have resulted in people coming to know Christ. But I don't personally witness or experience this, so more often than not I am left wondering if it is real. Instead, I tend to experience arguments and disgruntled individuals who pound the table trying to get what they think that they want. Somehow, this doesn't feel like ministry.

So, the question arises: Does effective ministry really have anything to do with how I feel about it? For something to work, do I have to glean benefit? Do I need to be fulfilled?

It's Monday, which means incessant meetings: producer meetings, production meetings, project meetings. I scurry to get my reports together and am just about to exit my office for the conference room downstairs when the phone rings.

THE VET:	Mr. Steele?
ME:	*Yes. This is Mr. Steele.*
THE VET:	This is the vet. We're terribly sorry.
ME:	*Why are you terribly sorry?*
THE VET:	We missed something when we last checked Hero.
ME:	*Missed something?*
THE VET:	She does not have gum disease.
ME:	*Well, that's good.*
THE VET:	No, it's not good. It's not good at all because she has something much worse.
ME:	*What does she have?*
THE VET:	Mister Steele, Hero has throat cancer.

There is an interminable silence on both sides of the phone. I am confused. I had not thought through this sort of diagnosis.

ME: *I don't understand. You said it was gum disease.*

THE VET: We said we thought it was gum disease, but it is not gum
               disease. It is throat cancer.

ME: *Maybe you just think it's throat cancer.*

THE VET: Mr. Steele, we are certain.

ME: *Well, you just checked her out a few months ago. It must be in
               the early stages.*

THE VET: I know we checked her recently, but it was not there then
               and it is there now.

I think this is all a ploy. Like when the guy fixing your car says you need a
new carburetor when really, there's a branch stuck in your undercarriage.

ME: *Fine. I get it. How much money are we talking?*

THE VET: Money? We're not talking money, Mr. Steele. She cannot
               be fixed.

ME: *I don't understand.*

THE VET: Any surgery we do would only make her more comfortable
               for the time being. But, she is very old, and probably
               would not make it through the surgery anyway.

ME: *Are you telling me that she is not going to make it?*

THE VET: We'll make her as comfortable as we can here until the end.

I stare at the phone. Literally stare at the phone. As if time will stand still and
the words that were spoken will force their way through the phone line back
into the mouth of the veterinarian who will suddenly realize the lie that those
words were and will state instead that my dog is fixed and ready for me to come
pick her up. But, the staring does nothing.

ME: *Forget it. I'm taking her home.*

THE VET: Mr. Steele?

ME: *We'll work it out some other way.*

THE VET: Mr. Steele. Please. She may not make it through the day.

She went on to tell me that there were three ways of doing this: 1) letting nature take its course at home, 2) letting them put her to sleep immediately, or 3) letting them give her drugs so that we could come and say good-bye before they put her to sleep. I can't imagine never seeing her again, but neither can I imagine taking my children in to see their beloved pet with full knowledge that it is the very last time.

This isn't the way it's supposed to happen. I've only been this emotionally connected to a pet one other time in my life. As a boy, we owned a collie named Lady and she lived with our family for over eleven years. When it was her time to die, she didn't let us say farewell. Instead, she ran away and was never seen again. This was incredibly difficult, but at least the last time I laid eyes on her, I had no idea it would be the last time. I was not required to deal with parting words.

I call Kaysie and we discuss the options, all negative.

We realize there is no other way to do this than allow the kids to make the decision themselves.

I hear sobs.

Absolute sobs in the background.

They want to see her again, even though it will be the last time.

I go back home and pick up the family. We ride to the vet in relative silence until Morgan speaks:

> **MORGAN:** Dad?
>
> **ME:** *Yes, sweetheart?*
>
> **MORGAN:** I'll bet she gets better.
>
> **ME:** *Uh.*
>
> **MORGAN:** I'll bet they're wrong.
>
> **ME:** *Morgan, Hero is very old and she's in a lot of pain. It sounds like it's her time to go.*
>
> **MORGAN:** But, they could be wrong. We should pray for God to heal her.

And there it is.

Things begin to get very very sticky.

Charlie just stares out the window. Gazing into the cold rain.

How does one explain this to a child? I wrestle. Can my sweet innocent children grapple with the fact that the dog may not be healed by a desperate prayer and yet that does not cancel out God's goodness? For most, the answer is simple: She's just a dog. But, in my kids' perspective, she is so much more. She is of grave importance and the thought that what is of enormous significance in their lives would not be valuable to God is an awful lot for their single-digit minds to wrestle through.

I tell myself that this is the only problem—that the children cannot process this well. But what do I do myself with the idea of death and loss? Yes, in the literal "physical life ends" sense, but also on a much deeper level: the kind of loss where one lives to suffer on. And a large part of the lump in my throat comes from seeing Charlie in the rearview mirror. Happy, unwavering Charlie cannot pull the corners of his mouth up. And I think to myself …

> *No. It is too soon. This damage is too soon. I want the unpolluted Charlie at least a little longer. I don't want doubt and fear and sadness to ease in just yet. I'm not ready for him to start becoming me.*

I remember being Morgan's age and laying in bed awake for hours, the fear of death throttling me by the throat. I was never really afraid of dying myself, but I was terrified of significant others being torn away from me. What if I woke up and my mother or father was gone forever? What if one of my brothers was killed? I began to picture Jesus standing outside our front door at night, guarding the entryway as death snuck in a back window I had forgotten to close. Faith became a protection against the scenarios found in those horror movies we would watch on HBO while Mom and Dad were at prayer meetings.

And now, as an adult, time after time my family has been forced to address major crisis. Crazy stuff. This is fresh on my mind because I've been doing a lot of radio interviews this month for my last book, which chronicles bouts I've had with some of the most bizarre physical maladies in recent memory. Most of the radio interviewers ask the same thing:

When did you first realize that you have bad luck?

Bad luck? I had never seen my life that way. In my opinion, all lives are filled with lame and glory and some people just choose to see one or the other instead of the collision of both. I have made my best attempt to see it all in order to figure out how it can all make me a better man.

But, bad luck? Hmm.

I don't believe that.

But it has caused me to doubt a bit. Especially in moments where my beloved dog, who just had a mouth checkup a matter of weeks ago, is suddenly dying from throat cancer. And so I pray.

I talk to God constantly—all day long, in fact. From the time I was a child, I've spent a great deal of time praying for things to happen or to not happen— for situations or events or people to be fixed. Of course, the definition of fixed was my own. I understood that I was not the best barometer for what I need, but I also believed that if it was important enough to me and if I was belligerent enough to God, God would feel obliged to do something about it.

Sometimes He did. Sometimes He didn't.

Once, when I was about seven years old, I needed ten dollars for something. I have no idea now what it was, but the ten dollars might as well have been ten unicorns. I prayed anyway. A few days later, I found my baby scrapbook under a stack in my closet. As I flipped through, I found a card that a family friend had written to me the day I was born. When I opened the card, ten dollars fell out. This was an extremely formative moment in my faith. It did not convince me that Jesus wanted me to have more material things, but it did make me believe that God could see and hear me. To me, that ten spot was God saying, "I notice you."

He always says something back.

But, it isn't always what I want.

So, I don't always believe it is Him speaking.

I have a difficult time surrendering when God doesn't give me the answer I want. I have, in different seasons, subscribed to one of two camps: the first being what I would label "surrender plus," which appears to be complete submission to God, but is mixed with moments of doing what I want to do anyway. At other times, I have resigned myself to "surrender anyway." My wife and I have a very close friend named Susan who lives this credo. Her son, Logan, died as a teenager of leukemia. We had all prayed so hard and shed so many tears, that it was a literal shock when rescue did not come. If anyone in my life has ever had reason to deny surrender, it is Susan, but she has chosen a different path. It is a path of daily wrestling, yes, but somehow that wrestling match has changed Kaysie and I as we have observed in awe. Susan doesn't serve God because everything has gone her way. She serves Him in spite of the chaos, tragedy, and unanswered conundrums. She surrenders anyway. And we are not the only ones watching her who have changed because of it.

My daily Bible reading today is a passage from the book of Job. I wouldn't normally recommend such a despairing portion of the Bible during the bleak midwinter, but I am attempting to read the entire Bible through chronologically this year. Whoop-dee-doo, that means Job comes early. And right now, I am in chapters 20 and 21, smack in the middle of ultimate misery. Every earthly thing that held value to Job has been stripped away, and Job's friends are trying to make sense of it. But some things just can't be made sense of. His friends attempt to chipper him up, making their best attempts to explain the situation, but Job exclaims:

> *How can your empty clichés comfort me? All your explanations are lies!*[†]

[†] Job 21:34 NLT

Fortunately, these chapters are balanced out with my daily New Testament assignment, which today is Matthew, chapter 11. Jesus has been healing the sick and the lame and raising the dead, and needless to say, it is causing quite the commotion. But the people keep doubting anyway.

So, in Job, people just like me doubt because God is doing nothing.

And in Matthew, people just like me doubt because God is doing everything.

But there are other people besides the ones who doubt and question. There are also the ones He heals. To those He heals, Jesus says this:

> *Come to me, all of you who are weary and carry heavy burdens, and I will give you rest. Take my yoke upon you. Let me teach you, because I am humble and gentle at heart, and you will find rest for your souls. For my yoke is easy to bear, and the burden I give you is light.*†

But to those who doubt, He says this:

> *O Father, Lord of heaven and earth, thank you for hiding the truth from those who think themselves wise and clever, and for revealing them to the childlike.*††

So I ask myself the obvious question: Am I the doubter or the weary? They both go through the exact same life crap, but some find answers while others find disillusionment—and the difference seems to be found in their own personal take on the matter. A provocative thought, yes, but it does not bring me any closer to knowing what I should say to my children about the impending death of their dog.

The problem in the crux where prayer meets tragedy is that so many people claim to have the final teaching on the subject. It seems those individuals find the Scripture passage that best reinforces their belief and then ride that sucker to the ground, but as is true of any subject, what the Bible has to say is not always neat and tidy. It is not one-dimensional. The Bible teaches that God answers prayer in the following passages:

---

† Matthew 11:28–30 NLT

††Matthew 11:25 NLT

When two of you get together on anything at all on earth and make a prayer of it, my Father in heaven goes into action. And when two or three of you are together because of me, you can be sure that I'll be there.[†]

But Jesus was matter-of-fact: "Yes—and if you embrace this kingdom life and don't doubt God, you'll not only do minor feats like I did to the fig tree, but also triumph over huge obstacles. This mountain, for instance, you'll tell, 'Go jump in the lake,' and it will jump. Absolutely everything, ranging from small to large, as you make it a part of your believing prayer, gets included as you lay hold of God.[††]

This is very exciting. We want to be able to ask "anything at all" and have our prayers "triumph over huge obstacles." But that isn't all the Bible has to say about prayer.

Going a little ahead, he fell on his face, praying, "My Father, if there is any way, get me out of this. But please, not what I want. You, what do you want?[†††]

The world is full of so-called prayer warriors who are prayer-ignorant. They're full of formulas and programs and advice, peddling techniques for getting what you want from God. Don't fall for that nonsense. This is your Father you are dealing with, and he knows better than you what you need[††††]

So perhaps the big question is not, "Why does prayer work sometimes and not work other times?" or "Why do bad things happen to good people, even though they pray?" Perhaps the big question is, "What is prayer really for?" We are quick to believe (hope) that prayer is for all of the magical things that prayer does if we think we can figure out the secret code. We want to keep the part about praying for "anything" but discard "not what I want. You, what do You want."

[†] Matthew 18:18b

[††] Matthew 21:21

[†††] Matthew 26:39

[††††] Matthew 6:7a

But, all of these passages (and others on the subject in the Bible) insinuate that the tangible benefits of prayer are mere by-products of a healthy prayer life. That prayer is not, in fact, for getting what we want and solving our problems.

Prayer's purpose is that we would know God. Real relationship. Real communication. For us to have this unprecedented two-way conversation with our Creator for the purpose of understanding Him better. Because the more we know Him, the more our prayers will coincide with His business. And the more the words out of our mouths reflect His heart, the more results we will see. So, how do we pray in the meantime?

> *Meanwhile, the moment we get tired in the waiting, God's Spirit is right alongside helping us along. If we don't know how or what to pray, it doesn't matter. He does our praying in and for us, making prayer out of our wordless sighs, our aching groans. He knows us far better than we know ourselves, knows our pregnant condition, and keeps us present before God. That's why we can be so sure that every detail in our lives of love for God is worked into something good.[†]*

This is me. My pregnant condition. Pain and turmoil without a visible conclusion. But, something is growing—and God assures that it will be worked out for good. Most of the time, I trust and believe that the Bible knows what it is talking about. But right now, as we park the car and begin walking into the building to see our dog for the last time?

It doesn't seem so good.

Still, I assure the kids that Hero will not know—that by the time we see her, the veterinarian will have given her painkillers and she will simply be glad to see all of us.

The kids ask me what they should say:

> **MORGAN:** Can we tell her that she was a great dog?
> **ME:**   *Yes.*
> **CHARLIE:** Can we tell hew she was the best dog evew?

[†] Romans 8:26

ME: *Of course.*

JACKSON: I think we should thank her for protecting us.

ME: *That's a great idea.*

We step inside a small room where Hero is about to be brought in. It is cold, and there are only two seats for the five of us. We are uncertain what to do with our hands, which are suddenly clumsy orbs of stone hanging at the ends of our arms. A lump forms in my throat.

WHY?! Why is this rattling me so deeply? For crying out loud, she's a dog!

But, I know she is more than that. She is the love I never had to work for. She is the affection that would remain unchanging regardless of how much I changed. Comfort, like a footstool, and yet—

A door opens and suddenly, with a burst of joy, Hero trots into the room.

It is as if we have loaded the family up into a time machine. She is spry and smiling. Her tail goes mad, slamming against the walls of the cubicle. It's as if the last five years have disappeared from her history. For a moment, I could picture her running up that mountain once again.

Suddenly, smiles on all three children. They love on her. Deep love. Laughter as she licks their faces. They are elated. I am thrilled that they are taking this so well until I realize that they are not taking it at all.

MORGAN: I told you, Dad! She's healed! God healed her!

Oh no. The woman vet explains that this is the intense medication. It has taken away all pain, but only momentarily. She wanted us to have the best possible final moment with Hero. The medication cannot last and the energy and joy we are witnessing is not, in fact, real.

Now, they are confused. How can their friend be dying when it is clear by looking at her that she is living more than ever before? As the half-hour comes to a close, Charlie, who has been most hesitant, speaks:

> **CHARLIE:** Can I hug her?
>
> **ME:**   *Of course, Charlie.*

Charlie takes her around the body and neck. And I could swear that I see her stare into his eyes. He looks at her for a while, studying her face, memorizing it—as if he understands remembering her will be a struggle. Suddenly, with a choke I have never heard in that boy's voice, he speaks.

> **CHARLIE:** I wuved you, Hewo.

Wuved. Past tense.

He embraces her hard as her wagging tail begins to slow its pace. He holds her, his face scrunched into the nappy fur at her neck. And as Charlie pulls away, we see them.

Big fat tears.

He is not whining or crying because he didn't get his way. For the first time in his little life, these big fat drops of water come from a broken heart. They roll down his cheeks as his lips quiver. The room heaves with emotion, and then, it is time to go.

Kaysie agrees to take the kids out to the car, so each says one final good-bye.

Hero continues to smile and wag that tail. They back out of the room, wanting every last eyeful they can muster, treasuring each second. And then the door closes.

I ask the woman when it will happen. She reassures me that Hero will feel no pain and confirms that as soon as I leave the building, the deed will be done. She decides to give us a moment alone. She exits. I stare into the eyes of my companion.

> *Hero, you've done a good job. You protected our family. You did what you were made to do. Your job is over now. You need to know that. Your job—it's finished—and you did good. You can go home now.*

The woman opens the door and takes her away, out of my sight and reach. I ask if she will please call me on my cell phone when it is over. She says that she will.

I return to work and attempt to focus, staring every thirty seconds at my non-ringing cell phone. She said she would call. Why doesn't she call? The day comes and goes and still, no call. I begin to reason with myself. Perhaps they realized a mistake? Maybe it wasn't as bad as they thought? I drive home at the end of the day and am just putting away my things when my cell phone rings. I see that it is the vet, so I step into the backyard to take the call.

ME:	*Yes?*
THE VET:	Mr. Steele? I see that you have left several messages.
ME:	*Um, yeah. You said you would call to let me know when Hero had passed?*
THE VET:	Yeah.
ME:	*Yeah, you called?*
THE VET:	Yeah, she's passed.

I stare down at the ground, holding the phone to my ear in silence. I hear the woman on the other line blathering on about the details, but my eyes are filling with tears. My vision is getting cloudy. All I can see is that hole under the fence that Hero was digging. I was so angry at her. She was digging furiously. Trying to escape.

Trying to get out.

Get out.

Get out.

She finally did.

Stank.

(Exhibit D)

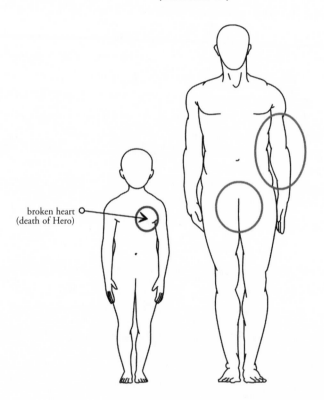

broken heart
(death of Hero)

VALENTINE'S DAY

Charlie is ill.

This is a problem because his birthday is in six days and he absolutely refuses to be sick on his birthday. We are planning a knights-themed birthday party, and Kaysie and I have been up to our ears in cardboard, aluminum foil, and fabric, making shields, swords, and tunics for every boy attending. We will have jousting events, a knighting ceremony, and a dragon piñata to slay.

ME:	*I don't understand what I'm making.*
KAYSIE:	It's a coat of arms.
ME:	*It looks like a pillowcase.*
KAYSIE:	That's because you haven't cut it in half. Cut it in half, and it's like a painting apron.
ME:	*Ah. Just like King Arthur's Knights of the Painting Aprons.*
KAYSIE:	You have to draw a cross on the front to turn the painting apron into a coat of arms.
ME:	*This is how Bibleman got started.*
KAYSIE:	Not a Jesus cross. A Red Cross cross.
ME:	*You mean a plus sign?*
KAYSIE:	Yes, but fancy.
ME:	*So, they'll look like walking flash cards.*
KAYSIE:	They will until you tie the sword holder around the waist.
ME:	*What sword holder?*
KAYSIE:	The one you're going to make out of this gold twine.
ME:	*I don't know how to make a sword holder.*
KAYSIE:	You're making twenty.

This is the way we Steeles do celebrations: with great intensity and a wealth of props. My mother's mother died when she was a little girl and from that point on, she decided that she would make every moment with her own children special. To this end: Every holiday was filled with tradition—every birthday stuffed to the bursting seams with merriment. She even had a way of turning the times we were short on money into adventures. We would regularly have "fun with a dollar" days. All in all, my childhood was marked with revelry that Kaysie and I have made great attempts to replicate in our own household.

Kaysie and I used to do this for each other, but most of that intention is now aimed at the children. This is why, on Monday, February 14, we are focused more on Charlie's party than our own romance. After all, Monday is not exactly the best day of the week for Valentine's. Nor is February the best month. I don't know who decided it would be optimal to celebrate our sweethearts in the aching cold, but I am suspicious that the decision was due to a first-quarter downturn in the greeting card industry.

And the winter outside is indeed aching. It gets so cold here. The temperatures alone aren't too bad. It's that slicing north wind. The gusts are so fierce, they plummet the thermometer down into its nether regions. When we lay asleep, we are able to hear the earth groan as the wind howls and the branches scrape against our bedroom wall from the outside. We attempt to block the cold with towels tucked under the doors, but somehow it trickles in like a ghost, waiting for a warm moment to attack with a shiver.

Kaysie is in the kitchen putting together the cake. This always astounds me. Over the years of birthdays, she has concocted some serious cakeage. And it is always in tandem with the event's theme. Once, we had a rocket party with two round planet cakes that sat on an icing pan of the solar system. She has created blue dogs, castles, and one year, for a "bug party" a wide array of cupcakes shaped like insects.

Kaysie is meticulous in her passion to make the children's fun carefree. And so I am wrapping sword-shaped cardboard with aluminum foil, then black-taping the handles. There are fourteen to be made. I thought they would take an hour or so.

I am on day two.

We used to take this sort of attention in surprising and impressing one another. Day trips and cooking special dinners and mix-tapes and whatnot. Of course, back in those days, we were the only ones around to impress. Courtship and early marriage is a lot like that first season of serving Christ, where you want to know everything about Him and spend your time, energies, and pursuits making Him the core of your existence.

But alas, over time, Jesus is no longer the only person in the room.

A few weeks after that fated Juarez trip, Kaysie came to visit me in Tulsa for the first time. That single weekend we went from "I can't live without this person" to "Will you marry me?" And I was indeed distracted—every spare thought was aimed at ways I could astonish her, entice her, make her heart permanently mine. I didn't have a ring to speak of that August week, so we planned for a more formal proposal to follow at a later date. For the next few months, we were on the phone every single night—two to three hours at a time. We let other relationships slide or implode completely. We became one another's everything.

Then, in the heart of winter—right around this time of year, in fact—I surprised Kaysie by flying her unexpectedly to Tulsa. She was brought to the Colorado Springs airport, thinking she was picking someone up. Instead, her bags had been checked and she was handed a ticket to be with me.

You may ask why I flew her to me instead of flying to her. The answer? Home field advantage. I did not have the friendships or financial resources to pull off a legendary proposal in her hometown, so I cheated. I took her away from everyone else she loved so that it would be easier on me. It was a proposal of Nora Ephronesque grandeur: limousine, candlelight dinner, gorgeous ring that the bank still owned.

That first Valentine's Day, we were separated by several states, but did special things for one another. We made each other a series of love notes, and Kaysie sent me a candy machine filled with tiny hearts: two for each day until we were wed.

My coworkers at the time did not respect the math and continually stole little sugar hearts from my desk when I wasn't looking. I believe the cavemen kept similar calendars with small coffee beans. This is why the age of the planet is such a mystery. Prehistoric man kept eating the Saturdays.

I created a Valentine's masterpiece for Kaysie: another mix-tape. It was entitled "Songs for Kaysie," and it made her swoon. It included songs like:

> "Hold on My Heart" Genesis (second song, side one)
> "True Companion" Marc Cohn (final song, side two)
> "Hold Me Now" Thompson Twins (next to final song, side two)
> "It Had to Be You" Harry Connick Jr. (first song, side one)
> "I'm Gonna Be (500 Miles)" The Proclaimers (third song, side one)
> "All About Soul" Billy Joel (first song, side two)

Those first few Valentine's Days, we really made elaborate attempts to surprise one another, go to unique eateries, and purchase gifts the other would not expect. But then bills came. And we would have to wait over an hour to eat at the restaurant. And we would be so tired after the workday/house-cleaning/barrage of noise/constant touching from our children. Eventually the thought of having a romantic evening out seemed more work than pleasure, so our Valentine's nights consisted of getting the kids to bed early, ordering food in, and falling asleep on the couch.

We are about to begin our twelfth year of marriage. And most Valentine's days are already on autopilot. This is the plan tonight: get the kids to bed early, order food in, and watch something romantic.

I don't know what makes a film romantic. The most romantic film of all time to me is *Sleepless in Seattle*, but it is by no means the most romantic film of all time to many others. I find it romantic, not because its story is better, but because I first saw it with Kaysie when we were first in love. Every Valentine's we do one of two things: we try a new romantic film we've never seen and are disappointed, or we watch *Sleepless* again. The new film is never romantic. *Sleepless* always is. Because *Sleepless* will always be stuck in that perfect window when love was fresh. And the new films are stuck in right now.

Ah. When love was fresh.

Back then, Kaysie and I could occasionally consider ourselves "well-rested." The relative stress of our jobs was nonexistent. We had spare hours and spare dollars to do with as we pleased. And we were in love. We are still in love, of course. Deeper now than then. But deeper love isn't nearly as much fun.

And most days—the despairing days—the thing that seems to bring me down is not that this day and this life aren't wonderful. The thing that seems to bring me down is the thought that at an earlier point in time, it was MORE wonderful than now and that time is over. So, without attempting to do so, I center most of my efforts around either remembering that early wonderful again or trying to recreate it. But this creates a problem. Because I was not created to live in yesterday. And every time I attempt to recreate then-wonderful, I ruin now-wonderful. I tamper with it, replacing it with a fraud. And it is ripping my heart apart.

I first started having heart pains in college. For a few semesters, I worked as a carpenter stagehand for the university theater. It was a great deal of manual labor, and I often felt strained. One day, standing in the theater, I was having a discussion with one of my professors when suddenly …

Thwang.

A heaviness. Instant dread. I clutched my chest. I went to the doctor to have this checked out, but they found nothing. My heart rate was fine. My bill of health clean. It must have been in my head. So, I went on with life.

Though the stagger in my heart continued to hit me on-and-off, I have never told Kaysie about it. I tend to go with what that first doctor said: Nothing is wrong. It's simply one of those inexplicable quirks about me. And hey, if I had to choose between my heart being broken physically or emotionally, I always assumed I would choose the body over the soul.

I had never had my heart broken by love before.

Because Kaysie was the first and only I had ever let in.

But now I am having second thoughts over which I would prefer because my body seems to be crumbling. I cannot pinpoint what is going on, but ever since last summer, I seem to be deteriorating. I suppose I attribute this to falling through the ceiling, but I don't know. Could there be more to it?

Ever since I fell through the ceiling, the pain down there has grown more substantial—not to mention it's painful to get romantic. This has caused a real disintegration of my confidence. At the same time, the anger I mentioned has been rising more often. I don't act out physically, but I tend to get frustrated and irritable with everyone around me. I have very little patience these days. I am always stressed, always maxed out, always overwhelmed, and to add even more concern, I have started feeling the pains in my heart again.

I have not painted the full picture to Kaysie, and yet, every time I wince when someone gets clocked with a softball in the nether region on *America's Funniest Home Videos*, she urges me to make an appointment with the doctor.

But I do not.

Because I don't want him to find anything.

And I don't want to pay for it.

All of these talks of aches and pains have caused Kaysie and I to do something we had never considered before. We begin to write our will. It is a "living will," which I suppose is a less abrasive way to say "do this when I die." It specifies, among other things, who is to take care of our children if Kaysie and I pass. And by "pass," I mean move to Barbados.

We don't feel old enough to be putting these thoughts down on paper. We're still young. We both turn thirty-six this year, and it seems that the paper in my hand shouldn't be something we have to consider for another decade—and yet here it is.

I have trouble imagining myself dead. For a long time, this was because I felt so filled with life. It is the very thing that drew Kaysie to me—that drew others to me. I was so in love with God and people. You could feel it, hear it, sense it when you spoke with me.

But that life has trickled.

It hasn't trickled toward death.

It has trickled toward numb.

The threat of death—that is something else entirely.

That is something that would startle me awake.

I know this because six months after Charlie was born, Kaysie was heading up the stairs in our home to get little Jackson (or Baby Jack as we called him at that time) out of his crib. Her pregnancy with Charlie had wreaked havoc on her back, and she was having intense pain. The doctors said this was because we had the two boys so close together and Kaysie's skeletal system literally did not have time to move itself back into support mode before it felt the hormone change of pregnancy once again. The skeleton, knowing another human would have to fit through soon enough, stayed put.

This particular day, Kaysie climbed to the top of the stairs and was just reaching into the crib for Jackson, when POP! She crumbled to the floor. She had thrown her back completely out, and she could not move from the pain. Jackson stood in his crib, sobbing, wondering what was wrong with his mommy. Kaysie could not stand up, much less lift him, so she had to talk him down—a two-year-old, discovering the way out of his crib on his own as his mother coaxed him out with her voice.

Once Jackson made it out of his crib, he and Kaysie slid on their bellies down the stairs. For Jackson, this was fun. For Kaysie, not so much. Finally near the phone, Kaysie called me in a panic. I hurried to pick up Kaysie's mother Dawn, who also worked downtown, and we made a beeline for the highway.

I remember Dawn and I chatting worriedly about Kaysie's condition. We intended to get home faster, but there was so much more traffic then normal on the highway for this time of the morning. I was about to call Kaysie to check in on her when, suddenly …

My life flashed before my eyes.

Directly in front of me was a large yellow moving van. I stared in disbelief as the world moved in slow motion. The back hatch to the van slowly raised. I was transfixed. It was as if my car was on autopilot.

Inside the van, there was only one object.

One of those four-foot-tall wheeled metal dollies you use to lift a piano.

I watched.

It began to move.

Rolling.

Towards me.

Then suddenly, life resumed normal speed as the dolly, clearly weighing at least a hundred pounds, rolled out of the back hatch of the van and came FLYING flipping head-over-wheels directly toward my front windshield not fifty feet in front of me. In one nanosecond, a half-dozen things happened simultaneously.

Dawn grabbed my arm and yelled for Jesus.

I grabbed the wheel and swerved hard and fast to my left, knowing that seconds ago there was another car in that lane.

I practically dug holes into the steering wheel with my fingers.

Swerve! BANG! Swerve!

Silence.

No crash. No horns. Silence.

I EXHALED. Somehow, in that life-threatening instant, God must have parted that highway like the Red Sea. Not only did I dodge the dolly, but all the cars behind me did as well. I had swerved into the left lane without incident between two other cars. The dolly smacked down onto the pavement exactly where my car had been, creating a trench of a hole. It then bounced high into the air and came down once again. Then, miraculously, without hitting the median itself, I swerved again back into the center lane.

I glanced around us on the highway.

Cars everywhere.

Absolutely everywhere.

I don't comprehend how it was possible that we (and everyone else) survived this incident. But, I do know one thing for certain: That morning, I was having a lousy day. But then I dodged death—and I can't imagine what could have possibly been such a big deal.

Dawn and I were so excited to enter our home and tell Kaysie all about the miracle. But Kaysie was still sprawled out on the floor in pain. Our lives had been saved.

But her tragedy had not changed one bit.

◉ ◉ ◉

Charlie, on the other hand, is far more resilient than we are. Take now, for instance. Charlie is sick. He is coming down with something, possibly the flu. But where you or I or anyone else with the flu would fall into a vegetative coma on the couch, Charlie lies on the floor and builds things. As I mentioned before, Charlie's love-language is dirt. But dirt is only available in the spring through the fall. In the winter, dirt is replaced with something else.

Legos.

Charlie is a master builder of Legos. He builds vehicles, architecture, *Star Wars* villains, contraptions, Machu Picchu, you name it. Even now, when he can barely lift his head off of the floor, Charlie takes bricks from a large pile to his right, builds, then places the constructed entity in a new pile to his left. He is an assembly line of fun.

Because Charlie not only refuses to play dead.

Charlie plays alive.

Where lately, I look at my living moments and somehow play possum, Charlie looks at a dead situation and wills it back to life. He is his own CPR. Yes, he has a high fever. Yes, he can hardly keep his eyes open, but Charlie is filled with faith. It isn't because Charlie believes the best will happen. It is because Charlie believes he can make whatever happens into the best.

CHARLIE: Whadda ya doing, Daddy?

ME: *I'm making the swords for your knight party.*

CHARLIE: Is da party gonna be at night?

ME: *No, the people at the party are going to turn into knights.*

CHARLIE: Gweat. Wook what I made.

ME: *What is it?*

CHARLIE: Da Taj Mahal. Are you making dose swords weawy sharp?

ME: *No. Not at all.*

CHARLIE: Den how will we win da fight?

ME: *We'll make other rules. Mom and I thought it would be best if your friends didn't leave your party mortally wounded.*

CHARLIE: Aw wight. Are dose shields weal metal?

ME: *They're cardboard and aluminum.*

CHARLIE: Sweeeeet. Daddy will you pway wid me?

ME: *Sure. Pray about what?*

CHARLIE: I wanna tell God dat I DO NOT want to be sick on my birfday.

ME: *Of course I'll pray—but He knows that.*

CHARLIE: Then why am I sick wight now?

ME: *To get it over with.*

And I find myself feeling awfully sad. That is a very good question. Why is he sick right now? I mean, why even make him bother with the stress of it? Why make a four-year-old (five next week) wonder if he's going to miss his own party? It seems so simple to stop and so cruel not to. Of course, it could be the party itself that makes him sick. Growing up, this is how Kaysie's body responded to anticipation. Impending fun always wore her out. She would get sick. So very sick. As a matter of fact, I feel even now that when something special is coming, she is afraid that someone will fall ill.

Maybe that's why we've made days like today less special each year. The less we anticipate an event, the better chance we will be well enough to enjoy it.

⊙ ◉ ◉

By the time we are finished working on the party, it is time to put the kids to bed and as Charlie is not feeling well, he needs to sleep on the floor of our bedroom.

So much for Valentine's Day.

It's probably for the best. After all, we are both exhausted. We decide I should just go pick up some dinner. Maybe we'll get the chance to celebrate the holiday another night.

We decide on sushi.

And, *Lord of the Rings.*

It doesn't feel like Valentine's.

We might as well pretend it isn't.

I step out to the car and am startled by the bitterness of the chill, which burns my lungs as I inhale. The forecast is for snow again. So bitter. So dark. The sun sets early and I can feel the clouds closing around us. The once-green grass snaps like a twig under my boot. Except for the smell of logs burning in fireplaces, this might as well be a ghost town.

I look into the sky, which, a few months ago, caused me to gasp at the grandeur of God's creation; now, I feel very alone. I wonder if the romance—not the love, mind you—but the romance between Kaysie and I is fading. But then I realize that the romance would be there—if only I were.

It is me.

I am fading.

Not my love.

My sanity.

And I don't know how it started.

A freight train barrels through my head and my heart leaving gaping holes and everything is trickling out: my memory, my confidence, my happiness, patience, peace. Where is it all going? What am I supposed to do to plug it up, and do I want to? Because if I just plug it up, then what is lost is still LOST and I am left only with what didn't quite make it down the drain.

All across this neighborhood, a hundred special someones are celebrating their love. But I stand here alone, uncertain of who I am anymore. It is a dark day. I clutch the collar of my coat as the clouds roll in. This sounds familiar.

Oh yes. My Bible-in-a-year reading assignment. Today, I'm at Exodus 19 and 20: the Ten Commandments. All the "how-tos" God gave so that His people would remember Him. That mention of the cloud was in chapter 19:

> GOD said to Moses, "Get ready. I'm about to come to you with a thick cloud so that the people can listen in and trust you completely when I speak to you."[†]

Is this what my winter is for? Though I see only confusion and despair, could God be hemming me in from all four directions so that I can step out of the chaos and become refined by His voice? I suppose a thick cloud would seem pretty dark—but it would also provide the padding of proof that He is here. And what was that other verse, I'd read?

> Moses spoke to the people: "Don't be afraid. God has come to test you and instill a deep and reverent awe within you so that you won't sin." The people kept their distance while Moses approached the thick cloud where God was[††]

So that's it.

I see the dark cloud.

I sense that it is filled with testing.

And I want to keep my distance.

I continue to resist while God expects me to approach.

It can be no coincidence that my New Testament reading today is Jesus' darkest hour. Matthew 27 chronicles the crucifixion. My reading began with the soldiers shoving a crown of thorns on Jesus' head and ended with Jesus crying

---

† Exodus 19:9

†† Exodus 20:20–21

loudly and breathing His last. It was the ultimate revelation of love. The resurrection of Christ revealed His power.

But the torture—the despair, the death—they prove His love.

I have no idea what is about to unfold over the next twelve months. I have no way of knowing that Charlie will experience overwhelming challenges and that his challenges will foreshadow the darkness I will myself experience. I have no idea that it is going to feel like a death around here. But, without knowing this, I am still able to realize that God is even now enshrouding me in a thick cloud, dark though it may seem.

At times, it will feel like abandonment because I will try to cling rather than let go. I only know enough right now to realize that I must commit something.

A living will.

That whatever is left of me after this impending death—will all go to God.

But, I do not know.

That Charlie would indeed be sick for his birthday.

And for the entire summer.

That I would be required to stare darkness in the face multiple times.

That my fears would be dug up and exposed.

That Kaysie and I would be faced with the choice to fight for one another.

Or run.

Had I known, we might have taken the opportunity to celebrate Valentine's Day—to celebrate our affection while it was still readily on display. Instead, I steady myself for the coming battle, having no idea that I am readying an aluminum foil sword to attack a dragon filled with a lot more than Tootsie Rolls.

But, right now, raw fish and hobbits await.

I button my coat tightly and steel myself for the thick clouds that are moving in faster than I expected.

SIX DECISIONS THAT MATTERED

decision #2:

SELFISH / SELFLESS

I never considered myself a selfish person because most of the thoughts I had about me were negative. It never dawned on me that my obsession with thinking poorly of myself never allowed any time to focus on others. To this end, I was the very definition of selfish: consumed with nothing but the capital I. Every life has a trajectory, an arrow, and mine was pointed directly at my sternum. I have determined that this not only feels lousy, but it is what the enemy of my soul most wants: for me to never broaden my focus outwardly enough to notice that there are plenty of things out there that would change me for the better, if I would only notice them. Those things, by the way, are people. But I have instead been consistently trapped in the current state of "me" and all the disappointments inherent. I have focused there, dwelled there. So overwhelmed with what I currently am or am not that I have refused to lift my eyes and see a world hurting all around me. A mission waiting to be accomplished. A mandate I have long ignored. Because I cannot see what God is doing through me if the arrow of my attention never points all the way through. I have navel-gazed for most of my adult life. Worried about my future. Despairing about my failure. Hopeful about my dreams. Angry about my hurts. At some point, I have to realize that I am not the point of my arrow. So I now turn the arrow the other direction. Extroverted. And I see for the first time that there are many waiting to be healed not only by seeing what I do right but by hearing what I have done wrong. And how somewhere in the collision of the two,

I am no longer the one

aiming my own

arrow.

THREE SPRING FEVERS

EASTER

We Christians are pretty freaky when you think about it. Our biggest celebration of the year revolves around the historic torture and murder of our Savior. I do not say this to be morbid. The resurrection of Christ is the single-most pivotal event in the history of humanity. I say it to point out the irony. Here we are, celebrating the conquering of sin through death, while we do anything we can to avoid the topic of death itself. Jesus' death makes us celebrate. The idea of our own makes us uncomfortable.

Why?

Do we not believe that Christ really conquered its eternal power?

The truth is: We like to cling. We like what we like and we don't want it to change, so we grab and squeeze at it desperately, never completely aware that every moment we clutch to keep what is around us, we insinuate that we don't believe what God has for us is actually better. We are afraid of death because we are afraid of losing control.

Every Easter (and Christmas, for that matter) for the past fifteen years, I have directed a passion play. Some years, I have directed several. And so I love Easter, but I also tend to view it as work.

I have certainly worked on my share of passion plays. I trained youth and mission groups for eight years to take a drama out that portrayed an allegory of Christ's life and death through toys and their maker. In a professional international tour of the same story, I was the narrator—God Himself, if you will.

For six years, I produced and directed one of those big arena epic, gladiator-style Jesus reenactments that included live animals, explosions, and vocal soloists. One of the years, the vocal soloist was Bob Carlisle and the live animals had lice.

Please don't confuse the two or "Butterfly Kisses" takes on a whole new meaning. This was the same season where I worked for a production company that required their male employees to grow hair and beards to the exact length of any one of the twelve disciples (longest hair: Peter; shortest hair: Thomas). As this was the early nineties, we looked like a Mötley Crüe cover band.

The audience members who witnessed these multimedia spectaculars were moved. However, those of us putting on the presentation had to fight to remain awake. Inevitably, every year we would need to construct the entire set and rehearse the show all in one evening's time. From Saturday at 9 p.m. to Sunday morning at 8 a.m., we would do nothing but carve Styrofoam chunks into Golgotha and teach volunteer church kids to wave palm branches in syncopation with the *Via Dolorosa*. We wanted to truly absorb the meaning of what we were doing, but had built a schedule so tight, we were able to do nothing but shove our way through the details. It is challenging to herd people while illustrating worship. You find yourself saying the strangest things:

> STOP! You three in the back of the crowd! Can you tone it down? You're worshipping Jesus a little too much.

> The verse to this song is only forty-five seconds. You centurions are going to have to get Jesus on that cross a lot faster than that.

> More blood! We need two more buckets of blood on Jesus' back.

> There's too much smoke coming out of the tomb. It looks like the Peter Frampton Alive Tour.

It was also a technical nightmare. This was never more evident than the year the actor who played Jesus (who also happened to be my boss at the time) was hooked into his harness onto the cross only to discover that the harness had not been secured at the right length. As the minister waxed eloquent and we saw the look on our boss' face, we realized that the harness was not holding him up, but rather the metal brackets that held his wrists in place to appear nailed were. The actor was actually being crucified. His wails could be heard from the back row of the 10,000 seat arena, but his comments were whispered. Sternly.

HIM:	Get me down!
ME:	*I think that would send the wrong message.*
HIM:	I can't breathe!
ME:	*You've got that half-inch of balsa to stand on. That should bring some relief.*
HIM:	How much longer?!
ME:	*He was almost done preaching, but your screams were so chilling, he branched off into a fourth point about the history of Jeremiah.*
HIM:	OOOH GOD!
ME:	*Good. Stay in character.*
HIM:	I. Can't. Breathe.
ME:	*About that raise…*
HIM:	AHHHHHHHH!

Best. Altar call. Ever.

There were scenes where the disciples were supposed to be asleep. This was the biggest challenge of the presentation because the disciples were also the crew, who had been awake all night. Many wives sent prayers up to heaven that at least two of the disciples would awaken in time to see Christ emerge from the smoke machine behind that prop rock.

This was how I experienced Easter for years.

Loving Jesus deeply.

But going through the habitual motions instead of truly experiencing the greatest moment in all history.

This year we have decided to change it up. Our pastor, Roger, asked my best friend Jason and I (he is the youth pastor and I am the college pastor) to take a new approach to our church's dramatic Good Friday and Easter presentations. Instead of making it about crosses, we will make it about tombs.

Our own tombs.

I live in a town that has seen the passion story done to death. We have seen *what Jesus did* on Easter dramatized a hundred times. But we have not seen *how that personally affects each of us.*

On Good Friday, Jason put together a stations of the cross experiential walk-through—an artistic five-senses interactive process where each attendee could pause and contemplate every detail of Christ's final hours. And on Sunday morning, we decided to illustrate our own tombs and reveal how Christ's death and resurrection cracked each one wide open. We also have a wildcard thrown in. In order to truly illustrate how Christ's resurrection breaks us out of our tombs, we have four different testimonies this morning. People we have known for years. Or—as most of the church is about to discover—people we only thought we knew.

I am a firm believer that the tomb that enshrines us most deeply is the fear of others knowing our stuff. Our garbage. The enemy does his best to convince us that if anyone ever knew the real truth, we would be unloved. What we are not so quick to discover is that there is power and healing in our story. Being truly known leads us to truth and clarity. This is how the power of sin is broken.

It is how stones are rolled away.

This morning, that will happen for four members of our church.

Just like it happened for me a year ago.

Among other things, my first book *Flashbang* delved deeply into my personal issues. Of the many it addressed, the most secret was my addiction to pornography. This was not an issue that I wanted revealed to my church friends when they read the book and so when it was released, my pastor asked me to preach on the subject. I revealed my story to those I held dear, though I was deeply concerned about how their new honest perspective of me would change things.

And it did change things.

But not at all in the way I expected.

Many of us had been a part of churches where each person did their best to cover up what they had done wrong in their lives and, instead, present a lily-white illusion. But our church was becoming a place of honesty. A place of vulnerability and accountability.

Others began to come forward with their own sin, and the church and the community were there for them. Now, as painful as it continues to be, we are a community of believers who understand that life can only be lived truthfully, warts and all. No more hiding, but instead becoming healed through leaning on those who are going through the same mess.

This morning's Easter presentation—these testimonies—are a direct result of all that. So, I am excited for those who are about to share. But, I am also a little hesitant. Though I experienced pats on the back after I shared my struggle, there were other ramifications. I had to deal with my history. Yes, victory has been a substantial part of my journey. God has given me the accountability and tools to fight against my proclivity toward sin in a way that makes Him proud. But, I have come to the conclusion that it will never be easy. My issues will remain a wrestling match for life. I don't get to announce my sin and then assume it a closed door.

So, my problem became public. And with publicity came attention.

This has caused some tension in our marriage. In the past, my issue had been something Kaysie and I rarely had to process together; suddenly it was the talk of the town. The collision of my past and present were instantly unavoidable. The debate and discussion that followed daily ripped open scars and made it very difficult to heal. This is where we are now.

Raw.

Kaysie is my biggest supporter, but I don't think I fully understand the damage I have done to her. It is ironic that now, when I am doing better, we find ourselves struggling to connect and forgive. I asked a friend of mine if he shared some of my struggles:

Of course I do. But, I'm not stupid enough to write about it.

⊙ ⊙ ◉

The kids began the morning by opening their Easter baskets—yet another way we turn God's suffering into our own accumulation of knickknacks. Easter baskets were a very big thing for me growing up. It was that one big-ticket item that sustained me between Christmas and my summer birthday. We would get the Peter Cottontail stop-motion-animation TV special and encore viewings of both *Jesus of Nazareth* and *The Ten Commandments*. These days, we're lucky if we get a *Sister Act* marathon on the USA Network.

And of course, Saturday evening. Memories of haircuts and new, stiffer collars on pastel-colored shirts. I would always struggle sleeping the evening before Easter because of the year I turned four. We spent that Saturday Easter Eve at a motel and at midnight, I was the only one awake as a man dressed in an enormous bunny outfit hopped by our sliding glass door. I'm certain now that this was an amenity of the hotel—a way to stir up belief in the children who were renting rooms. But, it was kind of freaky. *Donnie Darko* freaky. Haven't been a big fan of the Easter bunny since.

This does not insinuate that I wasn't perfectly happy receiving Easter baskets. I was hesitant. But, this was because Easter candy was a real crapshoot for me. For instance, the chocolate rabbit? I lived and breathed to receive one of those babies. But the yellow marshmallow chicks? Just dip me in black plague instead, won't you? I was coerced as a toddler to try one of those suckers and slap me silly if it did not usher in the concept of gag reflex.

One of my favorite and most shocking Easter gifts was the year that I awoke to discover a basket filled to the brim with Dunkin' Donut munchkins: the little doughnut holes that one could buy in bushels. I was so excited, I refused to open it until after church.

This is one of the many dysfunctions of the way I am built. I love to receive things, but I want them to remain pure and untouched for as long as possible. I love to stare at the pretty packaging of the freshly wrapped DVD. I know from experience that the moment I open up that basket, seemingly full of hundreds of doughy nuggets, I will realize that the hidden bottom half is a cardboard platform deceiving me into thinking the visible good stuff above the rim continues below the surface. But right now, it looks so awesome, so bursting with glazed goodness.

I left it on my desk until after church. Sadly, the sun shone in hard through that window and by the time I got home and pulled off the cellophane, the munchkins had merged with the Easter grass. The contents of the basket were no longer edible. This does not mean that I did not try. I sucked sugar and wheat off of strands of plastic for the remainder of the day—simultaneously snacking and flossing.

So another pattern in my life is revealed:

> Hope for the best (a good Easter basket).
>
> When I get the best, expect it to be the worst version of the best (a few treats on a cardboard façade).
>
> Delay opening the best, lest my expectations be confirmed.
>
> When I finally open the best, it has become the worst.

Why, why, why do I do this?

These days, this pattern has nothing to do with Easter baskets. It mostly affects my relationships. Take my friend Jason, for example. He has been having a bit of a hard go at things lately. He's deeply unsatisfied with where he has progressed in life, and he's uncertain what the next step should be.

Now, I have been in this same place many times and Jason is always there for me. But lately, as he has communicated his crisis, I just haven't known what to say. Because I hear his pain and I understand what he needs. But, I don't like the answer. Because the only thing that seems to make sense in the back of my mind is the worst-case scenario.

That he must leave.

That he and his wife, Sarah, must move away and begin again.

But this doesn't work.

I mean, it works for them, but it doesn't work for the universe.

Because it doesn't work for me.

I'm dead serious.

I know it's selfish. But, what I need more than anything else right now is for something SOMETHING that I know I can trust to STAY! I need at least one oasis, and the dog already died.

Jason and I worked together a bit this past week, and I would have to say that our relationship has become a bit strained. I cannot help but know why. Because I am imagining the worst. I know the elephant in the room. He knows the elephant in the room. And we each know the other knows it.

But I am finding myself unable to let go. I find myself praying for them to stay instead of praying for God's plan to be made clear. And worst of all, I do not pray this believing it is the right thing for him. I pray it believing it is the easiest thing for me.

◉ ◉ ◉

The spotlight is hitting me.

How much time has passed? Are we already starting the rehearsal?

Myself and the four other actors on stage begin to break into Greek-chorus style musings on what each of us would call our character's "tomb," the thing that holds us underground, keeps us from truly living. Each of us symbolizes an issue that, void of God's intervention, feels like the bitter end. Each character is given a number instead of a name. I am number two.

The tombs are (in order of performance):

Divorce.

Me.

Addiction.

Abuse.

Aloneness.

What is my tomb?

Death.

In my monologue, I play a man who has lost the love of his life. It has been a year since she died and he is still unable to take her clothes out of the closet. He ruminates on the unfairness of it all—that some who deserve much more are allowed to live while others waste away. The character's pain is unbearable and finally becomes a plea, a wish for someone to fill the void. But not just anyone.

The One.

All of these monologues and diatribes lead to the characters discovering that there is One who heals our pain and fills our heartbreak. These answers come primarily from the four testimonies:

> A couple who divorced, later discovering they are attending the same church and remarrying.
>
> A former addict who had successfully progressed through the church's recovery program and is now counseling others.
>
> A woman who was abused all her life until she found her solace in her heavenly Father and finally married a good man.
>
> A pastor who had lost his wife to cancer, grieved, and found new love all over again later in life.

And I realized that each had the same recurring theme: God opened their tombs, yes, but in each case, He did it through other people.

Kaysie and I had felt on display after coming clean with my struggles—like freaks ogled for a dime in the trailer parked next to the tilt-a-whirl—but it was in the coming clean that we allowed others to participate in our healing, and we became a part of their healing at the same time.

Painful? Yes.

Every single time it is spoken of.

Every single time it is addressed.

Every single time ground is lost and, yes, even when ground is gained.

The weight of our issues continues to press upon us, but the knowledge of those issues by our community has lifted some of the weight off. This has never been more clear than right now.

I stand, finishing the performance as I look out across the sea of faces (or in the case of our church, a small lake). They are not standing and cheering as one might applaud a light show with jets of smoke shooting out of a Styrofoam façade. Instead, they are changed. They see people they thought they knew in a different, truer context. This was not expected. The deepest struggles of life made known.

Suddenly church is unsafe.

It is no longer the best spot to hide.

Suddenly it's the place to stop playing dead.

It is unsettling.

And unsettling could make all the difference.

I congratulate the team of actors, dancers, and musicians and head home for the best part of the day: friends and family gathering for dinner. Kaysie and Dawn have been slaving over approximately thirty-eight courses for the last three days. This is what ladies from the South do. A holiday lunch is a feast of gargantuan proportions. There will be four salads, eight or nine sides, and at least three desserts.

Forget doughnut holes merged with plastic grass, Kaysie is making my favorite dessert: a sour-cream-chocolate cake with a white chocolate frosting that is impossible to describe. It tastes like the beginning of "Where the Streets Have No Name" sounds. The live version. It leaps for joy and throws its crutches to the ground in my mouth. I cannot prove this. You will simply have to come try some next year.

Our day will be filled with events that ring of religiosity:

1. Stuffing our faces.
2. Searching for eggs that contain sugar or money.
3. Watching *National Treasure* on DVD.

But the greatest thing about today is that friends will be with us and time will otherwise stop. Easter and Christmas are two of approximately four days a year that clients will not attempt to call.

One of my coworkers, Jeff, will be with us, as will Jason and Sarah and Kaysie's parents Dawn and Bill. My brother Dav will come by with Laura and the three boys after having lunch with her folks, and Dawn is bringing a woman from church, Miss Martha, who has been battling cancer.

Kaysie and I have a concern.

Kaysie's dad has been a part of the festivities of this day, and it has been hard on him because he has also just been diagnosed. The cancer he faced years ago is back. We are standing with him in this battle, but we know the battle is getting to him. And now, this day, this Easter Sunday normally filled with life, is a constant reminder to him of the threat of death. As much as I know Bill would like to ignore the issue, he is being bombarded with it. But Kaysie and I know that it cannot—and should not—be ignored.

Based on my life experience, I don't know why and when God heals and why and when He doesn't. I do know that my idea of healing is skewed and, just like my unspoken argument with Jason, has more to do with what I want than with what is right.

Everything dies. And for each of us, it could be now or much much later, but either way, something has to be—MUST BE—done about fear.

The crippling fear.

For me, that fear has always been the threat of change—the idea that something bad could not only happen but also bring a finality that does not fit in with my plans. I do not subscribe to the theory that God is looking for a magic healing formula to come out of our hearts and mouths before we are healed. I do believe that His deepest desire is for each of us to know Him well—and that in the knowing, to find peace and understanding in His outcome. That may be a healed body and it may not.

It is all so confusing. Susan's son Logan died of cancer.

Matt's mother just died of cancer.

Kaysie's college roommate Amy just died of cancer.

It is everywhere, and it is daunting, and it makes us very, very afraid because it is a word that rings of finality.

Cancer.

We are so quick to panic when we hear the word is in our bodies.

But it is already eating away our hearts and minds.

The most crippling cancers are fear and doubt—cancers that you and I deal with every day. They chew away at hope, spitting it out onto the ground. I remember Matt's mother at the bitter end. Her body was riddled with the disease, but her hope was sustained. Her trust in God the Father immeasurable. She left this world in great peace, free from the worst cancer of all—the cancer that most of us, including myself, continue to fight. At the time of her death, she was not held captive by anything except for her frailed earthly body. She was free. Freer and more healed than anyone I know right this moment who enjoys perfect bodily health.

Because we each remain diseased by what holds us captive.

This is the real tomb.

Not death itself.

But a life of despair.

And many who are physically dying continue to face this emotional death. For them, the final hours are ones of panic.

My own heart and mind are not at peace. It's like Gideon's army raging inside of me. I confuse myself by thinking that my goal is to make the good side of the battle stronger than the bad side, when actually what I need to do is weed the bad side out.

I know this because Judges 7 and 8 was today's Bible reading. Not necessarily a party book of the Bible, but enlightening nonetheless. These chapters chronicle Gideon's attempts to move on and fight the enemy—but God keeps whittling his army down. Gideon assumes what I do: that in order to win the battle, I need all-hands-on-deck. But to Gideon, God says, "No. You need best-hands-on-deck." So God proceeds to whittle Gideon's army down from thousands upon thousands to only three hundred. And how does He whittle? By cleaning house of anyone who was afraid or even the slightest bit hesitant. God considers an army of three hundred confident in Him much stronger than a multitude with commitment issues.

Now, three hundred people certainly do not seem capable of winning a battle. After all, in the film of the same name, they were all slaughtered to the tune of a prog-rock soundtrack. But to God, strength is measured by the neutering of fear and doubt in our lives. Because God knows that this cancer has no place in our fight for life. In fact, fear and doubt are the very road to death. Even worse, they turn the living into the walking dead.

But as my other reading today states:

> *"Put your mind on your life with God. The way to life—to God!—is vigorous and requires your total attention."*[†]

To Jesus, this is serious business and He does not pander. He makes no bones about the fact that the road to Him is not easy. Why? Because God wants to make it difficult? No.

Because the obstacles are numerous and will try to destroy us.

We panic when we think of losing our physical life.

But there is a much worse death already at work.

And we must fight it with everything inside of us.

We must choose God's army.

We must whittle what does not belong completely away.

Jason, Dav, Jeff, and I scramble about the yard, searching for nooks and crevices to hide eggs. The older the children get, the more difficult this task. Not only because the kids are getting better at searching, but also because we are running out of hiding spots they have not already uncovered. We fill some eggs with coupons good for family events like movie night or a trip to the chaotic pizza arcade joint that is probably a lot like the employee break room in hell. We put coins in a few, and jelly beans or chocolate in most.

I do not realize it now, but I will find this same chocolate egg I hold in my hand almost eight months from now. I love chocolate, but when I find this egg, I will want nothing to do with it, because it will be putrid, rotting, and filled with insects. A great thing hidden so long that it goes terribly wrong.

This is what God is requiring of my life. Where I would prefer to lay back and stare at the same hiding place declaring, "Hey God, here's that fear and doubt I keep seeing; fix it again," He would prefer that I move diligently from searching one hiding place on to hunting down the craftier crevices. He longs for me to get better and better at exposing my shortcomings to Him so that after a while I am so aware of my flaws, there are no hiding places left. And as for the good things that lay dormant? He wants me to keep an eagle eye out for them as well, constantly surrendering them—submitting them to His plan.

The kids have a field day and are each completely stoked at their sugar bounty, so we move them inside and begin watching the charming story of Nicholas Cage destroying patriotic tourist locales. As the kids sit and watch, the adults reconvene for dessert.

There is an announcement to be made. I steady myself. I am certain that the announcement is going to come from Bill or Dawn. Bill more than likely wants prayer for his malady and this is a great group to stand with in agreement. But, it is not Bill who has the announcement. It is Jason. He has been accepted to a school in Wilmore, Kentucky, where he will get his Masters in Divinity, paving the way for him to pastor his own church in a town far far away from here.

They are leaving.

It is final.

And instantly, I feel myself start slapping wet cement on the bricks. I'm like Charlie with his Legos. How high and how wide can I make this wall? I don't know what to do. This relationship I had invested so much time and energy and honesty and vulnerability into—is all about to disappear. All I know is that in this trying time, I have looked for an opportunity for Jason to be the same person I usually shared my struggles with, but something had been off.

This whole time, Jason had been searching for an answer to what was wrong. And the answer is leaving.

I ask when.

JASON: May 19.

ME: *May 19? That's Bill's surgery. That's only four weeks from now.*

JASON: I know. I'm sorry. It's when summer school starts.

ME: *Summer school? What happened to starting in the fall?*

JASON: We know it's the right thing to do.

Jason and Sarah live behind our house. We share a fence. We had assumed this would cause us to spend every waking moment together, but it has actually caused us to make time for everyone except one another. We were each other's default. We would always be here. Right here. Not only in proximity, but truly understanding the other, having all the answers. Ironically, this caused us to drift.

But, we knew it would always right itself.

Because we were right here.

Right here.

But not any more.

Two weeks ago, Jeff directed a video for our company that was laden with special effects. In it, a group of people are gathered on the streets of a large city filled with skyscrapers. As they go about their business, there is a faint, distant rumbling. One by one, holes appear in the ground. The people are swallowed whole. Cracks and crevices make their way across roads that had seemed safe. Windows begin to burst. Buildings begin to crumble.

The ground alone is not all that opens up. The entire world around them begins to implode, collapsing in on itself. Most are buried alive. Only a handful remain. In the end, they are left alone on a small island amid nothing but devastation. They look to the ground and see that, though the foundation had seemed solid, there was something brewing for a long time under the surface, slowly rising, ready to take each of them to their doom. They were left with next to nothing.

The video was a big hit.

And as I sit, stunned by the news, I see our guests embracing Jason and Sarah and wishing them congratulations. I look to Bill and see that he is distracted by hopelessness. I gaze at Kaysie and see tears in her eyes.

I can't be completely certain, but I vaguely hear the sound of something beginning to crumble deep down beneath my feet.

LAST DAY OF SCHOOL

Ah, impending summer.

I haven't had a three-month-long break since my junior year of college and yet I get excited all the same at the change of seasons. My kids can taste it—the end of another phase of learning leading directly into a well-deserved break. It hangs in the air. Summer means fun. Swimming. Movies. Parties. Vacations. Family time. Taking my shirt off without people screaming.

I have a thing for halfway, and summer is the perfect example. The uphill climb from January to May is a real pill, so I should be allowed a good ninety days to prep for the final push from September to December.

When I was young, summer meant trips to Florida. I grew up in Atlanta, and my aunt owns a place on Lake Butler in Windermere, a stone's throw from Orlando. We would drive down often and either do the parks or the beach. And I loved the beach. The undulation of the waves was so foreign, so other-worldly. It would transport me away from whatever lousy thing awaited onshore.

As an adult, time off in the summer has always been scarce at best, but we have managed to find ways to take the kids to some very cool places. One of the best spots we have ever taken the family is the Rocky Mountains. We ventured there a few years back with all of our camping gear and decided we would rough it for a few days in the wild.

When we arrived at our camping site, we were not disappointed. We had been assigned the furthest spot back, at the very tip of the woods. Woods that went on for miles and miles and miles. I knew Charlie would take one look at those woods and want to explore them.

I was a big explorer growing up—of course the only territory available was the one square block near my home that had not yet been turned into neighborhoods. And all we ever found there was the big rock where high school kids fornicated. At least that's what our church called it. Once I forged all the way through the brush to the other side of the neighborhood and discovered tennis courts. For a moment, I thought I was the first to unearth them.

But this! This was the Rocky Mountains! If we were to go exploring, who knows what we would find! A family of cougars, fossilized remains of mosquitoes containing T-Rex DNA, Desmond in the Dharma Swan Station—the possibilities were endless.

Oh, you don't want to do that.

It was the park ranger speaking.

ME:	*Of course I want to do that.*
RANGER:	I'll bet you do, Marshmallow, but once you get your spongy backside into that brush and lose sight of your tents, you won't know where the sam hill you are, and then you'll start screaming for Mama Ranger.
ME:	*I'm sorry. Are you a woman?*
RANGER:	Takes one to know one, Strawberry Shortcake. Once you get into the denseness of those trees, discombobulation sets in.
ME:	*Discombobulation?*
RANGER:	Look it up, Pansy Camp. You can't tell one direction from another. People get lost in there forever and whatnot.
ME:	*Well, that can't be good.*
RANGER:	Are you smart aleck'n me, Fudge Drawers? You best not let your young'ns wander. That there woods is a dark place, and once they set foot in, they might never come out.
ME:	*I'm sorry I've upset you, Miss.*
RANGER:	You cry and I'll slap you like fire.

She made me feel all shiny inside.

This was unexpected. Lucky me. I was the one who had the pleasure of informing Charlie that his dream trek would be canceled. Those woods out there? Those really awesome, attractive woods that you've drooled over in photos and are now a few inches from your feet? You can't go there. It's too dangerous. The unknown lives inside of them and we can't have that now, can we?

Charlie was, of course, devastated. There would be no crossing the line into the wilderness. So instead, he broke a branch off a tree and stood at the edge of the woods, as close as he could possibly get to the brush surrounding us.

And he paced.

Back and forth.

Back and forth.

Back and forth.

He looked like Moses unsure of what to do about this Red Sea. The woods were calling him and he could not answer.

◉ ◎ ◉

Summer is calling for Charlie. I know he is excited because he is asking if he can get on my shoulders—and as he asks me, he is already scaling my back and positioning himself atop Mount Father.

Charlie loves to sit on my shoulders. He requires, however, that I raise my arms and support his back as I do so. While I support, he rocks his body to and fro. It's a lot like holding a pummel horse over my head while a Russian wins gold. Slightly uncomfortable.

I cannot complain though. Because I carry Charlie on my shoulders so often, sometimes I forget he is there and I neglect to duck as I walk through doorways.

SMACK! Daaaaaad!

OHP! Sorry, big'n. You forgot to duck.

Big'n is one of the many masculine nicknames I have orchestrated for my sons. My dad used to call me *doodlebug* and I will not put my children through anything that humiliating. Instead, I have a list of acceptable names for each child:

MORGAN:	JACKSON:
Sweetness	Big'n
Princess	Big Man
Babydoll	J-Dude
Morgy Skorgy	J-Rock
Morgantua	Jacksonian
Morgoogly	Jack-a-lackin!

CHARLIE:
Big'n
Big Dude
Chachi
Chooch
Choochy
Chockochownin

Yeah. Much better than doodlebug.

CHARLIE: Stank! Dad, YOU fowgot to duck!

ME: *I'm already carrying you! Do I also have to be the one to remember to dodge all the doorjambs?!*

CHARLIE: Apowogize.

ME: *What?!*

CHARLIE: Apowogize fow hitting my head.

ME: *YOU hit your head! I'm hurt too. Every time you pull back on my neck, that place where I fell through the ceiling starts KILLING me!*

CHARLIE: Jesus wants you to apowogize.

It is the final night of Legacy, the home school co-op that my wife put together with a number of her friends. They meet every Wednesday and give all of the kids a classroom experience with each mom taking turns teaching subjects. This year, Kaysie taught history and creative writing while other moms taught everything from art to Latin. All in all, a brilliant idea, but extremely taxing on my already maxed-out wife.

Tonight, we get to see what they have been learning. I believe there is a dramatic presentation prepared to teach us about the planets. I'm certain something will be recited in Latin. We will see an art show and perhaps a living organism they have created out of their own DNA and toothpaste. When it is said and done, all of the children of our household will be FREE from their schoolwork for practically 100 days straight.

This is, officially, the greatest feeling in the world.

I think our planet would be much happier if everyone took the summer off. Like a yearly siesta, only moved up earlier due to daylight savings time. No one would make any money, but that's okay because for those three months—follow me here—everyone in a community would share everything. It would cause people to work harder the other nine months of the year to stock up their assignment. One family could be the bread team while another breeds cattle to slaughter around the Fourth of July. It would be great fun, because not only would we all get some rest, but we would be forced to interact—to get to know one another.

I see my kids running around the building screaming. They have so much pent up joy and anticipation. That, and they've each had a sip of my double espresso. I long for them to have the sort of summer experiences I embraced. Exploring the world with my bicycle. Meeting new friends. Attending that open-air concert where Mylon LeFevre forgot every word to every song he had ever written. Swimming after the sun had long since gone down. Being creative at my desk typewriter until I realized an entire day had passed. Getting stranded on a sandbar.

Oh yes. I forgot about that one.

I was twelve. Our family was in Bradenton and a friend and I decided to see if we were strong enough to swim out to a sandbar off shore. We dared each other to summon the courage, and the next thing you know, we were huffing and puffing, out in the water. Way, way out. I remember being concerned at the point of no return where we were exhausted, but closer to our destination than we were to our point of origin. It was that exhilarating sensation that sweeps over you when you realize that you may just surprise yourself and succeed. We made it all the way to the sandbar and decided to build some sandcastles there, where no one else could bother us. For at least an hour, it was our island. Population: two.

I want my kids to experience adventure. I want them to have this thing that I currently lack. This anticipation towards tomorrow. Bursting at the seams with potential—hungry for the next challenge. Crazy with vigor for anything and everything that is labeled "next."

Me? Still stuck.

I know. It seems like same book, next chapter. I have made great attempts. I really have, and though I am finding more and more windows of optimism and joy, some key things continue to linger: the lack of confidence, the muddled thinking, the anxiety, the anger, and of course, the physical pain.

It is getting worse. This doesn't make a lot of sense to me. It seems that this far removed from the fall—almost a year now—I should be feeling less pain. I've ignored it for eleven months. Shouldn't it be getting easier to ignore? And then, there is the new problem.

I cannot sleep.

I mean, I sleep a little here and there, but I don't ever feel like I have truly slept. There is a window: the middle of the night—2:37 a.m. to be exact—where I find myself the most riddled with anxiety, stress, and the previous day's details ravaging across me like bullet holes from an Uzi. I cannot get my mind to settle. And I am so sick of it.

I want to enjoy life.

I want to swim out to the sandbar.

I want to step across the line into the woods.

I want to run and laugh just like Charlie is doing right now in this hallway.

WHA-SLAM!

Charlie's legs come out from under him. They swing up, bringing him almost parallel to the floor, hovering in midair.

And then …

Headfirst into the concrete floor.

There is complete silence. Everyone in the room hesitates to breathe.

Screeeeeeeeeeeeeeeam!

I rush to Charlie. Kaysie breaks into a sprint. We cradle him. Our first instinct is relief as we see no blood. But then, we see it growing. Underneath the surface of the back of his head what appears to be a hard-boiled egg is rising. It is enormous, and there seems to be blood captured beneath it. His eyes get foggy. Something is definitely wrong. We rush him out the door and to the emergency room. The school year is suddenly over.

That second day in the Rocky Mountains, we took a long hike after driving one of those passes that is closed eleven and a half months out of the year due to snow. It was one of those creepy one-lane mountain roads above the tree line where you cannot see where the road ends and the deathly abyss begins. As we drove, a hush fell over the van until Jackson, our resident comedian, threw out in his best Daffy Duck voice:

Mother.

The tension was broken with laughter, and we quickly continued our ascent with renewed confidence. It was a great day. We hiked a mile-and-a-half to a snowy place just to prove that a snowball had a chance of surviving in July.

We returned to our campsite, exhausted and ready to roast some serious wieners. I was in the tent playing *Disney Princess Uno* with the kids (don't ask) when I saw Kaysie outside the tent. She was staring into the woods. She was not admiring God's creation.

She was frozen.

I look at her. *Baby?* Her eyes suddenly widened.

> That's a bear.

And it was.

Not twenty yards from our tent. Standing. Staring at us.

Big.

Black.

Hungry.

500 pounds.

BEAR!

The park rangers assure you that the first rule of a bear attack is to remain absolutely still. This is evidently so the animal can chew you whole without you poking out its eye.

We did not adhere to this rule. We scrambled, grabbing the children and running into the shower hut because those walls made of chopsticks are practically kryptonite. For an extra level of wildlife protection, I also hook-latched the screen door.

A BEAR! A freaking big black eat-your-head-and-use-your-large-intestine-as-a-straw-to-suck-all-the-marrow-out-of-your-feet-bones BEAR was standing right on the other edge of the woods, eyeing us as if we were the daily specials. I stared at the line I had told Charlie not to cross and thought to myself, *I hope the bear's mother told him not to cross that line either.*

◉ ⊙ ◙

We wait and wait and wait for the doctor to check on Charlie. It seems that, being an emergency room, the process should move along at a slightly brisker pace just in case, God forbid, anyone ever have an urgent medical need here. Charlie really wants to fall asleep and something in the back of my mind reminds me that this is a really bad thing after a head injury. Finally we are sent back and they take x-rays of our child.

Someday, we plan on filling a museum with the x-rays taken of Charlie and myself this summer. But at this moment in time, we don't realize that this is simply the first of many tragedies awaiting their turn.

His head looks just awful. I want to gag when I look at his head. It looks like the banana-shaped lump that rises out of Foghorn Leghorn's scalp before another character hammers it back down with a wooden mallet. I've never seen anything like it. Except, of course, on that one Foghorn Leghorn cartoon.

After a long night, the doctors slip in. Charlie is fast asleep from the pain medication they have given him, and we are told he is going to be fine. No internal bleeding, no fracture, no concussion—just an incredibly odd and freakish bruise. I realize this must look suspicious to the doctors and I begin to get paranoid.

> **DOCTOR:** How did it happen?
>
> **ME:** *How did what happen?*
>
> **DOCTOR:** How did he get such an enormous bruise? Was he struck with something?
>
> **ME:** *What?! No! No. Of course not. I didn't strike him with anything!*

DOCTOR: I didn't say "you."

ME: *The floor struck him.*

DOCTOR: The floor has no hands.

ME: *He fell.*

DOCTOR: He fell?

ME: *He fell.*

Wait a second. Isn't that the cover-up they always use in the movies when someone has been abused? Certainly the doctor doesn't think we've been abusive. I'd better straighten this out.

ME: *I know it looks like he's been abused. But he really did just fall.*

WHAT AM I SAYING?!

Now, he's really going to think something is fishy.

I am a monkey-chump. A sucker-punk monkey-chump.

Thankfully, the doctor sends us home to get some well-earned rest and to officially begin our summer. This is good news. Spring is ending and summer is beginning and, as we all know, that means everything else in our lives will transition to something better.

But then, one week later—to the day.

Charlie falls again.

Only this time, his head does indeed split open.

I hold a white rag tightly to his skull as I carry him into the emergency room. Great! It's the exact same woman checking us in. The inspection into our family history is about to begin. Blood flows from Charlie's head, and I ask if we need to hold things up and fill out the same paperwork we completed last week.

NURSE: You were here last week?

ME: *Of course! Remember us? It was even the same kid. The same head.*

NURSE:	That child has had two head injuries in one week?
ME:	*No, no, no, no, no. Eight days.*
NURSE:	Excuse me while I talk to the doctor.
ME:	*NO! Don't talk to the doctor!*
NURSE:	Your child is hurt and you DON'T want me to talk to the doctor?
ME:	*NO! I DO. I just don't want you to talk to him about what I thought you were about to talk to him about.*
NURSE:	And what might that be?
ME:	*The lovely ensemble you're wearing.*
NURSE:	Excuse me?
ME:	*Off with you, now.*

She asks me to please take a seat, which is nurse-speak for "I am more powerful than you right this moment. Behave before I give you a bonus catheter."

We wait and wait and wait. Thank God for iPods. Charlie remains settled due to a constant flow of *Clone Wars*. It's practically Novocain. Props go out to George Lucas for this. It's been quite a year for Charlie so far. He was sick for so long that we had to postpone his birthday party a full week. Now, two massive head wounds in eight-days time.

Two!

How does this happen?

I've always known that Charlie pushes himself to the limit—leaping from one furniture piece to another, seeing how many steps he can jump down from, launching off of the swingset as if it were a rocket. But how do I protect him from himself? How do I give him the freedom to push his physical limits and boundaries but keep him from lopping off an appendage? He is just so aggressive in his joy for life. It is a wonderful thing to behold and it is a powerful thing to behold.

These days, I don't have that kind of joy.

I think I left it on that sandbar.

My friend and I had played for about an hour when we started to hear the faint sounds of adults yelling. It was our parents. They had no idea where we were and the sun was setting. We realized that it was time to swim back, tired though we were. For the first time in sixty minutes, we looked back toward the direction we came. It seemed farther. Much farther.

For that matter, the island where we stood now seemed tiny, bearing no resemblance to the adventurous locale we had spotted from the other shore. Suddenly, it dawned on us that the island actually *was* smaller and the swim actually *was* longer.

Because the tide was coming in.

Fear began to grip us. It was an exhausting trek to swim here in the first place, and at that time, we weren't going nearly as far. We dove in and began to dog paddle, keeping our heads above water so that we could make certain the other person was still there. We pushed and kicked as the tide rocked us forward and back, wearing out the muscles on our little legs. I was growing weary. I struggled.

And then, at just about the same place where I had felt invigorated on the journey to the sandbar, I felt something entirely different.

Fear.

Despair.

Judging by what it had taken to achieve the accomplishment the first time, and taking into account my level of exhaustion, I suddenly did not believe I was going to make it. I thought I was going to drown. And my friend thought that he would as well.

What do you do when the person you thought you were holding on to for dear life thought he or she was holding on to you for the same reason?

As we both despaired for ourselves, another stronger thought took hold. Though neither of us thought we ourselves could succeed, we each firmly believed the other could. So, instead of dwelling on what we could not, we each urged the other forward.

We moaned and kept pushing, continually hearing our parents' voices growing louder. They still did not know what had happened to us. My legs were battery acid, my arms the tentacles of jellyfish.

And just as I knew I had no choice but to give up …

I suddenly felt sand beneath my feet.

We had made it.

Barely.

We waded up to the shore, ready to collapse, only to discover that the waves had pushed us so far off course, we had quite a bit of walking to do to get back to our families. I was scolded for running off. But I did not tell anyone where or how far I had gone.

I simply decided that pushing boundaries was no longer for me.

The nurse finally calls us in.

Same doctor. Whoop-dee-freaking-doo. This time, the wound is large and Charlie needs seven stitches. He won't be able to swim for a few weeks. Perfect. The kid lives for the water in the summer and, now, no swimming.

Why can't this sort of accident happen when it would come with benefits— when it would mean that Charlie gets to skip a series of exams or a broccoli-eating competition? Why must it occur smack in the middle of the time that he most needs a healed head?

The same thing happened to Kaysie when she was a girl. She was so excited about the pogo stick she received for Christmas that she didn't notice the oil slick in the driveway. When she came down hard on her chin, her head practically exploded with pain. Teeth were knocked out. Her face was ripped. She would spend the remainder of her Christmas holiday able to do very little due to the overwhelming pain.

I cannot help but wonder if these things happen to develop our patience. Of course, the question that follows is whether or not that patience is needed in

Charlie's life or his father's. If it is indeed for my own personal growth, then it certainly seems that Charlie gets the raw end of this deal.

I look at this wonderful kid, with all of his charisma and lovable eccentricities. I see that his life causes much joy, but puts his body constantly in harm's way. What do I do about this? I want to protect him, but I do not want to batter the champion out of him like the waves did to me.

I feel a bit over my head.

Where did I just read that?

Oh yeah.

In my daily reading, David was pleading to God in Psalm 69: "God! God save me! I'm over my head!" He continued a few verses later to entreat, "God, it's time for a break!" Preach it, Dave.

YES! A break. David was a man after Your own heart, God, and even he admitted that we can't do this beat-down called life without a halftime. Right? Am I right? So, when's that bell gonna ring, huh?

I often feel like my life reflects many of the psalms—pleading with God for eleven verses with the chapter ending before an answer comes. David often presented his case before his Maker, chronicling the plea in writing. He did not always reach a resolution. Instead, we read that he consistently chose to serve the Lord anyway—regardless of when or how the answer would come and regardless of what the answer might be.

And so the Bible seems to make it clear that the pursuit of answers is very important, regardless of whether or not we discover the specifics of what those answers might be. In the meantime, I need to assess what my view of God is, because that empowers my level of trust. Do I believe God is good? Yes. Do I believe that He knows what He is doing? Yes.

Does that mean I will be comfortable with what comes of it?

Probably not.

I do not know how and I may never know how. All I know is what it says in my other reading today. My New Testament reading in John 4. A man is very concerned for the well-being of his son. It is a life-or-death matter. He begs Jesus to help his son. Jesus does not tell him how, why, or even when. He simply states what to Jesus was a foregone conclusion:

Go home. Your son lives.

In my current state of turmoil, God is clearly stating, "Trust Me" while I continue to argue, "But, but, but HOW?!" I have a sneaking suspicion that the only way I will be able to get out of my state of stuck is by trusting even when I don't have answers. This is a problem, because in my life, the dread of the unknown has always made me want to run.

◉ ◉ ◉

In the Rocky Mountains, when that bear finally left, we resumed our fun with a new exciting story to tell. That is, until Ranger Marge came back.

> **ME:**   *Pretty big bear, huh?*
>
> **RANGER:** Eh.
>
> **ME:**   *What do you mean?! He was huge!*
>
> **RANGER:** SHE was huge. That was a momma bear looking for food for her young'ns. Don't wanna mess with a mama, Sugarplum. But I've seen bigger.
>
> **KAYSIE:** What do we do if she comes back?
>
> **ME:**   *She won't come back, baby. She's too frightened.*
>
> **RANGER:** Oh, she'll be back tonight.

We paused for a moment as we did not believe we could have possibly heard Marge correctly.

> **ME:**   *Say what?*
>
> **RANGER:** She's definitely coming back. She was just scoping out your site for snacks. She's coming back later to grocery shop, Tater Tot.
>
> **ME:**   *THEN WE'RE LEAVING!*
>
> **RANGER:** You don't have to leave, Sissy Shorts. You just got to put all

your food and cleaning supplies in your car overnight so there is absolutely nothing for her to smell.

ME: *What will she do to something she smells?*

RANGER: Eventually, she'll digest it.

KAYSIE: Thank you for your help.

RANGER: Scream if you see her.

ME: *Will do.*

RANGER: Have a good sleep, honey.

ME: *That's the first nice thing you've called me.*

RANGER: Well, bears eat honey.

Now, I'm a man, but I know that there is absolutely nothing I can do to stop a kodiak who wants to enjoy me open-faced on a hoagie roll, so I was definitely prepared to RETREAT.

We argued with the couple of friends we were camping with. The other wife and myself were of one mind (depart before being chewed upon) while the other husband and Kaysie were of the opposite mind (just wait and see what happens). Remember what I said about Kaysie being fueled by projects never ending? Kaysie was beginning to find herself disappointed in me. Realizing this felt worse than being torn to bits by wildlife, I caved and joined her side.

That night, in the darkness, with only our flashlights for illumination, we turned to the woods every time a twig snapped—as if staring into the darkness would erase the danger there. We laughed—not necessarily at our own fear—but at our own ridiculousness. A little past eleven, we climbed into our tents and drew our sleeping children close. I lay awake for hours, nervous at every sound. Eventually, it dawned on me that Marge was probably pulling my chain and I found myself drifting into one of those deep outdoor sleeps.

Until 2:37 a.m.

SNOOOOORT.

My eyes opened.

Rustle, rustle. Claw, claw. Chew, chew.

Raccoons, right? Got to be raccoons.

And then the shadow on the side of the tent became clear.

Mother.

Kaysie heard the bear. Our friends heard the bear. The children remained sleeping, motionless. We held our breath. What was it Marge had said? *Don't let her smell your toiletries or she'll try to eat them.* I suddenly realized I was wearing deodorant and pictured this silhouette clawing a hole in my tent and then consuming me whole from the starting point of my armpit.

And then, salvation.

A car horn began blaring as lights flashed on and off aimed directly at our tents. One of the other campers saw what was happening, and jumped into his car, honking and flashing to scare the bear back into the woods. It worked. We were saved.

The next morning, there were no arguments. It was time to leave.

As we drove, I wrestled with my thoughts. I felt so disappointed in myself for having not been brave enough to want to stay the night before. But, at the same time, the fear that emasculated me had also proven correct. I have no idea where this balance is supposed to land. I know God has charged me with protecting my family. But I also know that life is not supposed to be safe. I understand that as a man, I am supposed to have caution yet lack fear. I am supposed to be a father while being one of the boys, and I am supposed to be a husband while being one of her friends. And, darn it all, if these things don't all constantly oppose one another.

Should we have left the night before?

Should I have been brave enough to choose to stay in the first place?

Was what we did courageous or stupid?

I do not know.

All I know is that the tests keep coming. There is no way to truly run and there is no way to stop the assault. The moment we try to keep ourselves from straying into the woods, we discover the woods moving towards us.

There is no safe place in this life.

I've been uncertain about all of this for a long time.

And it has caused me to remain on the sandbar, never forging into the deeper waters.

But, whether I choose to move or not …

the tide is coming in.

Looks like I'd better start swimming.

(Exhibit E)

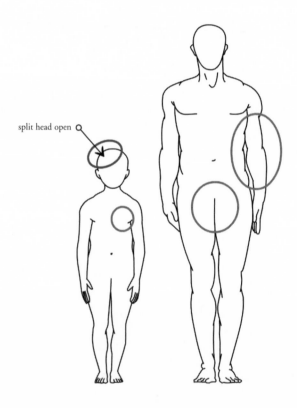

split head open

MAY 19

It's a hospital.

You would think that would make it the most inviting location of all time. Shouldn't people desire to be where healing takes place? Wouldn't it make sense for them to flock here, vacation here—for the lines for treatment to wrap around the building like Disney World?

But no. Somewhere in the bureaucracy of politics and insurance and disgruntled employees, this human attempt to do what God does best—to bring life—seems so lifeless.

I am waiting in a large antiseptic room that smells of mothballs. Kaysie and her mother, Dawn, are here beside me. They are watching a travel program about Italy on my iPod (imagining themselves in a better place, a different life) while I sip what I could have sworn the vending machine labeled as coffee and drudge through a Sudoku to keep myself awake.

I love Sudoku for three reasons:

> 1) It is an opportunity to put everything in its place.
> 2) Everything in Sudoku has an absolute definite place.
> 3) I know it will be finished after 81 numbers and 81 blocks.

I really like knowing when something is going to be over. I can wade through very difficult circumstances if I know when they are going to be finished. To this end, it is practically the middle of the night and I am counting the minutes, waiting for the moment where they stop climbing uphill towards the darkest hour and begin cascading downhill toward morning.

Kaysie's father, Bill, is recovering from lung surgery to attempt to remove the cancer. We've been here a very long time. And this is after a stressful week of strained schedules, shuffling the kids to-and-fro so that Kaysie could be at the hospital, and an inordinate amount of random client needs.

No, not a stressful week.

A stressful year.

Every time we think we're just about to close out the continuing chain of crises, a child's head is burst open or a pet dies or a friend leaves or a father goes into surgery—our hopes for peace dashed upon the shore by a tidal wave. It never ends. Kaysie worries so I encourage her. Of course, she takes that encouragement to mean that I am not listening to her, while I try to show her that I am.

I feel like I'm helping.

She feels like I'm not hearing.

So I feel like she's not hearing me.

Of course, all of this is heightened by the stress of simultaneously taking care of the father above us and the children beneath us. It seems a rational prayer that these sort of things could at least happen one-at-a-time instead of in-collision. But, then again, maybe there is something we need to learn that only a pile-on can provide.

Or maybe God isn't the one piling it all on.

Whenever I get this stressed, I think back to earlier seasons in my life when I thought I was stressed and I practically fall out of my seat laughing at the irony. I remember prepping for exams in high school and thinking to myself that I just couldn't wait until I was out of school and in the real world: married with children and my own money to spend and my own home. I just knew that the real world's stress would pale in comparison to my need to quickly absorb the periodic table of elements.

Hardy har har.

It never dawned on me that life would get more and more stressful. That I would witness a society that works more, does more, spends more, moves faster and faster and faster—and that I, along with the rest of the world, would leap onto that same gerbil wheel and chase the parsley treat dangling from the string. I would say that I was doing it for Jesus, but it would cause the same damage, the same trauma, the same life-spinning-out-of-control feeling as it did for those chasing money or fame or freedom.

Because Jesus doesn't hang from a string. He hung from a cross, which means He isn't dangling there with a list of demands that a human can never attain. He stands. Firmly. With love. Love that changes the way we run and gets us off of that gerbil wheel. Love that makes us want to run for Him, but run healthy, with purpose, and bear real fruit. Jesus' plan is one that allows us to be the kind of people we want to be—and yet so few of us are those kinds of people. Instead, we are spent. Restless. Tired. Disillusioned. Grumpy. And we say we are doing it for Jesus.

We are clearly running the wrong way on the wrong wheel. Jesus isn't the dad in the pool scooting backward every inch that we swim, never quite rescuing us. He is the Father of the prodigal son who runs TO us and says, "Stop running— Just stop."

And then He embraces us. We are healed by Him. We are restored by His embrace. And then we start moving. But not towards the cheese at the end of the maze. The Bible offers a different perspective:

> But those who wait upon God get fresh strength. They spread
> their wings and soar like eagles. They run and don't get tired,
> they walk and don't lag behind.[†]

Yes, God tells us to run.

But not until after we *wait*.

We don't find Jesus in the run.

We find Jesus in the wait.

Finding Jesus is what makes us want to run. Sometimes to Him, and sometimes to the plan He has before us. Right now, I find myself running for my

---

† Isaiah 40:31

life from all of the chaos. But, God is asking me to stop the running *from* and instead run *to*.

Today's Old Testament reading was Psalm 18:

> *"God is bedrock under my feet, the castle in which I live, my rescuing knight … where I run for dear life."*

Man, do I ever need that right this moment. A stable place where my running ends. Bedrock. A knight to save me instead of me finding my worth in desperately trying to rescue others. Maybe it's because it's the middle of the night, but I'm not feeling like very much of a hero. I need a hero, bedrock.

The iPod is still playing, but Kaysie and Dawn are asleep in the chair next to me. Me? I can't sleep. I drift off, but then something startles me awake. I've been told that this means I should begin praying for people, but all that goes through my mind at the witching hour of 2:37 a.m. is the stress. All the things I haven't done. All the things I haven't become. All the tasks ahead of me. And it all seems so much worse, so much darker, so impossible and despairing at 2:37 in the morning.

At that moment, I want to run to my bedrock.

But my feet are paralyzed.

◉ ◉ ◉

I've known two people who never had trouble sleeping: my brother Dav and my best friend Jason. Both could fall asleep anywhere in any position for as long as necessary and awaken refreshed.

I shared a room with Dav growing up, and I have to say that he was a slob. Dav would fall asleep to his alarm-clock radio blaring Ratt's "Round and Round" while sleeping with his head resting gently against half a sandwich wrapped in aluminum foil. I would have to wait until I heard him snoring to turn off the radio. Then and only then could I fall asleep. I've seen Dav fall asleep with his arms folded, leaning against a wall. I've seen Dav sleep on an airplane with his head resting nowhere, as though it were suspended in space, supported by imaginary pillows. Most impressively, Dav slept on the floor of my parents' living room as our nephew Lanning upchucked all over him. Impressive. The only thing that will wake Dav up from a nap is if you change the channel of the Braves game he is watching. Even on mute. Fascinating.

Jason and I went to South Africa together, where he discovered extraordinary new positions to slumber. He slept almost eight solid hours in his airplane seat, flailing the entire time. He slept in a van on unpaved roads that rattled the vehicle like it was in a paint mixer. He slept outdoors as the sound of lions emanated out of the brush nearby.

On the surface, both Dav and Jason seem to have just as much to worry about as I do. So, why is it that they can shut their minds off and disappear into unconsciousness while I cannot? I carry the weight of my stress and it continues to paralyze me.

On that same South Africa trip, Jason and I were given an opportunity to join a soccer team on their safari in Swaziland—definitely a once-in-a-lifetime experience. We leapt at the chance. We stayed the night in a hut with no walls and enjoyed the sounds of nearby wildlife and a bowl of wildebeest stew before getting a brief night's sleep. The next morning, we were awakened well before dawn to board the open-air jeep that would take us across the Savannah. As we sped along, the sun rose to our left. There, silhouetted against the blazing rising sphere were giraffe running at the pace of our vehicle in the distance. It was a moment of grandeur and I thought to myself, *God made something stunning out of something goofy. I wonder if He can do that with me.*

The primary warning we were given was to beware of the rhinoceros. This was the most vicious creature out there and, if we were to see one as close as fifty yards away, we were to stand absolutely still. I absorbed this information knowing full well that if I saw a creature the size of a Miata coming at me, I was NOT going to stand still.

THEM: But if you run it will enrage him.

ME: *And if I am killed it will not matter to me that the rhino did so without rage.*

THEM:	You cannot outrun a rhino.
ME:	*This is equally true if I do not move at all.*
THEM:	I know rhinos. You do not know rhinos.
ME:	*What is the best thing that could happen if I stand still?*
THEM:	He will stand still and stare at you.
ME:	*Yes. Much better. Maybe we will fall in love.*
THEM:	It is possible he will eventually lose interest.
ME:	*Remarkably like my old girlfriends.*

So, thoroughly freaked out, we began our excursion. We had not been driving for very long before we passed an elephant rubbing his tusks against a tree. It was fascinating up until the point that he began pushing the tree over onto our vehicle. We sped away. After a short drive, our guide slowly began creeping the truck down a dirt path shadowed by overgrown branches. He stared, not at the road ahead, but at the side of the road. He crept slower and slower. Suddenly, he eased to a halt.

He stepped out of the truck and entered the brush.

What? Are we supposed to follow him? Is he letting nature take its course?

Next thing we know, he stuck his head back out.

THEM:	Shhhhh.
ME:	*We weren't saying anything.*
THEM:	Follow me.

We stepped out of the truck, as quiet as mice, and followed his footsteps—taking great care to not step where he hadn't. I don't know why I did this. It was Swaziland, not a minefield. But, something about a place so foreign insinuated: *You don't belong here, Mark, and when you go where you don't belong, bad things happen.*

We stopped walking as he pointed to a very large log in front of us.

The log was unlike any log I had ever seen because directly in front of us, the log abruptly expanded, as if it were a piñata housing a living room ottoman.

The log moved.

ME:	*THE LOG MOVED.*
THEM:	Yes, this is a snake.
ME:	*There's a snake in that log?!*
THEM:	The log is a snake. There's not a snake in that log. There's a kudu in that snake.
ME:	*THAT LOG IS A SNAKE?!*

I surveyed further down and saw the tail. Unbelievable. We had stumbled upon a boa constrictor. It was the largest reptile I had ever seen. It had fallen from a high limb in this tree, pouncing upon a kudu (which is about the size of a deer) and swallowed it whole. We were observing the beginning stages of digestion. Neat.

ME:	*Shouldn't we do something?*
THEM:	Like what?
ME:	*Leave?*
THEM:	You are in no danger.
ME:	*Tell that to the kudu.*
THEM:	The kudu is why we are in no danger. After swallowing it whole, the snake hides itself here because until the animal is digested, the snake is unable to move.
ME:	*Unable to move?*
THEM:	Unable to move.
ME:	*I'm like that at Thanksgiving.*
THEM:	So, thanks to this victim, we can stand here as long as we like.
ME:	*YEAH. In your face, loser kudu.*
THEM:	There's the snake's head.
ME:	*How long will it take to digest?*
THEM:	A few months.
ME:	*Wow. That's like bubble gum.*

It was both disturbing and fascinating to me that the snake's actions and instincts caused it to acquire this large burden that would have to fully work its way through the snake before the snake could do anything at all. In the meantime, the boa did not have to feed itself, but neither could it shield itself from the elements or fight away any predators that might attempt to eat it. He was in the ultimate state of stuck—and it came from his own actions.

The doctor is here now.

I awaken Kaysie and Dawn.

There is a concern.

The first surgery had seemed to conclude well, but in the middle of the night a stitch burst.

Bill is bleeding.

He has lost seven pints of blood.

He is now back in emergency surgery. The doctor promises to keep us up-to-date with any new developments, but for now, we need to wait patiently.

And with that, the doctor is gone.

Jason and Sarah have already left for Kentucky. Yesterday was their last night in town. They are gone and we are here. They are driving and we are waiting. I remember Jason being rocked more than I at that boa constrictor—not at the threat of the animal—rather at the prospect of having to sit still that long. To Jason, that would be hell on earth.

Over the last month together, Jason and I worked things out. I ate a little crow and allowed myself to get a little selfless (just a smidge). I realized it would be a good move for them and that there was always the possibility of finding a new confidante, though the thought of the effort it would take to establish that trust still makes me want to dry heave.

I didn't really know how to say good-bye.

So, I made a mix CD with songs like:

> "The Adventure" Angels & Airwaves
> "One Moment More" Mindy Smith
> "What Susan Said" Rich Mullins
> "How Did You Find Me Here" David Wilcox
> "Next Year" Foo Fighters
> "Better Together" Jack Johnson
> "Somewhere Only We Know" Keane
> "Closing Time" Semisonic
> "Bad/40/Where the Streets Have No Name" (Live from Boston) – U2

The last song was the apex of the best live concert Jason and I ever attended together. The track was twelve-and-a-half minutes long, so I apologized to Sarah in advance for the half-dozen times Jason would inevitably play it on the drive to Wilmore. For better or worse, mix CDs have become my way to say "good-bye," "I'm sorry," "I love you," and "I care about what you're going through but don't know what to say so I will give you music that serves well for me as catharsis." They have also become my way of saying, "When are you going to make me a mix CD?" and "You really need better taste in music."

Of course, the best one ever was that one I made Kaysie in 1994.

Man, we should have never sold that in the garage sale.

Jason and Sarah are listening to theirs at this moment, and it is only now that I realize exactly why I made it for them. One last-ditch effort to remain important in their memory for a few hours longer.

⊙ ⊙ ⊙

Kaysie and Dawn and I pray for Bill. I pray with every ounce of faith I can muster, but it is so hard to do right now because I have experienced an undulating wave of "sometimes good / sometimes bad / sometimes answered / sometimes clueless" in my own prayer life.

I am continually astounded at how my daily Bible reading meshes irrevocably into what I am going through in a single day. It is a comfort, like God nudging my shoulder saying, "See? See? Huh?" whenever I am suspicious that I have done something that made Him stop listening to me.

My other reading today is the passage in John 6 where the people keep coming back to Jesus because He gave them free food, but Jesus wants them to understand that they will never be filled unless they understand that He is their sustenance—their Bread of Life. Of course, they don't want to take this offer at face value. They need proof.

> They waffled: "Why don't you give us a clue about who you are, just a hint of what's going on? When we see what's up, we'll commit ourselves. Show us what you can do. Moses fed our ancestors with bread in the desert. It says so in the Scriptures: 'He gave them bread from heaven to eat.'"[†]

They have already seen Him in action—and still, they are asking for proof. Oh God, this is so me.

I stress and I strain in the answer for today, but You have already answered me so many times. Why can't I see it? What am I not learning?

That morning in Swaziland, we continued driving to a waterhole where we were told we would be likely to see birds we had never laid eyes upon. As we parked, several of us stepped out of the truck and I began taking photographs. As I glanced through my telephoto lens, I heard our guide speak.

---

† John 6:30–31

THEM:	Shhhhh.
ME:	*We weren't saying anything.*
THEM:	Remain absolutely still.
ME:	*Why?*
THEM:	Rhino.

I saw his pointed finger and followed it with my eyes. There, standing on the other side of the shrub was a very large, very angry-looking rhinoceros.

Not fifty yards away.

Five yards away. I was stunned frozen.

ME:	*Rhino.*
THEM:	Yes.
ME:	*Rhino.*
THEM:	Yes.
ME:	*Right there.*
THEM:	Don't look into his eyes.
ME:	*Oh. You think that's the trigger point, do you? What am I supposed to do?*
THEM:	Run.
ME:	*WHAT?!*
THEM:	Shhhhh.
ME:	*You just got done schooling me on how NOT to run.*
THEM:	Yes. Forget what I said. Run.

But, I could not run.

Every instinct went into reverse.

I stood there, stunned, as if I were trying to digest a kudu.

And then, the guide said what I most needed him to say.

THEM:	Mr. Steele. Run … or die.

There. That did it.

I ran. The rhino didn't chase. We sped away.

◉ ⊙ ◙

I recalled this moment last night with Jason in our final time together and we laughed. But of course, it was a bittersweet moment.

I say that I like endings, but I did not particularly care for this one. We said all the things that one says—about how the relationship will remain the same, how the brotherhood that we shared was strong enough to endure the lack of time together. But we both knew as we spoke those words that the road beneath us was changing.

I lean heavily on the few people I trust deeply. It is more than sad. It is despairing.

Like a large, unsettling lump in my belly. The question remains, will I lay motionless, or will I make a next move?

> *God.*
> *I don't want to need proof.*
> *You have been there for me so many times.*
> *You have been the Bread I needed while I asked for the bread I craved.*
> *Help me trust that whatever comes next will not be too much.*
> *Help me trust without the how.*
> *Help me.*
> *Help.*

The doctor makes his way to where we are seated and we can tell by the look on his face that the urgency has dissipated. He confirms that the surgery went well. They have repaired the stitches, stopped the bleeding, and Bill is now stable. An answer to prayer. I breathe an enormous sigh of relief. Bill is now on a breathing tube, and the best thing we can do is attempt to get some rest ourselves.

I see one weight fall off of Kaysie and Dawn's shoulders. But there are so many weights remaining. The dilemmas keep coming like Tetris blocks. We sweat and scurry to line up little boxes of crisis into neat little rows so that they will disappear, but by the time we finish a row, eight more are already coming.

Kaysie's father is going to live. But I've still lost my dog and my best friend.

I cannot trudge uphill much longer. It's enough to make me want to freeze in my tracks.

I'm going to lean back in this chair, remain still, and attempt to sleep the witching hour away.

Although something in the back of my mind keeps whispering …

Run or die.

SIX DECISIONS THAT MATTERED

decision #3:

PROTECTED / VULNERABLE

Be a man. It is battered into every male from day one. We are supposed to take certain attitudes. Certain things we should automatically know. Certain things we are to leave to the women. But the key identifier for the man is the wall—the cone of silence that we wrap around ourselves to keep us protected. We each know good and well that men are more flawed than women, but it is our job to keep up the hero façade. To make everything look easy. To make everything feel safe. To never seem like we are uncertain. This is why we don't ask for directions. Why we build the Christmas toys without looking at the instructions. Why so many things we attempt to fix break. We are protectors. It is in our DNA. There is a tortoise shell around each of us that had better not crush, because the moment it does, the soft green goo inside is exposed.

But the shell is killing us.

Society expects us to be something impossible: unscathable. Unaffected. The world expects hurt not to matter to a man. But hurt does matter and every time we experience it, we have to bury it under a layer of dirt. This is why there is so much dirt in so many men's lives. They must keep shoveling the manure or else seem unmanly. In the meantime, our wives need us to be the spiritual leaders, to have all the answers. But no man has all the answers. God says that He is strong when we are weak, but there don't seem to be a whole lot of people out there excited to witness a man's weak moments. So, we—the men of the world—do our best never to be weak. And in the process, we never allow God to be strong.

This is a mother of a burden to carry.

The men in the world don't say this out loud, but we are about to implode from all this flexing. We have weakness and we need the freedom to let it be known without the threat of the awareness of it emasculating us. We must be able to drop the burden. To start allowing the dirt to be shoveled out so that the godliness in us can finally come up for air. It's time for us to get vulnerable and lean on God. Deep down inside, there's a lot of pain. We must go to the Doctor. And when we do, we need for you to see us as even better men.

FOUR SUMMER STORMS

FATHER'S DAY

It's supposed to be my day.

I'm not that picky. I'm not looking for parades in my honor or statues unveiled in the park. Brownies engraved in my likeness would be nifty, but I'm really just aiming for an afternoon nap and spending the day with a healthy family.

And yet today, out of nowhere, my son's eye is falling apart.

Charlie. Of course, Charlie.

It began a week ago when Kaysie took the kids to the local water park, or as I like to call it "Sewage City." That place is nasty. It would not at all surprise me if they discovered a human spleen clogging the wave pool. Unfortunately, there is no other competition for entertainment, which means there is no real need for diligent upkeep. We would complain, but we can only imagine how fruitless it would be.

ME:	*You think maybe the water could be blue some days?*
THEM:	Is there a family of possums in your pizza slice?
ME:	*Not today.*
THEM:	Then be grateful for what you do have.

Before visiting this park, I didn't know that water could have a smell. But we still go, because in the summer months, it can get up to 110 degrees around here and, after all, the black plague is better than being slowly cooked to death.

Kaysie took the kids last week because she desperately needed the break. She had just successfully organized the week-long Cub Scout Day Camp with our friend Shelley. This made her into a hero for our children, but a basket-case on all other fronts. Kaysie is a genius organizer but so much had to be done so quickly with so little guidance for Day Camp that the word *vacation* flew rapidly out the window. For the past month, she has done nothing but scramble to prepare the camp in time. Couple this with the stress she is feeling about her recovering father, and it's simply too much for a human being to carry.

Dav's wife, Laura, brought their three boys to the water park and Kaysie joined them for a day of relaxing in the cool of the water. But just as Charlie began playing with his cousins, one of them accidentally kicked Charlie in the eye while he was under water. Charlie came running to Kaysie and she took a good look at it. It was very red, but that was about all. No real harm done. We left it at that.

As the week passed, Charlie's eye began to look worse and worse. This, of course, made no sense. We called the doctor who assumed his retina had been scratched by a toenail. Not a pretty thought. How were we going to explain this to the clinic where they already wonder why Charlie's had two head wounds this summer? The doctor told us to wait it out a little longer.

But, then, Charlie woke up the next day with a fever.

A fever.

What on earth? Kaysie took him in to the doctor, and they peered and prodded and took cultures and determined that it must be pink eye.

Pink eye?

US:	*From a child's toe?*
THEM:	It's possible that the kick underwater scratched his eye and that the scratch made him more susceptible to catch pink eye somewhere over the past week.
US:	*But wouldn't we all have pink eye? We've been fooling with his eye all week, even kissing it better.*
THEM:	What can I say? Some maladies affect some people while not affecting others.
US:	*Yes. But history would tell us that if it is possible for me to catch something, I will.*
THEM:	Not this time.

So we were given medication to bring down the fever and an ointment to help with the pain of pink eye. Kaysie nursed Charlie for a few days.

And then, in the middle of the night—

Screaming.

When Charlie screams from pain, he screeeeams. He is able to internalize a great amount of suffering, so when it comes out verbally, it's fairly horrible. The kid can wail. Banshee-style. He becomes a tiny Marv Albert. You would think the noise alone would chase germs out of the house. He was squeezing his wounded eye shut, gunk all around it. When Kaysie was finally able to get a good look at it, she discovered the trouble.

Open sores.

Open sores all around our poor little five-year-old's eye. Ridiculous blisters all around the edge. Clearly burning like wildfire. For a parent, this causes two simultaneous responses: enormous empathy and dry heaving.

Kaysie took him back to the doctor. The new visible signs alerted our physician to new tests, and the culprit was finally identified.

Are you ready for this?

Herpes.

HERPES.

In his EYE.

My little boy had a volatile strain of herpes in his little eye, burning and doing damage and causing open sores that would make a grown man scream like a wild dog.

How did this happen? Did the kick to my child's eye allow water in, causing whatever was IN that water to do its thing to my five-year-old? That is a theory up for debate. All I know is that from now on, when we go to that water park, we're going to wear protective eye-gear to dodge all the STDs floating in the kiddie pool.

But now it is Father's Day. I want to be with my family, but instead I have to make an announcement for college group at church while my wife stays home with our miserable pirate-patched tot.

Getting to stay home sick is not always a negative reality. During the school year (and with an optimal not-all-that-bad ailment), staying home can rock and rule. Staying home means the television is on. Staying home means drinking Sprite and being waited on with warm soup set on a portable tray. It means napping only when you feel like it and more than likely getting to spend the evenings sleeping between Mom and Dad. If the sick is not TOO sick, it's actually quite like a spa weekend.

But this is the summer. In fact, it's only the middle of June, and Charlie has already been sick far too long and missed far too much. Once again, for another two weeks, Charlie is unable to swim. And swimming in the summer is practically all the boy lives for. He's a little dolphin. You would realize this if you saw our bathroom floor after he has spent ten minutes in the tub.

So, on Father's Day, they remain home.

This shouldn't be that big of a deal to me, but I must say that my favorite Father's Day thing in the world is the little craft that my children make in Sunday school to give me on Father's Day afternoon. I have more tchotchkes than I can count hanging up on the wall of my office—little construction-paper picture frames, artistic renderings of myself, and homemade coupon books. I have done the math and I realize that there are not that many Father's Days left where these will be constructed for me.

I am very proud of myself this year because I actually got my dad's Father's Day card in the mail on time for him to receive it yesterday. This is, I believe, a first. He usually receives my Father's Day card either the Tuesday after, or sometime closer to Independence Day. I mean well, I do. I even do a good job of thinking about Father's Day ahead of time. It's simply never ahead enough. I normally realize Father's Day is coming the previous Thursday. That's when I scramble to choose the card, sign it, and get it in the mail on time for him to receive it late. But this year, by some miracle of the Lord, I realized it on Tuesday because I was craving Chick-fil-A and the Chick-fil-A faces a Hallmark store. Hence, on-time arrival.

I am simply not built like all the people with floating-holiday-radar. I mean, I can remember special days like birthdays, anniversaries, and Christmas because they are on the SAME FREAKING DAY every year. Who is the moron that based the floating date of holidays on "Second Monday of the Winter Solstice" or "Ninth Equinox after Strawberries ripen in Toledo" or "Windiest Thursday of the Third Moon Cycle unless the square root of Mondays is carried and subtracted from the sum of X and Y"? Floating holidays do not announce themselves. I only know they are coming if I happen to catch a Target commercial, but we have TiVo, so I fast-forward through those. Somehow, this makes me unsentimental. There's simply no way to win.

Jackson came with me to church today. He's my big man, and he loves church. He gets very disappointed if he cannot attend. I would like to believe this is because he wants to make something special for his father, but I know good and well that today is the day they take coupons they have earned by memorizing Scripture and trade them for toys that would take three weeks to earn playing skeeball at Chuck E. Cheese.

I think about this big six-year-old (almost seven) and cannot believe so much time has passed. I remember the day he was born with such dramatic detail. Jackson's birth was very different from Morgan's or Charlie's on two accounts: 1) unlike the first and third child where we wanted to be surprised, we found out Jackson's gender ahead of time, and 2) we had registered for an epidural. We were elated about the epidural because Kaysie had Morgan without one and that was a place we did not want to go again. We looked forward to a labor with less pain.

We did not expect the back labor. Kaysie was in excruciating pain for twenty hours as her back heaved and pounded every time a contraction came. For Kaysie, the labor pains have always been deeply intense, resonating all throughout her skeletal system. She is the strongest woman I have ever met because she has had to carry so much in her lifetime. As Jackson attempted to break his way into this world, I held her up as her knees buckled again and again.

If there was a battle for any one of our three children to begin life, it was Jackson. The night was very, very long and every moment, it felt as if the boy who did not yet have a name was kicking down the point of entry. Jackson came into this planet hard. With great force. But he also came slowly. True to his nature.

As the pain intensified, we begged for the epidural multiple times, but the nurse continued to assure us that we didn't know what we were talking about.

ME:	*She's dilated to a four! Didn't you say she could have the epidural when she was dilated to a four?*
THEM:	Yes. But, we need to just watch and wait.
KAYSIE:	GLUNG HAR!
ME:	*HOW is watching and waiting anything like giving her the epidural?!*
THEM:	Your first child came slowly from this point. We need to make certain we aren't giving it too early.
KAYSIE:	MLOOOF!
ME:	*Does she SOUND like it's too early?!*
THEM:	I know it feels like he's coming fast, but we've been doing this for twenty years.
ME:	*You've been having THIS BABY for twenty years?!*
THEM:	Trust us.

This was enraging.

Not on a personal level, mind you. We understood that the nurse was just doing her job the best she could based on the hundreds of experiences she had before us.

But that wasn't what we needed. We needed someone who would base this job on US. Someone who would realize that, if all births are indeed different, perhaps we should be the ones listened to at this moment, as Kaysie was the only one with the predicament INSIDE her, and I was the only one in the room who understood KAYSIE.

We begged her to call the anesthesiologist. Finally, she caved.

Another hour later, the anesthesiologist had not arrived. Turned out, he was busy.

ME:	*BUSY?!*
THEM:	Well, it's Sunday.
ME:	*What's that supposed to mean?*
THEM:	There's another mother. Another baby.
ME:	*So?*
THEM:	So, you're next.
KAYSIE:	PHFLPFHLP FRAAAAANG!
ME:	*Are you telling me that in this entire hospital, there is only ONE anesthesiologist?!*
THEM:	On Sunday, yes.
ME:	*And that, knowing this, you waited until the last possible moment to contact him?!*
THEM:	Who knew?

Another hour passed and Kaysie was about to eat the metal guardrail of her bed just to clamp her teeth down on something to ease the back labor.

ME:	*We need you to give her this epidural NOW! This baby is coming!*
THEM:	I don't know where he is. He should have been finished by now.
ME:	*Should have been?! Do you not know? After two hours, have you not called him back?!*
THEM:	Perhaps I'll call him.
ME:	*She's ready to push now!*
THEM:	I know she feels like she's ready to push, but we know that it's not quite time for her to push.
ME:	*You don't understand. I know my wife. When the pain gets this severe, she's about to have the baby.*
THEM:	And we've done more of these than you. There is still plenty of time.

ME: *PLEASE CALL OUR FAMILY DOCTOR.*

THEM: In due time. We wouldn't want to wake him now, would
             we?

By calling, they discovered that the anesthesiologist had gone back to sleep after his last procedure. It had not been made clear to him that the need was urgent. So, he arrived within thirty minutes, a little groggy and more than a little put out. He prepped Kaysie and leaned her over as he held the large needle in his hand.

HIM: Okay. You're going to feel something here.

KAYSIE: UNNNGH!

HIM: Miss, I haven't put the needle in yet.

KAYSIE: IT'S TOO LATE!

HIM: It's not too late. Just hold still.

KAYSIE: IT'S COMING OUT!

THEM: Miss, I know it feels like the baby is coming out, but trust
             us. The baby is not coming out.

HIM: Just hold still.

KAYSIE: THE BABY IS COMING OUT!

ME: Honey, why do you think the baby is coming out?

KAYSIE: BECAUSE ITS HEAD IS BETWEEN MY LEGS!!!

THEM: Miss, it only feels that way because …
             (The Nurse feels for herself.)
             OH MY WORD! THIS BABY IS COMING OUT!

And in that moment, every single medical professional RAN OUT OF THE ROOM. I kid you not. I am certain they each had some urgent detail to take care of for this imminent birth, but they left us literally hanging. I held whatever sterile covering they just threw into my arms as Kaysie lay on the bed, her head hanging over the side. I could see the child coming out. The three of us: my bewildered self, my vulnerable wife, and my half-born child were utterly alone.

I pulled Kaysie to the position I remembered her in for the birth of Morgan and screamed …

ME: *HELP!! HELP!! Can we get some PEOPLE in here, please?!*

Suddenly, the room burst with activity. All of the doctors and nurses were back, fully outfitted for the labor. I asked where our doctor was. The nurse replied that they had waited too long to call him. There was no way he would be able to arrive in time. This baby would be born in a matter of moments. We would have to forge ahead without him.

At that exact moment, I finally heard a voice of rescue.

Why didn't anybody wake me?

It was our family doctor. He knew that once Kaysie progressed to an eight, she would move rapidly, so he had come to the hospital in the middle of the night and was asleep in the next room, waiting to be alerted that it was time.

So, in the next few whirlwind minutes, without the epidural that Kaysie had so longed for, Jackson hurled his way into this world like a freight train barreling off the tracks and into a barn.

Here, finally, was our boy.

We named him Jackson, after the city where Kaysie was born.

His middle name is Mark.

And just as Kaysie shed tears of joy, holding her first son, the pain medication she had been given an hour too late began to kick in and make her groggy. Not in time to help. Just in time to ruin the moment. We had wanted the protection from pain of the epidural so badly, but somehow ended up more vulnerable than we had ever been in our lives. Our preparation seemed to hardly matter as we helplessly watched the road change underneath our feet. The miraculous moment at the end came, not because of anything we had done to attempt to set ourselves up for success, but because our doctor anticipated the mistakes enough to make his bed as close as possible to the impending crisis.

And here he is now, my little genius.

Jackson bombarded his way into life on that August evening almost seven years ago, and he has lived every day since with just as much gusto. He moves at his own pace, yes, but it is always with flair, certainty, and enough creative genius to tempt Rupert Murdoch to purchase him.

⊙ ⊙ ⊙

It's time to head home from church, and Jackson is presenting me with a necktie made entirely out of purple construction paper and sheep stickers that state I am a "member of God's flock." I consider this flocking awesome and fawn over the Post-it notes he has attached to the tie so that I can jot daily reminders on my own torso.

> **JACKSON:** Happy Father's Day, Dad!
>
> **ME:** *Well, thank you! Happy Father's Day to you, too.*
>
> **JACKSON:** Why?
>
> **ME:** *Why what?*
>
> **JACKSON:** Why did you say that? I'm not a father.
>
> **ME:** *Right. Just habit, I guess.*
>
> **JACKSON:** I love you.
>
> **ME:** *I love you, too.*
>
> **JACKSON:** There's tape on the back so you can put it on your shirt.
>
> **ME:** *I see.*
>
> **JACKSON:** So put it on your shirt.
>
> **ME:** *Ah. Good idea.*
>
> **JACKSON:** And Dad?
>
> **ME:** *What is it, Big Man?*
>
> **JACKSON:** Close your eyes and open your mouth.

I am a trusting person.

I really am.

And I trust my wife and my children above all.

But, let's be serious here. When has this request ever ended well?

> **ME:** *No way.*
>
> **JACKSON:** WHY NOT?!
>
> **ME:** *You're gonna put something disgusting in my mouth.*
>
> **JACKSON:** Nuh uh.
>
> **ME:** *Then why can't I keep my eyes open?*
>
> **JACKSON:** You'll see.
>
> **ME:** *Technically, seeing is what I will NOT do and that is precisely the problem.*
>
> **JACKSON:** Daa-haaaaaad!

The whining response of "Daa-haaaaad" is kryptonite. There is no parental follow-up argument. There are only two options: 1) shut the proceedings down or 2) oblige. I can think of no valid reason to go with number one, so I do, indeed, close my eyes and open my mouth.

I taste dirty fingers and something hard inside.

> **ME:** *What is this?*
>
> **JACKSON:** Candy corn.
>
> **ME:** *Where did you get candy corn in June?*
>
> **JACKSON:** Found 'em. Happy Father's Day.

Salmonella averted, Jackson now wants me to pick him up, hug him, and carry him to the car. This is, on one hand, awesome. It is, on the other hand, causing my insides to explode. The pain below the belt is worse than ever and has had a serious deteriorating effect on my plumbing. I know that it is time to give in and see the doctor. But I really thought it would have improved by now. Loving on my child is both euphoric and excruciating, but I, of course, choose to suffer through the pain rather than eliminate both.

Even with Charlie's illness, I have been inspired today to move forward strong. My reading today was Proverbs chapters 22 through 24. These are called the Thirty Precepts of the Sages and they are perfect wisdom for Father's Day. At first glance, they seem scattered, but on closer introspection, I realize how many of them apply to our crises:

> Soak yourself in the Fear-of-God – that's where your future lies. Then you won't be left with an armload of nothing.
>
> God wants your full attention.
>
> It is better to be wise than strong.
>
> If you fall to pieces in a crisis, there wasn't much to you in the first place.
>
> No matter how many times you trip them up, God-loyal people don't stay down long; soon they're up on their feet, while the wicked end up flat on their faces.

Yes! I can grab onto these. In all the effort to push through these hard times, it is refreshing to be reminded that this is not about Kaysie and me summoning human strength. It is about us remaining connected to God—fearing Him, remaining loyal to Him, giving Him our full attention. This is the only thing that can keep us from falling to pieces. And we are assured that if we stay loyal to Him, though we may be tripped up many times, we will not stay down.

Man, am I ever ready to stand back up.

That is, if it didn't hurt my groin so much to stand.

We are home now, and with all obligations complete, I lean back and prepare myself for a relaxing day alone with my family.

Ding Dong.

No. It can't be.

Ding Dong.

DingDongDingDongDingDongDingDongDingDongDingDongDingDong.

I attempt to dive behind the couch before the inevitable, but I am not fast enough. Suddenly, the silhouette of a four-foot sandy blond-haired boy appears in the living room window, standing on our begonias and pressing his nose against the glass.

I KNOW YOU'RE IN THERE! I CAN SEE YOU MOVING!

It's Zachary.

The British Invasion.

Zachary is a maelstrom of a child—a joyful, perpetual-motion seven-year-old with free reign over the entire neighborhood. Everyone knows Zachary and, if one were to compare stories with the neighbors, it would become clear that he has found a way to be in multiple locations at the same time. He was born and bred in England and therefore has a charming little accent that causes him to be immensely likable even though he gives no regard to personal space or family time and can only speak at the volume of eleven. My kids love Zachary and I find him fascinating in the same way I find used-car commercials fascinating—in thirty-second doses with the mute button close by. There is no denying that when Zachary arrives, there is mandatory FUN. He simply tends to arrive at the most inopportune moments. You would think that, as a parent, it would not be a problem for me to send him home. You clearly have not met Zachary.

ZACHARY: LET ME IN! I SEE YOU! GUESS WHAT!

(I open the door just enough so that he cannot fit through.)

ME: *Hey Zachary. It's family day today.*

ZACHARY: WRONG. It's FAHTHER'S Day today. Guess what?

ME: *I don't know Zachary, but it's time for you to go home.*

ZACHARY: WRONG AGAIN. You are a teddible guesser. I made my
              fahther a picture of MYself.

ME: *That's awesome. But, since it's Father's Day, I'm going to just
              be with my kids today.*

ZACHARY: Of course. And I will just be with your kids, also.

ME: *NO. That's not what I mean.*

ZACHARY: But it IS what you just said.

ME: *I meant that only our family will be together.*

ZACHARY: I don't mind. HEY! That's Xbox *Star Wars* Legos!

ME: *Zachary, you need to go home.*

ZACHARY: No I don't. I just came from there. I LOVE Xbox *Star Wars* Lego's!

ME: *Zachary, Charlie has an infection in his eye and can't have other kids over.*

ZACHARY: What other kids are coming over?

ME: *None. That's the point.*

ZACHARY: Is his eye CATCHING?

ME: *Well, no.*

ZACHARY: Then why cahn't I come over?

ME: *Go home, Zachary.*

ZACHARY: Can I HAVE your Xbox?

ME: *Closing the door now.*

ZACHARY: I'm thiiiiiirsty.

ME: *Your house is down that way.*

ZACHARY: When CAN your kids play?

ME: *Maybe tomorrow.*

ZACHARY: I'll just wait on your steps then.

And he sits out there, head-in-hands, little British puppy-dog eyes aimed at our living room window.

Fifteen minutes later, I cave. I always cave. It looks like I will be spending my special day with my tired wife, my incapacitated son, and Parliament. Of course, this is wonderful for Charlie, but not for me.

I first met Zachary a month ago when Kaysie and the kids were out of town and I was arriving home from work. I stepped out of my SUV onto my own driveway, and he was right there, two inches from my face.

> **ZACHARY:** HEY! You have CHILDREN! I've SEEN them! Where ARE they?!

A most unique introduction.

Since that moment, Zachary shows up at practically every meal, weekend, holiday, and family reunion. Zachary, as an individual, bewilders me because he is so many things that I am not and cannot fathom becoming. First of all, he is completely free in who he is. He befriends everyone and will not hesitate to tell you exactly what he thinks of you and what you can do for him. But Zachary is also very loving and very giving. I have never seen him have a selfish moment. He is so passionate about every moment and every person in that moment, that sometimes it gets a little overwhelming. But overall, the kid is awesome. Deeply awesome. So awesome, that I can't handle the awesomeness for more than ten minutes at a time. The awesomeness quickly spikes, and I inevitably send the awesomeness home. Because, to be honest, I don't always want love and joy and effervescence. Sometimes, I just want quiet.

So, I send Zachary home.

And I see Charlie deflate.

ME:	*What's the matter, buddy?*
CHARLIE:	Zachawy went home.
ME:	*Yeah. But I'm here.*
CHARLIE:	But we were pwaying a game.
ME:	*Well, I'll play a game with you.*
CHARLIE:	Weawy?
ME:	*Sure.*
CHARLIE:	YAY!
ME:	*Just let me lay down for a while first.*

This is clearly not my children's vision. What am I thinking? Lay down? I just sent their friend home so that I can sleep?! You've got to be kidding me.

I see it on their faces.

Bad decision.

ME:	*Tell you what. I can sleep later—when I die. Let's play a game!*
CHARLIE:	YAAAAAAY!
ME:	*What do you want to play? Checkers? Connect Four?*
CHARLIE:	Nope.
ME:	*Then, what?*
CHARLIE:	I wanna WESTLE!

Yeesh. Wrestling. Something I simply cannot do.

Don't get me wrong. Ten years ago, I would battle challengers just for the ninja points alone, but every activity these days has to be registered on the fell-through-the-roof-and-landed-on-my-manhood-Pritchard-scale. However, this activity is one of the ways my boys know Daddy loves them—by rolling on the floor and getting dirty and wounded so that they can have a rough-and-tumble time.

I thought I had dodged this bullet when we started the college ministry at church and men in the prime of life came over at least once a week to run our boys ragged. I fallibly believed that if I timed our meetings right, my kids could get wrestled out on a regular basis without me ever having to stoop down again.

Nope. All it means is that now, they get more practice.

ME:	*I don't know about wrestling, Charlie.*
CHARLIE:	Pweeeeeease!
ME:	*Daddy's got a little scrambled-egg action in his trousers and has to be careful not to ruin anything that might come in handy later.*
CHARLIE:	Pwihddy pweeeeeease!
ME:	*I know you really want me to wrestle, but don't you also want me to be able to stand up in future years?*
CHARLIE:	Just a wittle bit?

This is always Charlie's final argument. "Come on, Dad! Does it have to be all or nothing? Can't we meet halfway? Can't you suffer just a little so that I can be just a little bit happy?"

And I consider this. Because I don't want to be one of those breakable fathers. I don't want to be remembered for all the brilliant excuses why I would not or could not try or push or do so many things. I want my children to have joyous memories rather than a vast lexicon of verbal escape routes. And let's face it: This may very well be the only true way to finally escape my physical, mental, and emotional funk.

To finally just DO something.

Caution to the wind. So what if it hurts a wittle bit?

I decide to be the man.

I decide to be the FATHER.

And I firmly and agreeably respond.

Okay.

Charlie is overjoyed.

He is smiling ear-to-ear.

And he is coming at me like a FREAKING FREIGHT TRAIN!

He runs lickety-split, head jutted out as if he is the bull I am running with in Pamplona. I see him coming, but I have no time to protect myself. He is seismic.

He sprints.

He collides.

He SLAMS.

I am down.

Happy.

Father's

Daaaay.

Stars.

Lots and lots of stars.

My stomach upturns. I feel nausea. I believe I am about to toss my candy corn.

Charlie stops laughing. He glances down and sees me, a crumbled man, lying on the floor by the ottoman.

Eyes closed and mouth open.

Kaysie asks if I am all right, but I am an agonized heap. I can barely emit a moan.

Charlie stares.

> **KAYSIE:** Kids, why don't you give Daddy a minute. Go play outside.
>
> **CHARLIE:** What happened?
>
> **KAYSIE:** You won the wrestling match.
>
> **CHARLIE:** SWEET!

The kids make their way into the backyard. I see them (sideways and blurry) as I lay, attempting to remain immobile. They swing back-and-forth on the swing set. I feel more nausea. I turn my head slowly toward Kaysie, my eyes opening fully for the first time.

I take it you haven't gotten any better.

It dawns on me how long I have kept this pain to myself. Secret. Partly because I did not want to do anything about it, but partly because I wanted to seem strong. Resilient. I didn't want to be a breakable husband. I didn't want to need anything. I wanted to be one of those husbands who doesn't constantly look for an escape route.

But, for almost a year now, I have been trying to escape the truth.

It's so funny. When Jackson was born, I was infuriated by the medical professionals who told us that what we were feeling was not as bad as we thought—those who refused to contact the physician in the next room. And now, I have become them. I am the one pushing myself to ignore the symptoms, to say no, it's not all that bad. No sense going to the trouble. You can always keep waiting.

And now I am the one curled up in the most vulnerable position I can imagine, feeling like it is too late for help. Hopefully, the Help who knows me best is ready in the next room, just waiting for me to call out His name.

Kaysie kneels down next to me, deeply concerned.

That does it.

Day after tomorrow, you're going to the doctor.

(Exhibit F)

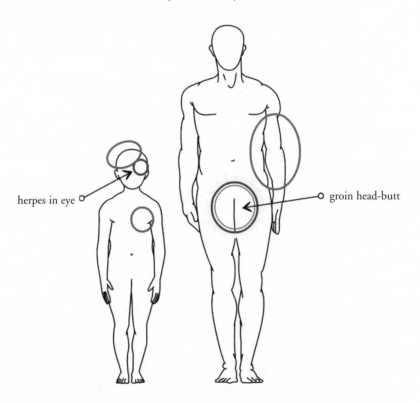

herpes in eye

groin head-butt

JULY 5

With Kaysie's father's recuperation and the weeks and weeks of Charlie attempting to recover from his eye, the tension at home has reached Threat Level Orange. We need a change of pace, so we travel to Atlanta, where I was born and raised, to celebrate our family's yearly "party week."

Our nation's birthday, my daughter's birthday, and my own birthday fall on three consecutive days in July, so we normally take vacation just to sort it all out. This year, we need relief from reality so badly that we escape from town altogether, assuming that all would be well. But last night, we went to Stone Mountain to enjoy the fireworks and laser show only to be rained out after being rained upon for more than four hours.

Not feeling very celebratory right now.

I thought this would be a great thing to do. Get out of town. I thought it would help cheer Kaysie up.

But she is in a funk.

A deep funk.

I'm also in this funk, but as I am by nature an optimist, I am choosing to do any activity I can that I believe might dissolve her funk. This is because the dissolution of Kaysie's funk is the only thing that will cure my funk. I don't just need joy. I need the one I love to find joy in the joy I am finding. In this same manner, she needs for me to find joy in the places she finds it. But, with the exception of our children, our joy rarely collides.

We learned this when my job first required me to travel. I would go away to comedy dates, mission trips, training seminars, film shoots, and speaking engagements and come back refueled and filled with confidence over a job well done. I would come home gloating about all the fabulous places I was able to dine or sightsee. Kaysie would then show me the exact seven places where the baby threw up on her.

Our joy was not shared.

I stopped talking about my work.

I did not want the fact that I loved it to make her feel that she was not as emotionally fulfilled.

I stopped talking about what I loved.

And then I started loving it less.

Because I felt guilty for loving it.

And I felt guilty for putting her in the middle of a life that she wasn't loving.

It wasn't that she didn't appreciate what I did. She just couldn't see it. And I couldn't show it to her because I was afraid it would make her love it even less and then maybe I would too.

But, then came a problem.

I started loving me less.

This was not my wife's problem. It was my own dysfunction. As I became less impressed with what I was doing, I became less impressed with who I was because though I hadn't realized it, my impression of who I was WAS what I did. If there were applause and compliments, I felt joy. If there were hands raised at the altar call, I felt validated. If there were "thank-yous" and "that-was-exactly-what-I-neededs," I felt I had earned a spot on this planet.

And when those things were not there, I felt empty.

Now I find myself badgering Kaysie for approval or confirmation that she is still somewhat fond of me. I know that she is, of course. But, it certainly doesn't feel the same. It does not feel like applause. There is no ankle-licking.

She used to love my jokes. Now, she rolls her eyes. She used to reach for my hand. Now, I grab hers so people will see. I used to listen to her pain. Now, I am so self-absorbed that I personalize everything she does or says as if it is aimed negatively at me without any thought of what else might be the actual problem.

And here is the rub. I see this. I actually see it. And deep inside, I want to change. It's as though I'm hovering over my body, looking down on my actions screaming: "You fool! You're losing everything! Don't do THAT. Do THIS." But THAT remains while THIS takes a hike. I yell at my kids for nothing, lecturing on proper stillness in a bath so that no drops get on the mirror. And as the wrong words come out of my mouth, I talk to myself in third person, telling myself to get a grip and let them be children—to just love them. But I can't stop.

I am losing it.

And every night now—every single night, I stare at the ceiling, wide awake. There are many, many things going right with my life. But, at 2:37 in the morning, I am completely blinded to anything but the devastation. At 2:37, I am disgusted with myself—so very disappointed at the schmuck I have become. So overwhelmed at my need for change. Angry at my tiredness. Ashamed of my fat. Perplexed at the way the life force has been sucked out of me. I wonder where that guy went who made everyone laugh—the one they all called *people-pleaser*. Where the Hello Kitty did that guy go?

2:37 is the point of no return. It's the moment when, if you are unfortunate enough to still be lucid and staring at the clock, you realize that you are no longer crawling into the night. You are now creeping toward morning. Rest seems impossible, clarity futile. It is the half-life of the darkness. And I find myself visiting there more and more often.

It's different in the morning. In the morning, I can suddenly see that there is so much good. But, in the witching hour, I cannot feel it. I keep trying to feel it, but then before I know it, I am reaching desperately in the dark for my wife's withdrawn hand. My stomach churns. Some nights I want to vomit. Other nights, I just want to die.

And then the sun.

Clarity.

Hope.

This week, I'm going to buy a clock that skips 2:37.

The real irony is that you would never know any of this by observing me in day-to-day life. I run a creative media business. Kaysie and I minister to college kids. We engage with people on a daily basis who would probably talk about our confidence and peace of mind, and it's not an act. It's difficult to explain. There are simply moments when things click, but there are also moments of panic.

I don't share this with my coworkers.

I don't share it with my friends.

Actually, I don't share it with anyone at all.

Just you, really.

My doctor has a name for all this.

You see, I actually did it.

I went to our family physician with the agony between my legs and you know what he gave me?

Paperwork.

Pages and pages of tests and paperwork.

ME: *What's all this?*

DOCTOR: Just a little pop quiz.

ME: *These are questions about my emotions.*

DOCTOR: Are they? Huh. How 'bout that?

ME: *This is not in my head. This is in my pants.*

DOCTOR: Sure.

ME: *No. Really. I fell through a roof.*

DOCTOR: Haven't we all?

ME: *I don't think we have.*

DOCTOR: What I mean to say is that every man faces his own roof and some fall through it.

ME: *You do realize I literally fell through a roof.*

DOCTOR: Certainly. But, let's deal with the real problem.

ME: *My lack of motor skills?*

DOCTOR: No. You said that you were feeling angry, lacking confidence, unable to sleep …

ME: *How is any of that related to falling through the roof?*

DOCTOR: It isn't—unless it is.

ME: *I'm confused. Did you give me medication without telling me again?*

DOCTOR: You see, the thing you see isn't always the thing that is. Sometimes you have to look at the thing you cannot see to discover what is behind the thing you can. Medicine isn't an exact science.

ME: *Actually, medicine is the only exact science.*

DOCTOR: Eh. Figure of speech.

ME: *Say. While you figure out what I cannot see from this questionnaire, why don't you give me some Ibuprofen to take the edge off what we can see—that is, when they're not shriveled.*

This is when he began inspecting.

Down there.

Now, let's be honest. There's no easy way to do this: my doctor checking under the hood—taking the Silly Putty out of the egg. It's simply not the recipe for a happy morning. He says things like "just relax" and "sorry my hands are cold" but that doesn't make the moment any more chit-chatty. It is the most vulnerable a man can get.

DOCTOR: Well, they look normal.

ME: *I didn't say they relocated to my ear. I said I crash-landed on them.*

DOCTOR: There was clearly some intense soreness.

ME: *How did you know that?*

DOCTOR: You pulled a little of my hair out.

ME: *Sorry. I never know what to do with my hands.*

DOCTOR: Happens all the time.

ME: *So is it fixable?*

DOCTOR: I'll run some tests. You think the pain may just be in your head?

In my head?!

What was he talking about? Certainly the test had just proven that there was deep bruising—perhaps even permanent damage. How could he think this was in my head?

It seems that he believes all of my problems are interconnected. The pain. The broken parts. The lack of sleep. The angry outbursts. The disappearing confidence. All of it. But he does not give me medicine. He gives me the next best thing: a multiple-choice pop quiz. And the answers to that quiz have given him a word for what I am feeling.

Depression.

Now, he made it sound a little more pleasant. He calls it "mild depression."

This is like calling it a "brisk plague" or a "quaint tsunami" or a "brief Macarena." No matter how you slice it, the adjective is not milquetoast enough to neuter the wallop of the noun.

My first response to his prediagnosis (an approach he takes quite often) is shock. Not the sort of shock where it makes no sense, but rather the sort of shock where it makes perfect sense but you would like it be untrue. But the word is not final. The tests haven't been completely assessed. My multiple-choice answers have not been fully graded. All of this will happen once we get home from this vacation that is supposed to catapult me back into jollyworld—a process that would have begun yesterday at Stone Mountain had our merriment not been drowned by a quaint tsunami.

But today is a new day and the sun is up. No sadness is allowed because today is Morgan's birthday. She is nine, which means this is the last year that she will want anything even remotely little-girlish. We're starting to get into tweener

territory now and want to treasure every innocent moment left. That is why we
are currently waiting in one of the longest lines ever formed in order to get inside
the new Atlanta aquarium. We just finished shopping at Ikea, which is a Dutch
word that translates to mean "you-will-no-longer-want-this-by-the-time-you-get-
home." Every room in Ikea looks like it should be inhabited by the cast of *Logan's
Run*. It's not so much a store as it is an Epcot attraction. I was slapped because I
assumed the saleslady was animatronic. We ate lunch in the cafeteria, where all
the food was Danish except ironically for the danishes, which were American. We
bought eleven items that I no longer want. How fickle we Americans are. One
moment: excited by antiseptic cubicles; the next: staring at live fish.

We are loading this week with frivolity. Overloading it really, because we
are attempting to shield our children from the myriad of family crises that we are
currently experiencing. As challenging as my life has been lately, it is far more
daunting to imagine my children suffering because of it. This has been an
anxiety of mine since they were born. To this end, when Morgan was a baby, I
used to dream of her calling out for rescue. One night, I had a vivid dream that
she cried out for me and I leapt out of my bed to save her. I awakened with a
start to discover myself prostrate on the bed, my hand grabbing my bleeding
scalp. While asleep, I had literally thrown my own unconscious body out of bed
and into the wall, ramming it with my face. I left a dent in the wall and a
slightly smaller one in my head.

Kaysie laughed a lot.

Oh, do I miss that free in-love laughter. I had noticed it dwindling, but it
wasn't until this month that I noticed it completely missing—as if being held for
ransom. But by what, I have not yet taken the time to investigate. Instead, I am
continually taken aback by seeing despair in her eyes in moments I hoped would
bring her at least fleeting joy. Even here on vacation. I keep asking her if
everything is all right and she keeps saying the same thing:

Don't you know what week this is?

Yeah. I do know. Vacation week. My birthday week. All the more reason I expect her to smile, even if there is no truth at all behind it.

The doors are opening to the aquarium. It is a staggering vision, but we are unable to experience it just yet because we have to go through three rounds of security checkpoints before they allow us inside. I know the puffer fish are rare and it would be a shame if they were harmed, but I still think a cavity search is a bit much.

The first exhibit is one of those hands-on dealios where the kids can reach in and stroke a sea urchin. If we weren't shelling out a hundred bucks to experience it, I would consider it punishment. Why would I want to wait in line to touch something slimy? I can do that for free inside my own nose round the clock. In fact, most of the children standing in this line just finished doing that to their own nose and all I can think about is how my hands are going to touch the same urchin as theirs.

Charlie, being the shortest of the bunch, cannot get more than the tip of his fingers into that water. This is not enough for him. Technically, it won't be enough for Charlie until he is squeezing the urchin with both fists and goo pops out several of the creature's orifices. To this end, Charlie decides he wants a better grip and lunges upward over the wall toward the water.

I grab him by the waist before he actually topples.

There is no real danger here, but I still feel that flipping of my intestines. For a moment, I had a serious flashback.

Morgan.

She couldn't have been more than two-years-old at the time and Kaysie and I lived in a small quaint rental house with a swimming pool in the backyard. It was a weekday and I was home for lunch. I know this because I remember random details. I had the mail in one hand and my cell phone in the other. I was wearing a dress shirt and khakis. I was sticking my head out the back door to tell Kaysie I was heading back to the office.

Sploosh.

Subtle like nothing. Practically calm.

My little girl sank to the bottom of the pool.

There was a split second that felt like dragging minutes as Kaysie and I stared at each other, absorbing what had just happened. Suddenly, I dropped the mail, gripped the cell phone more tightly and dove into the water. As I swam towards Morgan through water that was suddenly made of oatmeal, I beheld the strangest thing.

She didn't breathe in water.

She didn't panic or flail.

She just kept staring.

Straight into my eyes as she plummeted fast toward the concrete floor ten feet beneath the surface. Her eyes were confused and wild. Like I had let her down. Like I was the one killing her.

I snagged her with my phone-free hand and pumped my legs toward the surface.

We broke through to oxygen and she suddenly sputtered, coughing up water and screaming to alert the media.

I lay her into Kaysie's arms as Kaysie, sobbing and rocking back and forth, clutched Morgan's soaked form. The panic raced through my mind. *What if? What if? What if?* A matter of nanoseconds separated rescue from tragedy. It seemed so easy, so effortless for death to arrive. Safety was out of reach. Life suddenly seemed like nothing more than a lengthy sequence of days where I would do my best to swerve around doom and yank my loved ones toward rescue.

My hand was suddenly blistering hot. I looked down and realized that I was still clutching my cell phone and it was frying in my palm. I gazed at my only daughter, breathing heavily but beginning now to fall asleep in Kaysie's grasp. I had never saved anyone's life before. And as I allowed myself to consider the devastation that would have occurred in my soul had my baby girl not survived that moment, I began to realize that the life I saved might have just been my own.

⊙ ◉ ◉

Thirty-seven.

That is the number. Tomorrow I will be thirty-seven. And yet I feel decades older than when I turned thirty-six.

I don't know what it is about these last twelve months. It's like when you buy a house that isn't actually new, but is new to you. Everything has been touched up, and you live there about three years getting used to the moderate upkeep required in a house that someone recently spit-and-polished.

Then, suddenly, year four arrives like a quaint tsunami. Everything begins dissolving at once. Paint peels revealing layers of color that would have never been a good idea on any wall. Plumbing starts to leak. Burning smells turn up more frequently. The termite fumigation guarantee expires. Something dies in the walls, and you have no idea how to even begin to consider how to fix it.

That's thirty-seven.

That's me tomorrow.

Over the course of the past year, Kaysie and I have repeatedly hit a wall. This wall is not foreign to us, yet it suddenly seems impenetrable. Things that used to bother us moderately now seem insurmountable. Arguments grow more personal. The misunderstandings longer. The making-up shorter.

I know what is at the root of it.

As I have grown older, I have slowly become less of a man.

As my anxiety has increased and my confidence decreased, I have felt her distancing herself—finding solace in friends where she used to draw toward me. And the more she pulls away, the more I grab at her. I know this seems desperate. It is emasculating, and I don't know how to remedy it. I want to hold her like we used to hold one another—those moments where it was painful to let go. But I see it in her eyes when she looks at me. She still loves me; I know this. But, where she used to see her hero, she now sees the one thing that I wish I were not.

Fat.

I do not only mean in a bodily sense, though this is also true.

It should come as no surprise to me that I am fat. As far back as I remember, I have always been told that I will be fat. And I believed it, because I loved food. But more than that, I hated pain, and exercise was always pain.

Fat is where I got my sense of humor. I couldn't retaliate from the horrible names I was called by physical force, but I could turn my tongue into a heartless weapon, wielding sarcasm and insults as both shield and dagger to protect myself from seeming the loser that I knew I was.

Finally, one summer, when I was fourteen, I decided I was sick of my friends calling me lardo. I was tired of being informed that fat was my destiny. I began to diet and exercise diligently, and by the end of the summer, I had lost almost twenty-five pounds. But it didn't change anything. The girls that I liked still thought of me as the kid who used to be fat. I was still informed that it didn't matter what I did—fat was in my genes. And my insecurity grew and grew to paramount proportions.

I knew that a man was supposed to have confidence.

Maybe this is why the girls didn't want me.

I didn't have confidence.

I decided then and there to live as an actor.

To pretend that I had confidence.

This is when I left home and went away to college. Suddenly, I was known as the thin guy, the talented guy, the confident guy. One man apologized to me my first year of college because, before getting to know me, he assumed I was cocky. I told him I forgave him, but deep down, I relished it as a compliment.

Suddenly, girls liked me. Lots of girls. And for a moment, I felt as if the confidence might be real because it was becoming more and more effortless to seem the fictional self.

But the confidence was not actual because every single day of my life—including the half of my life I was thin—every single day I have felt fat. I had considered my fit appearance temporary, like a girdle that was about to burst open exposing skin folds of the truth. I was never talented in any sport, so I strove to seem manly on the outside, while inside I was being crushed by my perspective of myself.

After marriage, I kept the weight off for years, but then I grew tired. Up until now, it has been a moderate fat. It hasn't kept me from playing with the children or engaging in activity. But, now, thirty-seven. The paint is starting to peel. The plumbing just burst. I can feel it.

And I see it in my Kaysie's eyes.

It seems so petulant to dwell on such a thing. So childish. Until I realize how intertwined it all is. As the body goes, so goes the mind. The heart. The spirit.

My entire being is out of whack.

Fat.

People continually say to me, "What are you talking about? You're not fat."

But I know the truth. Not because I know how fat looks. Rather, I know how fat feels.

I smell the scent of selfishness, fleshliness in my life—not simply committing overt sins, but making sure I get what I want the moment I want it. There is very little denying myself at this stage of my life, and I don't do it because I feel good. I do it because I feel horrible. I find myself in a vicious cycle of downcast emotions, and my natural reaction is to gratify those emotions with a bite of doughnut or media or spending or a half-truth that makes me appear better than I am or God only knows what. A taste of this. A glimpse of that. An ignoring of the truth. Suddenly, I am obese. Round like a snowball gaining momentum down the hill, amassing inches at every rotation. And I don't simply mean the circle around my belly, because I know a lot of thin people who are just as fat as I am.

I see this same despair in my marriage and I WANT to fix it. I do! I am DESPERATE to fix it! But, I haven't the foggiest idea how to begin. It seems too painful.

So, instead of sitting it down and getting to the root ...

I take it on vacation.

● ○ ◉

ME: *Can't we just enjoy the vacation?*

KAYSIE: I'm trying to enjoy the vacation. But it's a hard week for me.

ME: *Well, it's also my birthday.*

KAYSIE: I know it's your birthday. I can't help it. Are you going to do what the doctor said?

ME: *What do you mean?*

KAYSIE: Are you going to take the antidepressants?

ME: *You think I'm depressed?*

KAYSIE: The doctor thinks you're depressed.

ME: *I don't know. Do we have to talk about this now?*

KAYSIE: We never talk about it.

ME: *It's my birthday week.*

KAYSIE: Do you realize what it says to me that you aren't willing to take the antidepressants?

ME: *How does me taking the antidepressants have anything to do with my feelings for you?*

KAYSIE: It's like you don't want to be fixed.

ME: *OF COURSE I want to be fixed! You know what; let's not do this now. Can we not do this now?*

KAYSIE: Fine.

ME: *What?*

KAYSIE: What do you mean what?

ME: *You said fine but you didn't sound fine.*

KAYSIE: Let's just drop it. It's almost your birthday.

ME: *Are you okay?*

KAYSIE: I'm FINE. Stop asking.

ME: *I just want to know if you're okay*

KAYSIE: I'm doing the best I can. It's a hard week.

ME: *Yeah. It's also my birthday week.*

A pause. A life-shattering pause.

KAYSIE: You really don't know what week it is, do you?

My face goes red.

ME: *What do you mean? It's the week of July fourth.*

And my mind begins to race. July Fourth. Was that when I fell through the roof? No. It couldn't be. What were we doing a year ago? July Fourth. We didn't do much of anything if I recall. We were lazy that week.

No. Not lazy.

Sad.

Wait. We were alone. The kids were away.

Why were they away?

Why were we sad?

No. Not sad.

Devastated.

No.

No. No. No.

God help me.

We had decided that three was probably enough. After Kaysie's back went out that one time, the doctor encouraged us not to put Kaysie's body through another pregnancy. But, there it was: that stick with the very pronounced straight line announcing a birth was imminent. We were both almost thirty-six with a house too small for the three gymnasts already in our care. It took a few days to absorb the information fully, but we were going to have a FOURTH child.

Morgan, Jackson, and Charlie had all been praying for a new baby for quite some time. We wanted desperately to tell them, but we thought we should wait for confirmation from the doctor. It wasn't long before it was clear that we were, indeed, going to have another baby. It had taken a while to acclimate to the idea, but now we were ecstatic. We knew it would be a challenge with space and finances, but how could we feel anything but radical joy?

We decided it had been long enough. We called a family meeting and asked the age-old question: "Guess what is in Mommy's tummy?" The third guess was correct (the first two guesses being Transformers and poop) and the room literally swelled with the elation of three kids rocking out to Europe's "The Final Countdown." We went to bed a happy family.

Then came 2:37 in the morning.

It was July 2 and Kaysie awoke with a start. She had been in and out of sleep all night with pains that seemed strange at best. Then, she was buckled over in agony. Moaning out loud in anguish and fear.

The next morning, we waited in the lobby of the hospital for a very long time until tests were done and it was clear that we had, indeed, lost the baby.

A miscarriage.

Nothing could have made less sense. Doesn't God want us to be fruitful and multiply? Aren't we supposed to bring more people into this world? Why bring us such unparalleled joy just to smash it against the rocks of the shore? If this baby was bound for death, why did the baby hold on just until we had told the children and then die mere hours later? Why allow those three precious hearts to know if it was already secretly lost?

I was angry. Freaking furious.

Why? WHY on earth were we losing our baby?

I was silent. Kaysie was silent.

The doctor left us alone as we looked at each other.

Then, looked away.

I knew Kaysie needed me to say something, but I couldn't for the life of me think of anything that wasn't trite. My job was that of the optimist and nothing came.

Kaysie softly sobbed.

Kaysie sobbed and I stared at the television.

The G8 Summit Concert was playing and Madonna was standing next to a beautiful African woman who had barely escaped starvation and the AIDS epidemic. Madonna shed a tear for the woman, and I remember wondering what the spectrum of sadness must look like. Somewhere on the scale between that African woman's fight to survive and Madonna's remorse over how far removed her life had been from helping her—somewhere in between lay these tears of mine and Kaysie's. Tears for our little one who would never know life. And tears for the three innocent hearts we would be required to crush in three hours time.

When the children were brought home that evening, they rushed in to see us, smiling ear-to-ear, thrilled for more stories about the coming brother or sister.

But their questions were met with silence.

We sat them down—four, five, and a day away from eight—and told them that we did not understand why, but the baby was in heaven now.

There was grave confusion.

Charlie's lip quivered hard.

Tears began to roll.

And Morgan begged to know why.

I did not have an answer.

Something broke in our household that evening. Something in our family. An uncertainty crept in–the awareness that we were no longer immune from devastation. We huddled into a mass of five and wept and wept.

I don't know why, Morgan.

Oh God.

This is what started it. The descent into the abyss.

Kaysie thinks I have forgotten this moment.

That I deemed it unimportant.

But she doesn't understand. It was not forgotten. It was buried.

I had pushed it away—shoved it into the thick manila folder in my heart labeled "unfixable."

This week marks one year since we lost the baby.

One year since our children's hearts were broken in half.

One year since we began to question God.

All of that emotion—the grief and despair—all of it has flooded back to Kaysie. And I didn't even realize what week it was.

◉ ◉ ◉

Hours after the argument, Kaysie lays next to me asleep. I stare at her as I hold my Bible, hoping my daily reading will bring me enough peace to fall asleep. I brush the hair from her eyes. She's so beautiful. So quiet. My heart is filled to the brim with sadness. It's not as if the words we threw at each other were that harmful. It's more the fact that there is an ongoing electric wire of tension that traverses from my spoken words to hers. Every sentence seems to be misunderstood. Every breath or sigh or pause in the midst of conversation translated into assumptions of revulsion. I carry this weight of disappointment. I carry an unspoken feeling that in Juarez she saw the man I was capable of becoming and then I never quite did.

She exhales and stirs, causing her to roll over, away from me, against the darkness. I stare at the back of her head. I want to whisper to her …

> *Let's run. Let's escape. Everything. The people we have become. The damage. The baggage. The history. The myriad of reasons we have disappointed and dismantled one another. Let's run and start over. We'll find a beach or a desert or another Mexican orphanage and we'll rewind to the best version of ourselves and begin again with the awareness of what never ever to say to each other. We'll pray and we'll really listen this time instead of assuming it will be a cakewalk. I'll never roll my eyes and sigh and you'll never say "forget it" and we will have a*

second chance to have the perfect marriage that everyone
assumed we would.

But I don't whisper anything at all. Instead, I look at the clock as it strikes midnight. I am now thirty-seven years old. I weigh our future. Could this year perhaps be different? Can I stop this downward emotional spiral? After all, I'm practically middle-aged now. Two times thirty-seven. That's seventy-four. I hope to outlast that, but it's certainly not guaranteed. I've always said I have a thing for halfway. For that top of the hill moment when I finally stop pedaling and start coasting. Maybe this is it. My half-life. Thirty-seven. Why not? I weigh these thoughts carefully and am about to drift off to sleep when the Old Testament passage on the page draws my attention:

> *[Elijah] came to a lone broom bush and collapsed in its shade,*
> *wanting in the worst way to be done with it all—to just die:*
> *"Enough of this, GOD! Take my life—I'm ready to join my*
> *ancestors in the grave!"*[†]

Yes! This, I can identify with. That Elijah. He was a godly man—crazy, but godly. And if he felt the way I feel, certainly there is hope for change. I read on:

> *Exhausted, he fell asleep under the lone broom bush. Suddenly*
> *an angel shook him awake and said, "Get up and eat!" He looked*
> *around and, to his surprise, right by his head were a loaf of bread*
> *baked on some coals and a jug of water. He ate the meal and*
> *went back to sleep.*[††]

And there it is. This is what I believe: that it is possible for me to come to the very end of myself—sheer hopelessness—but that God will not abandon me there. Regardless of whether I find answers, God will find a way to bring me sustenance. This is something I can hold on to. I glance over at the back of Kaysie's head and realize that this epiphany might just push me over the apex of the hill in question.

[†] 1 Kings 19:3
[††] 1 Kings 19:5–6

I am so preoccupied with the miracle of God's provision for Elijah in the moment of despair, it takes me a second to realize that the sustenance was there for a reason. I read one more sentence:

> The angel of God came back, shook [Elijah] awake again, and said, "Get up and eat some more."[†]

Wait a second. Where exactly is this going? Why does God want Elijah to eat more?

> You've got a long journey ahead of you.[††]

I drop the book in my lap and stare into space.

This may not be the top of the hill after all.

---

† 1 Kings 19:7a
†† 1 Kings 19:7b

(Exhibit G)

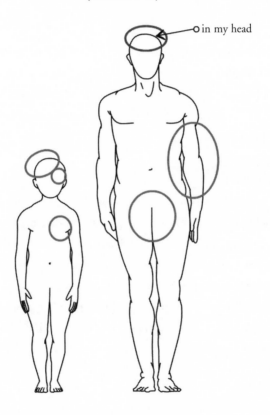

in my head

KAYSIE

The reward is ready.

After a melee of a summer, especially for Charlie and his recurring maimings, Kaysie and I decided that a bonus was in order. School is forthcoming and it breaks our hearts to think that our kids have lost it all to sickness. So, now, August 26, the day before Kaysie's birthday, we are unveiling a backyard bombshell of gargantuan proportions.

We bought a trampoline.

YES! I was never allowed to have one growing up because it was assumed that one leap would vault me into a nearby dogwood, impaling me upon a branch and piercing a spleen. But now, in adulthood, Kaysie and I finally have the opportunity to be children. We bought the trampoline as a surprise and set it up last night with my friend Jeff. As we constructed, the kids stood a half-inch from us, salivating and constantly requesting updates regarding progress. We finished building it too late for them to experience it last night, and so this morning, they are on top of the world.

> **CHARLIE:** Dad?
> **ME:** *Yeeees.*
> **CHARLIE:** Can I jump on da twampoween?
> **ME:** *It's 6:30 in the morning.*
> **CHARLIE:** Dat's wight.
> **ME:** *Is the moon out?*
> **CHARLIE:** No. I can see a wittle of da sun.
> **ME:** *Go ahead.*

CHARLIE: Gweat.

(A moment of silence.)

CHARLIE: Dad?
ME: *Yeeees.*
CHARLIE: Will you jump wiff me?

I knew this question would arise.

And I knew the answer would have to be a thudding "no."

When we returned from vacation, I went back to my doctor. The results from my written "this guy is crazy" exam were back and my suspicions—though not clarified—were at least confirmed.

DOCTOR: Well.
ME: *What do you mean "Well."*
DOCTOR: I beg your pardon?
ME: *Most people say "Well?" with a question mark but you said "Well." with a period.*
DOCTOR: I wasn't asking a question. I was making a statement.
ME: *A statement that I am well?*
DOCTOR: A statement that you are not well.
ME: *Then why did you say "well"?*
DOCTOR: I meant "Well." As in "Ah." Or "Hmm."
ME: *As opposed to "well" as in "well."*
DOCTOR: Correct.
ME: *Well?*

The truth was, I was unwell. Very unwell. And the doctor did not bother to disguise his inability to make sense of it all. The different pains, maladies, and anxieties I was experiencing didn't add up to one complete diagnosis. Every time one diagnosis seemed to click, it did nothing to explain the rest of what ailed me.

ME: *So, this is all because I'm depressed then.*

DOCTOR: No.

ME: *Great!*

DOCTOR: I mean, yes. You are depressed. But, that doesn't explain a lot of what we are finding.

ME: *You mean depression alone doesn't account for the thudding ache I constantly feel down in boy's town?*

DOCTOR: Precisely.

ME: *Wow. It's almost as if I mentioned that theory before.*

DOCTOR: Have you had any severe trauma down there?

ME: *Severe trauma? Hmm. Not that I can think of. Unless of course, you're referring to the falling-through-the-roof-onto-a-crossbeam-incident I've mentioned TWELVE times.*

DOCTOR: No. Other than that.

ME: *Other than that?*

DOCTOR: Maybe they're twisted. Do they feel twisted?

ME: *That depends. Like a pretzel or a twizzler?*

DOCTOR: Could they have been twisted?

ME: *You mean did I squat over a bread mixer? No. Just the fall through the ceiling.*

DOCTOR: I really don't think that's it.

ME: *And why would that be?*

DOCTOR: Either way, I have concerns and I don't want to have to take one or both.

ME: *One or both what?*

DOCTOR: One or both of those.

ME: *These those?*

DOCTOR: Those those.

ME: *Stank.*

DOCTOR: Just to be safe, I'm going to schedule an appointment for you at the clinic.

ME: *The twisted boys' clinic?*

DOCTOR: No. No. No. No. No.

He jots down a few bullet points onto his doctor's pad.

DOCTOR: I'm ordering you an ultrasound.

An ultrasound.

I was not completely unaware of this process. I had experienced it multiple times when Kaysie was pregnant with our three children. Kaysie would put on one of those gowns that covers every inch of the human anatomy except for the entirety of the butt crack because, let's face it, you need a good laugh in the hospital. The doctor would come in and spread what appeared to be alien secretions all over her belly, squeezing it out of one of those ketchup bottles that they use at truck stops. He would then take a wand that gave off a radioactive hum and slowly rub it across her belly like a tractor tilling the fields until he could see the moving form of our unborn child. Like so much in life, it was a perfect blend of the miraculous and the disgusting.

I never expected to experience one myself.

DOCTOR: There are other problems I am having more trouble explaining.

ME: *Which ones?*

DOCTOR: Well, the anxiety. The fear. The anger. The lack of confidence.

ME: *Just that?*

DOCTOR: It makes me wonder.

ME: *I thought the depression was the thing destroying me.*

DOCTOR: But what if it isn't?

ME: *What do you mean?*

DOCTOR: What if something else is causing the depression, and that something else is the thing that is destroying you?

ME: *I don't understand.*

DOCTOR: Answer one question for me, Mark.

ME: *What is it?*

DOCTOR: Do you often have trouble sleeping?

Whampow.

He handed me another, smaller questionnaire that asked me very specific questions about my sleeping patterns. I answered quite honestly.

> Do you have trouble falling asleep? *YES.*
> Do you wake up repeatedly throughout the night? *YES.*
> Do you use the bathroom repeatedly through the night? *YES.*
> Do you snore? *YES.*
> Do you wake up with headaches? *YES.*
> Sore throat? *AND YES.*
> Dry mouth? *You people have been spying on me.*
> Do you wake up suddenly? *Again: YES.*
> Sometimes gasping for breath? *Is that not normal?*
> Do you feel unrested after a night's sleep? *YES!*

I'm fairly certain I passed the test.

The doctor reviewed my answers.

> **DOCTOR:** Well, I'll be.
>
> **ME:** *You'll be what?*
>
> **DOCTOR:** Not, what I'll be. What you'll be.
>
> **ME:** *What will I be?*
>
> **DOCTOR:** Mark, I need to put you through some intense studies in the next few months to make certain, but based on your answers, if you're being truthful …
>
> **ME:** *Nothing more fun than fibbing about sleeping patterns.*
>
> **DOCTOR:** I am quite certain that you suffer from sleep apnea.
>
> **ME:** *And ten bucks for you if you can guess my next question.*
>
> **DOCTOR:** It means that when you sleep, you can't breathe.

I allow this to soak in for a moment.

> **DOCTOR:** It's why you snore. Your body is struggling to get oxygen. Every time it is unable to seize a breath, it wakes you up.
>
> **ME:** *What does that mean?*
>
> **DOCTOR:** Well, it's very serious. People die from this. We need to put

you through a sleep study to determine whether or not my
suspicions are accurate.

ME: *Does a nap count as prep for a sleep study?*

DOCTOR: Mark, think about what I am saying. If this is your
          problem, and we are able to figure that out, we can remedy
          it. And your whole life will change.

ME: *How's that?*

He begins to draw diagrams on his notepad.

DOCTOR: This is you sleeping. You attempt to breathe and it doesn't
          happen, so your heart kick-starts you awake. This means
          that the few hours you do sleep, you are only getting to
          levels one or two. That's not very deep. My guess is that
          you practically never reach REM sleep, because that's where
          testosterone is developed.

ME: *Did you just call me a girly-man?*

DOCTOR: No. No. Think about this. Your testosterone. That's where
          you get your confidence, your strength. Once that is gone,
          you're emasculated—a worrying mess. Add to that what
          the lack of level three and four sleep would do to your
          body: constant exhaustion. It would explain the fear, the
          explosions of anger, and it would ABSOLUTELY explain
          the depression that comes from it all.

ME: *Why would it explain the depression?*

DOCTOR: Mark, your body is starving for oxygen. Without it, your
          heart is dying a little bit every night.

ME: *So, what you're saying is that the wreck that I currently am is
          all because—*

DOCTOR: All because you are unable to find real rest. And I think I
          can help you find it.

I have been at the bottom for a long time.

It never dawned on me that there might be an actual reason. I knew I was
disintegrating, devolving, but I was convinced that this was the result of my
choices—the chemical reaction to my good and bad decisions colliding. I had
believed that God had continual answers for others, even that He intended to

utilize me to communicate those answers to them. But for myself? I believed I was stuck with darkness.

Suddenly, renewed hope.

What if all of this is accurate? What if I can get some or all of the good back? I could find myself again.

Love myself again.

And perhaps Kaysie could too.

I resolved to pursue these answers and I asked the doctor what it was that I needed to do. His response? First things first. There was still my mystery pain. I needed to go get that ultrasound.

A couple of days later, I showed up at a clinic where I was greeted by a girl fresh out of college.

HER:	Good morning, Mr. Steele. I will be performing your ultrasound.
ME:	*Excuse me?*
HER:	Excuse you, what?
ME:	*You, you, you can't be.*
HER:	I assure you, I will be more than professional.
ME:	*Have you read the card?*
HER:	What?
ME:	*It's not your average ultrasound.*
HER:	I beg your pardon?
ME:	*It's sort of a mega-ultrasound.*
HER:	I don't understand.
ME:	*My doctor wrote it down on the card.*

Annoyed, she read the card.

And suddenly turned beet red.

HER:	Oh.
ME:	*Uh huh.*

HER:	Ooooh.
ME:	*Mmhm.*
HER:	WHOA!
ME:	*Yeah. That last sentence is a whopper.*
HER:	Oooookay.
ME:	*Unique.*
HER:	Hmmm.
ME:	*Suppose I'll take a raincheck.*
HER:	No worries, Mr. Steele. I'll just get a man to help us with our dilemma.

I felt much better about the situation knowing I had averted this train wreck. She showed up a few moments later with a gentleman wearing what appeared to be a janitor's coverall.

ME:	*Who's this?*
HER:	He's new, but he'll do in a pinch.
ME:	*The CUSTODIAN is gonna do my ultrasound?*
HER:	Oh! Heavens no.
ME:	*Thank God.*
HER:	I'm going to do it. He's just going to chaperone.
ME:	*What?!*
HER:	I'm a professional, Mr. Steele. There's nothing to be nervous about. Now drop those pants and stick your legs in these stirrups while the cleaning guy plays Tetris on his laptop.

The next thing I knew, I was doing my best to imagine nuns taking care of wounded puppies while the female facilitator slowly navigated the circumference of my Tater Tots with the equivalent of a Hot Wheels van coated in lime Jell-O. Needless to say, it was humiliating. The janitor seemed uninterested, alternating yawns in between attempts at computer hangman. I thought she was almost finished.

Then came the kicker.

HER:	Now, I'm going to need you to push.

I stared at her. Here I thought I was already as exposed as humanly possible and she suddenly introduces me to all new, even more degrading opportunities.

ME:	*You have got to be pulling my leg.*
HER:	No, sir. That is strictly against the rules.
ME:	*No. I mean you can't be serious.*
HER:	Just bear down like you're going to the bathroom.
ME:	*If I bear down in this position, it won't be like I'm going to the bathroom. It will be immensely realistic.*
HER:	Sir, don't be embarrassed. This is my job.
ME:	*How sad for you.*
HER:	I need you to bear down so that I can make certain the blood is flowing down there.
ME:	*And what if it isn't?*
HER:	Then, we may have to remove them.

No problem. Bearing down.

Within a span of time that couldn't have been more than seven minutes, but felt like the Peter Jackson director's cut of *The Lord of the Rings* trilogy, she was finished and I was dressed. She came back into the room and handed me a folder as I asked her for the results of the ultrasound.

HER:	Congratulations. It's a boy.
ME:	*I'll bet you've waited your whole life to make that joke.*
HER:	Who knew such a perfect scenario would arise?
ME:	*So, what is it?*
HER:	What is what?
ME:	*What is causing the pain?*
HER:	Oh. That's not my job.
ME:	*What isn't your job?*
HER:	To say what I found.

ME:	*Your job is to find something but not to say the something.*
HER:	No, I say the something. I just don't say the something to you. I say the something to your doctor.
ME:	*And then my doctor says your something to me.*
HER:	That's right.
ME:	*So you can't say your something to me. You have to say your something to the someone who is going to turn right around and say your something to me as if it were his own something.*
HER:	Bingo.
ME:	*An exercise in patience.*
HER:	And redundant co-pays.

And here we are. August 26. Two weeks since the ultrasound. And I still have not been told the something.

An exercise in patience.

But today is a different focus. Because today, I am making all the final preparations for Kaysie's birthday. I love Kaysie's birthday because it gives me the opportunity to show her how much I love her. I suppose I could do this on other days, but who has the time?

The plan? Get those kids on the trampoline so they can exercise their day away. In the meantime, I will get the last presents and rehearse tonight with the band. You see, tomorrow I have been asked to preach the Sunday morning service. Regardless of the turmoil going on in my personal life, Kaysie and I continue to have a desire to minister out of our frailty—to help others in the midst of our hurt. It doesn't make us experts, but it does give us perspective. As tomorrow is my wife's birthday, I have seized the opportunity of being on stage in front of her to plan a song.

Yes, I will be singing.

And not just any song.

A country song.

Now, all of my friends fall into one of two camps. They either: a) tolerate country music on a sappy sentimental level, or b) want to cut off their own ears when it comes on the radio.

I personally find the emotional honesty of country music appealing. It is not afraid to be schmaltzy. If the singer loves his wife, he will sing so. If he wants his enemies dead, he will probably throw that into the lyrics as well. Clarity. The cowboys know what they want and how to set it to a tune you can yodel by.

Tomorrow morning, this will be me. I will be a cowboy to my wife. I know she will love it. After all, we've been on a bit of an upswing in the past month—a tiny one, but progress nonetheless. We are starting to communicate more, laugh occasionally. I expect the birthday hoopla to throw us over this hump. Still looking for that apex. Still ready to coast down that easy second stage of our marriage that has just got to be starting any moment now.

I am beginning to have more clarity. The prediagnosis that I just might have sleep apnea has given me something to focus my efforts upon: a solution. My malady is no longer a meandering whatnot. It is mere days away from being defined. With this newfound lucidity, I am beginning to realize what a monkeychump I have been.

Today, I've been reading 2 Chronicles four through six, which records King Solomon's work on the temple of God. In the past, these sorts of passages would bore me to tears, but now, I am seeing myself in the worn pages.

Solomon begins his work with practically nothing—damaged goods brought by damaged people. But under Solomon's supervision, the people work to refine those damaged goods. In the process of choosing to celebrate God and remember His goodness, they become less and less damaged themselves. King Solomon chooses to remember God by making beautiful things out of things that seem useless.

I have been frustrated that God has not been making more of my days beautiful, while all the while I have remained stagnant, dull clay. I was dwelling so much on the pain around me that I was neglecting to see what was laying dormant inside—resisting any attempt to mold it into something worthwhile. Dwelling on the dross that I had become instead of seeing the fire as refinement.

As a climax to the rebuilding of the temple, Solomon got all the chiefs of tribes and family patriarchs together in Jerusalem and began to install the ark of the covenant inside. Then, after the grueling task, they sang praise to God in perfect harmony.

*"Yes! God is good! His loyal love goes on forever!" Then, a
billowing cloud filled the Temple of GOD. The priests couldn't even
carry out their duties because of the cloud—the glory of GOD!—
that filled The Temple of God."†*

I have a tendency to beg God to change my situation so that I can be freer
to worship Him. But that is not what Solomon did. He worshipped God first.
Honored Him. Remembered Him. Made the very best out of what he had
already been given.

And then … the situation changed.

Once God shows up, Solomon starts asking Him some pretty bold things.
Solomon goes through a litany of personal requests. My favorite is verse 27
where Solomon asks for a fresh start if the people repent.

*Listen from your home in heaven, forgive the sins of your
servants, your people Israel. Then start over with them; train them
to live right and well; Send rain on the land you gave as
inheritance to your people.††*

Wow.

Start over.

Can I have that, God?

Can I finally drag my lifeless body over this hump, learning from all the
damage done, but moving on to something brighter? Can I live right and well?
Can I somehow change from the dark clay into a refined beauty?

The answer seems to be right in front of me. In today's other reading:

*All praise to the God and Father of our Master, Jesus the
Messiah! Father of all mercy! God of all healing counsel! He
comes alongside us when we go through hard times, and before
you know it, he brings us alongside someone else who is going
through hard times so that we can be there for that person just
as God was there for us. We have plenty of hard times that come*

---

† 2 Chronicles 5:12–14
†† 2 Chronicles 6:26–27

> *from following the Messiah, but no more so than the good times*
> *of his healing comfort—we get a full measure of that, too.* [†]

And then it continues,

> *Instead of trusting in our own strength or wits to get out of it, we*
> *were forced to trust God totally—not a bad idea since he's the God*
> *who raises the dead! And he did it, rescued us from certain doom.* [††]

Whoa Nelly.

The answer has been here all along. It is not my own strength or my own wits that are failing here, because they are simply not strong enough to get me out of this pit. The answer is God and God alone. He is the only possible strength, and the clear next step is to get my selfish heart off of my own aches and pains and saddle alongside someone else instead.

Help someone else through.

Stop grabbing for my own comfort and freaking provide some for somebody else.

Of course!

And I finally can. Because the clouds are beginning to clear.

The kids are well.

Kaysie is smiling.

My diagnosis is coming.

It's as if the sun is shining again.

The kids love this trampoline. They are bonkers over it. Especially Charlie. His entire life, he has bounced off the walls. It's about time we found a way for him to make it literal. They jump, jump, jump. All day long and into the late, hot August afternoon.

I can tell they are beginning to wear out, which is perfect because this evening I finally have time to get the rest of the details together for the celebration

---

† 2 Corinthians 1:3–5
†† 2 Corinthians 1:9

tomorrow. Not that my wife wants much. If you asked her what she really wanted for her birthday, she would answer "sleep" and "to be with my family."

Kaysie has just left with her mother and Morgan to go shopping, so I am scurrying to get out the door while Papa watches the boys.

Ding dong.

No. Please no.

Ding dong ding dong ding dong ding dong ding dong ding dong!

I take a moment and glance about the room.

The kids are on the trampoline out back.

Papa is asleep on the couch.

If I time it right—

I leap behind the living room armchair, catching a glimpse of Zachary's silhouette as he presses his face against the window. I don't think he saw me.

    ZACHARY: Hellooo! Ah you there?!

I remain still.

    ZACHARY: I theenk you ah. Your automobile is pahked in the
        driveway.
    (silence)
    I'm VEEEEERY thirsty.
    (silence)
    I cahn't see anything. If you ah hiding, you ah very GOOD.

I am hiding in my own living room from a seven-year-old British boy. Why don't I just go over there and tell him "not today"? I know why. Because every time I say that to him, I crush him. But hey, I'm trying to change, right?

I open the door abruptly.

He is not surprised. He is smiling ear to ear.

> **ZACHARY:** Where were you HIDING?! Can I play?!
>
> **ME:** *Zachary, don't press your face against the window.*
>
> **ZACHARY:** How else will I know if you ah here?
>
> **ME:** *Just knock on the door.*
>
> **ZACHARY:** But that's when you hide.
>
> **ME:** *The kids can't play right now, Zachary.*
>
> **ZACHARY:** Of COURSE they cahn! They ah ALREADY playing!
>
> **ME:** *I mean, you can't come over right now.*
>
> **ZACHARY:** Why on EARTH not?
>
> **ME:** *Because I have to run some errands.*
>
> **ZACHARY:** Will they be here alone?
>
> **ME:** *They will be with their grandfather.*
>
> **ZACHARY:** And why cahn't HE watch me?
>
> **ME:** *Because he is old.*

Zachary stands there, hands on his hips, and takes a very large exhale as if he is about to scold me.

> **ZACHARY:** Okay. I don't mean to be RUDE, but you CERTAINLY come up with a LAWT of reasons for me NAWT to come inside your house.

And with that, the British Invasion retreats.

I grab my keys and am about to bolt out the front door.

> *Daddy?*

It is Charlie.

> **ME:** *Yeah, bud. What is it?*
>
> **CHARLIE:** Will you jump on da twampoween wid me?
>
> **ME:** *I already told you I can't do that, Charlie.*
>
> **CHARLIE:** Pwease?

ME: *Charlie, Daddy's hurt—and I'm way too big to jump on the trampoline with you. You'd rocket sky high.*

CHARLIE: Weawy?!

ME: *I've gotta run. Come hug me.*

CHARLIE: Pweeease pweeeease?! Pwetty pwease? Just a wittle bit?

ME: *Charlie …*

CHARLIE: Just ONE jump.

ME: *Charlie …*

CHARLIE: Juuuust one? Dat's all. Just one wittle jump. One tiny jump.

ME: *I really have to—*

CHARLIE: Pweeeeeease.

And then it hit me.

Change.

I'm not gonna be "that Dad" anymore. I'm not going to be the father who never does anything because of the possibility that something might go wrong. It's just a trampoline. It's just one jump.

And it will mean the world to Charlie.

I sigh.

You know what, Charlie? Absolutely.

Charlie emits a squeal that is unparalleled in its euphoria. I watch as he skips—I am not kidding, literally skips—to the trampoline. He kicks off his shoes and climbs up onto the black stretchy mat.

I finagle my way on the circular tarp and take a look at my elated five-year-old.

ME: *You ready?*

CHARLIE: JUUUUUUUMP!

I jump twice.

And break Charlie's upper leg bone in half.

(Exhibit H)

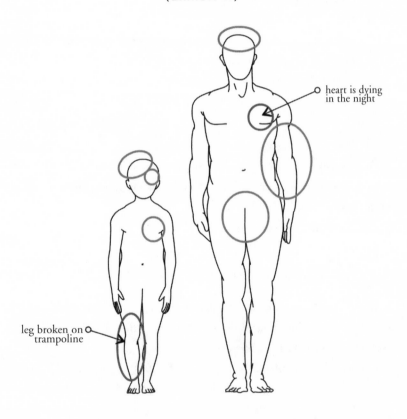

heart is dying
in the night

leg broken on
trampoline

2:37 A.M.
APEX BECOMES NADIR

Awake again.

Back-and-forth, back-and-forth.

Stop it.

We do this every night, Mark. You make an attempt at sleep only to have the thoughts come back.

I can't help it.

Right. You can't help it.

I lay here trying not to worry, not to be fearful, but everything in my life that seems to be falling apart rushes into my head like Attila the Hun.

That's because your problems are the center of your life.

What's that supposed to mean?

God isn't the center of your life. Worry is. Anxiety is.

That's ridiculous. Don't go blaming this on me. I have been diagnosed! I have sleep apnea! I can't help this!

You tell yourself that. Whatever helps you sleep at night.

Nothing helps me sleep at night.

Exactly.

How can you say God is not the center of my life when I am constantly bringing all of these anxieties to Him, begging Him to change them?

Yeah. You consider God for a fleeting moment just before you spend the next three hours obsessing over the unfairness of it all.

What would you think? My head is a mess, my marriage is stale, my children are constantly bludgeoned by this and that—just look at Charlie down there at the foot of my bed.

I know.

The cast is all the way up to his hip! He's in a wheelchair, for crying out loud! He can't walk, can't swim—all I can picture are those few seconds when he was skipping happily right before the screaming.

Lots of screaming.

He thought his awful summer was finished. We all thought it was finished. He was hurt so badly. I can't imagine the next time he will skip like that.

You've got to stop replaying it in your head.

Do you know what he said while I was carrying him to the car?

Stop.

He said, "YOU SHOULDN'T HAVE JUMPED WITH ME!"

You've got to stop.

And I said, "But you asked," and he screamed "I DIDN'T KNOW IT WOULD HURT SO BAD!"

Mark?

I just know that clinic is going to think we're doing something awful to him.

MARK!

What?

You're stuck in the circular.

Huh?

You're still not learning. This is the way you've always lived. Sure, it's ramped-up this time. It's suddenly a melodramatic version, but it's still the same garbage over and over with no change or growth in your reaction to it.

Oh. So, this is all about me, then.

Nothing is all about you. But, you seem to think everything is all about you. That is exactly my point.

Well, I don't care what you think, because my life is not circular. I am pushing through all of this rough stuff and I just know that any moment, I'm going to reach my half-point.

What are you talking about?

My life—my faith has felt like an uphill climb and I'm ready now.

Ready for what?

For my half-life.

Your what?

The apex of my experience where learning turns to application and the circular path finally gives way to the straight and narrow.

Where did you hear that?

It's in the introduction.

So. Let me get this straight. Your life has been a challenge.

Yes.

So, your perspective is—expend all your energies attempting to get to the point where the challenges are suddenly over?

I wouldn't exactly ...

You really think there is supposed to be some euphoric summit that cancels the climb and begins a slide?

Of course not.

Well, you've been living that way. You've been living as if all of your pursuits are grasping at easy.

Have not.

Have so. It's a lame duck way to live. That's you, Mark. You're the Lame Duck Christian.

I resent that.

Think about it. Think about what you've missed spinning your wheels just to escape lousy. Life isn't rosy, but it's certainly not all eye herpes either. It's a collision of the two and you've missed the better half trying to scrape your way out of the stink. There is no top of the hill—and you have most certainly not been climbing. There is only you facing the fact that joy can definitely be found on this path, but you've got to fight for it because the fight builds character. It turns you into something beautiful. You really thought you were at your apex?

Well, it's just a theory.

You do realize what an apex is, don't you?

It's the half-point.

No, Steele. It's the high point. The high point doesn't change you—and that's a good thing, because this moment is certainly not the high point.

Then, what is it?

The nadir.

The nadir?

The lowest point possible. It's where you come to the end of yourself. Where you die to your selfishness and surrender to God. But, you won't do that if you are pretending you've scaled some triumphant peak. You are not a martyr, Mark. You're just figuring out that life can be hard, but that is okay.

The nadir.

If you're looking for a halfway point—this is it, baby.

The low point of my life.

Embrace it, brother! It's a great thing to come to the end of yourself because it's the only place you can truly rely on God's power. Accept it. Surrender.

It's the only way to truly tackle your grief. Die to yourself, and you'll start rolling despair over and spanking it in public.

But I've been through so much.

And, you're going to go through more, but your perspective on what you're going through could change everything. Take a moment and look at your wife.

I can't. Her face is covered with pillows.

Well, take some action—lift them off of her. Look at her. Do you remember?

Of course I remember!

Well, then FIGHT for her! Get off your fat patoot and live in a way that will get her and keep her. FIGHT for you. Get yourself back.

I keep TRYING to get myself back!

No. You keep trying to get comfortable back. Trying to get the past back. The naïve, undisciplined you back. Forget that garbage. You've got to die to that.

That's exactly what I've been avoiding.

Of course it is, because it's even more painful than what you've been wallowing in this past year, but it's just going to keep getting worse until you decide to dive in and face what is down in the darkest depths.

You say that as if it is easy. I am at the end of myself here.

No. You just think you are. If you were really at the end of yourself, you would start seeing what God is doing. You're actually quite full of yourself and all the agony that comes with constantly staring in the mirror. You aren't even close to the end of yourself. You keep saying you are ready for all God wants to do inside you, but you're not letting any old garbage out to make new space.

You're telling me this year—all this pain—has been selfishness?!

I'm telling you that you know the one thing you have to do and you keep refusing to do it.

I've done everything I know to do!

Have not.

Have too!

Have not.

Okay, wise guy, what is this one thing left that I have not done.

Die already.

Die already?

Die already.

You mean—now?

Yes. Now. You've been stretching this angst out a bit, don't you think? Make a move. Stomp on that despair. Kill that suckerpunk monkeychump.

But, death is what I've been doing my best to avoid.

Exactly.

I don't understand.

You think you've been clinging to God because you love Him and you want to be who He has created you to be, but the moment that becomes painful, you decide that you love comfort more. So, you try to pray the pain away, refusing to acknowledge that the pain itself might actually be a part of the way out of the pain. Everybody hurts, Mark. Everybody dies. But there is much to embrace, to find joy in, to hold onto throughout that very same path. You're in agony every single day. And you will be until you finally decide to die already. Until then, you're only living half a life.

But, how on earth do I do that?

You really want to know?

Of course I do!

You cannot possibly really want to know it unless you are really ready to do it.

I'M READY! JUST TELL ME!

Okay ...

Open your mouth and close your eyes.

And what is that supposed to mean?

Don't worry.

You'll figure it out.

SIX DECISIONS THAT MATTERED

decision #4:

PRETENDING / LEGIT

It's the half-truths that kill you.

The ones you tell to those you love.

The ones you tell to yourself.

The ones that you believe without them ever being spoken.

The half-truths mold you—shape you into the worst version of them.

They slowly kick out the truth-half

and mold you into the half that began as deception.

It is the thin line crossed.

The variation so small that it becomes

difficult for you to see the truth yourself.

But eventually, so many half-truths

become a half-life.

No more pretending.

No more fudging in the name of encouragement.

Smoothing over for the sake of optimism.

Dodging details so as not to disappoint.

No more pretending.

It is time to acknowledge the truth.

The whole truth.

Time to become legit.

And face whatever pain might come along with it.

FIVE FALL BACK

SEPTEMBER 18

DOCTOR: And then what?

ME: *Then, I contacted you.*

DOCTOR: After the bleeding.

ME: *After three days of bleeding.*

DOCTOR: That must have been frightening.

ME: *You mean going to the bathroom in the middle of the night, and then turning on the light to see that it was all blood? Yes. It was frightening.*

DOCTOR: Why didn't you come to see me sooner?

ME: *I was on a job in Chicago. I just got back.*

He looks at his notepad a while.

DOCTOR: And you're still having the pain in your abdomen?

ME: *Yes sir.*

DOCTOR: You've had an awful lot happen to your family this year, haven't you, Mark.

ME: *Yes, but I have a peace.*

DOCTOR: A piece of what.

ME: *No. A peace. A peace that this will all work out—in the end.*

He changes the subject.

DOCTOR: You ready for that sleep study tonight?

ME: *Remind me exactly why I have to do it again?*

DOCTOR: Well, these things often require one night of testing and another night of fitting.

ME: *But you had said that we'd do both in one night, and last time, it was reeeeeally expensive.*

DOCTOR: You can't put a price tag on health, son.

ME: *Well, you certainly did.*

DOCTOR: We were unable to complete both last time because you barely slept.

ME: *I thought barely sleeping was the reason I was taking the test.*

DOCTOR: You slept a lot less than everyone else.

He had not verbalized this before, but I knew that it had to be true because I woke up just about every five minutes two weeks ago when I took sleep study #1. It was three days after Kaysie and I celebrated our twelfth anniversary. We were certain that a new year would clear out the old garbage and ring in the healthy new. Good old year thirteen. What could be easier?

The evening began as I enrolled in the emergency waiting area of a hospital on the other side of downtown. I was then ushered into what my college dorm room would have looked like, had someone been murdered there. A very pleasant young woman entered the room.

WOMAN: Are you ready to go to sleep?

It was 9:30.

ME: *No. I tend to wait until the sun passes the tree line.*

WOMAN: Well, not right this second, Snappy Stewart.

ME: *My name is Mark.*

WOMAN: You don't think I've got that written on your file right here in my hand? Nice try, Willy Whiskers.

ME: *I take it we won't be using my actual name.*

WOMAN: Why don't I slip out while you go ahead and do whatever it is you do to get ready for bed.

ME: *Just the basics: brush teeth, change my clothes, debone a flounder.*

WOMAN: Well, you'll want to change clothes in there.

ME: *In the hazardous materials closet?*

WOMAN: That's a bathroom. Ignore the sign on the door.

ME: *Why can't I just change clothes out here?*

WOMAN: Because of the camera.

She points to a device aimed squarely at the bed.

WOMAN: It's night-vision, so we can see if anything happens while
            you sleep.

ME: *You're going to stare at me while I sleep?*

WOMAN: Call it a perk of the job.

ME: *That seems weird.*

WOMAN: I KNOW! Do it here, get paid. Do it at my apartment
            complex, get a restraining order. It's all about location.

ME: *So many things are these days.*

WOMAN: Gotta watch you closely. You never know.

ME: *You never know what?*

WOMAN: Nobody ever knows. That's why it's a study,
            Frankendoodle.

ME: *Can we maybe vote on one nickname and stay there?*

She leaves the room and shuts the door as I prepare myself for what cannot
possibly be a healthy night of rest. I glance about the room. Cameras. Monitors.
Devices that go beep with a lot of flashing warning lights. Everything seems
daunting including the carpet stains. Once I have my pajamas on, she pops her
head back in. She ushers me into a wooden chair and makes one last request.

WOMAN: You're not going to need to go to the bathroom, are you?

ME: *You mean ever?*

WOMAN: Did you just go?

ME: *I'm going now.*

WOMAN: Zip the one-liners, Sassafras Sassypants!

ME: *Sorry. Yes, I went before you came back in.*

WOMAN:	Good. Because it will be virtually impossible to untangle in the night.
ME:	*Oh, I sleep pretty still.*
WOMAN:	Not your body. The wires.

She then proceeded to wrap a very tight Velcro belt around my abdomen.

WOMAN:	Is that too tight?
ME:	*No. I think I'm good.*
WOMAN:	You sure now?
ME:	*Fairly sure.*
WOMAN:	Good. Because the other two will cut off the circulation.
ME:	*The other two?*
WOMAN:	One Velcro belt around the tummy and one Velcro belt around the nipples. Just like connect-the-dots.
ME:	*Ahhhh.*
WOMAN:	Yes. Cold. An unfortunate side effect.
ME:	*I think that's going to chafe.*
WOMAN:	Of course. It's a nipple. But you won't mind in about five minutes. You'll be way too distracted by the wires sticking out of your head.

She began wiping clear paste all over my chest and face, affixing wires to every few inches of my body. First, the chest.

WOMAN:	Oh. You're a hairy one. Not gonna enjoy that coming off, are you?

Then, the face, and finally—the hair.

ME:	*I don't understand what you are doing.*
WOMAN:	I'm spiking your hair, Slapcracker.
ME:	*The doctor said nothing about my sleep being improved by transforming me into Dream Into Action era Howard Jones.*
WOMAN:	I have to affix these wires every inch or so along your scalp,

and the only way to do that is to spike your hair upward, creating crevices.

ME: *Just like the parting of the Red Sea.*

WOMAN: If Moses had pomade.

Now that I looked like Yahoo Serious, it was time for me to lie down on the mattress. This was easier said than done.

WOMAN: Tell you what: you grab this group of wires with your left hand, the red group with your right, and then squeeze the green group against your free hip. I'll carry these twenty larger cables and we'll see if we can scoot you onto the mattress without having to redo this sucker.

MAN: *I'm supposed to sleep like this?*

WOMAN: Heaven's no! That would be simple. We haven't even started working on your nose.

The next thing I knew, I was laying face upward (tricky, as I always sleep on my side), holding a device in my right hand that would contact the nurse in the rare instance that she was not sleeping through my alertness. I was literally covered in wires.

But, the affixing was not finished.

A strap was fastened to my head that held a small, sharp plastic U, which cut under the skin between my nostrils and stuck a rod up into each airway. A squeezing mechanism was then clasped onto a finger on my left hand and another onto a finger on my right.

I lay there—motionless—finally understanding all this talk of how technology was taking over our lives. I heard a scuffle and attempted to peek out of the corner of my eye to see what she was doing.

CLICK!

WOMAN: Nighty night.

It was 10:15.

This was undoubtedly going to be the worst night of sleep in my life. I lay there, wanting to toss and turn the way someone in a body cast needs to scratch that itch. But I couldn't move.

Tick tock. Tick tock.

All night long.

I nodded in and out of sleep perhaps ten times, only to awaken within minutes.

And then, I gave in.

I thought to myself ...

> *So, it may not get better than this.*
>
> *So what?*
>
> *Just deal with it.*
>
> *If this is what sleep needs to look like tonight, then this is what sleep will look like tonight. I'm going to stop dwelling on how I could have changed it or whether or not I should have submitted myself to this test in the first place and I am just going to choose to sleep.*
>
> *I began to drift.*
>
> *The blinking lights faded.*
>
> *I began to ease into unconsciousness.*
>
> *CLICK!*

WOMAN: Wakey wakey! Four in the morning! Test's over.

I was fairly certain that I had not passed.

But, I had no idea how badly I had failed.

My doctor broke the news that I had severe sleep apnea. My body was waking up over one hundred times every night because my breathing was stopping at least ten times every hour.

TEN TIMES EVERY HOUR!

And every time it happened, my brain and my heart were dying just a little bit.

DOCTOR: It's no wonder that you are so stressed, depressed, and anxious. Your body is in radical upheaval. You can't survive this. You've got to start sleeping.

ME: *What do you think started this?*

DOCTOR: Started this?

ME: *Yeah. Did something happen to cause me to sleep so poorly?*

DOCTOR: Mark, when I say that you stop breathing ten times a night in your sleep, I mean that you always have.

ME: *You can't be serious.*

DOCTOR: It is highly possible that you have NEVER had a good night of sleep. Your entire life, you have never found rest. Every day you've lived, your body has been killing you.

Never.

Not at all the diagnosis I expected.

This created all new possibilities of hope. All this time, I have existed in a world where I thought I was living my way through life and sleeping at night. Instead, I have been sleeping my way through life and dying at night. Not so much a tit-for-tat trade.

Tonight, the problem is supposed to be remedied. I have been told that this evening I will be fitted with a breathing machine that will not only keep me from dying but will change my life. I will finally understand what it means to get a healthy night of sleep. I am told that this will bring me more peace, make me more confident, even boost my creativity. It almost makes all this ridiculousness worth it.

> **ME:** *Yes. I'm ready for Sleep Test #2 tonight.*
>
> **DOCTOR:** You don't think it will be too hard to get your mind off of all this?
>
> **ME:** *What "all this"?*
>
> **DOCTOR:** This. The bleeding. The pain in the abdomen.
>
> **ME:** *Why would I have trouble getting my mind off of this?*
>
> **DOCTOR:** Oh. Right. I suppose you wouldn't.

He jots something down on his pad. A moment of silence passes.

> **ME:** *Doctor?*
>
> **DOCTOR:** Mmhm.
>
> **ME:** *What do you think I have?*

He answers without even inhaling first.

> **DOCTOR:** Oh. I'm pretty sure you have colon cancer.

Foom.

A thousand thoughts race and collide through my mind. Grandparents and uncles and friends who have suffered and died at the hands of this word. The life choked out of them. The joy.

He's—well—he's wrong.

How could he say such a thing, toss the comment aside so casually? Cancer? Not just cancer but colon cancer? That would be—well, painful—and so unbelievably humiliating. Colon cancer. It rolls around in my brain. I realize that the doctor has been saying things now for some time and that I have, evidently, been answering him with an incessant droning of "uh huh sure."

He's been saying that he just can't imagine what else would cause these two distinct symptoms: the bleeding and the abdominal pain. He is making these things sound very official. I know he cares but he seems distracted.

Colon cancer.

> **ME:** *Doctor, that's fine, but for a moment, let's just brainstorm. Out of all possibilities, regardless of how extreme, what else could this be?*
>
> **DOCTOR:** I'm sorry, Mark.
> But if I'm being honest …
> I can't imagine anything else.

I walk silently to my truck and sit for a moment in silence behind my steering wheel. I look at my hands. They seem to be the hands of the same person who drove here an hour ago. But it does not feel like they are. I check the time. Eleven minutes ago, I was concerned about the time. I needed to speed out of here and get to a meeting.

A meeting? What's a meeting?

I do not start the ignition, but I grip the steering wheel.

I stare at my cell phone and wonder if I should call.

I do not call just yet.

I look at my fingers.

I breathe in. I breathe out.

I close my eyes—and I think of the falling leaves.

Last week, the children were out shopping with Kaysie and I was in the front yard, raking the freshly fallen leaves. Autumn is my favorite season and it has a lot to do with these leaves and their dignified, beautiful death. After the torrent of a Tulsa summer, the cool breeze shoves its way in like the Coast Guard, reminding us that the outdoors are supposed to be an inviting place.

In Tulsa, the turning of the leaves is gorgeous. Stunning. Oranges and yellows and rich wine reds that make it seem as if the leaf has bled itself off of that limb. I love to smell the earth and feel the crisp wind as I gather them together into bags. Their death makes me feel very much alive.

Just as I was enjoying my quiet nature moment …

I can rake AHL these leeves FAHSTER than you! Ready, set, GO!

Zachary hacks into my neatly rounded pile of leaves with a garden hoe, clearly attempting to chop the leaves into dust so they would evaporate in the breeze.

ME: *ZACHARY!*
ZACHARY: Your pile is nawt veddy good.
ME: *Well, it was.*
ZACHARY: I am GOING to help!
ME: *Zachary. Really. This is me time.*
ZACHARY: But you ah doing a jawb.

I sigh. Very loudly. I am hoping that he picks up on the sigh. He does not.

ME: *Yes. Fine. You know what? You can help.*
ZACHARY: I am AHLREADY helping.
ME: *Why do you want to help? Wouldn't you rather be playing with other kids?*
ZACHARY: I like playing with you.
ME: *Well … uh … thank you.*
ZACHARY: And, also, there ah not many who ah nice to me.
ME: *There aren't? Why?*
ZACHARY: HEY! I'm hungry! Can I have, can I have, can I have, can I have, can I have …
ME: *You might as well say it, because it's going to be a no.*

ZACHARY: Can I have your bicycle?

ME: *No.*

ZACHARY: All right. A cupcake?

ME: *I don't have cupcakes. But, if I had cupcakes, no.*

ZACHARY: I LOVE cupcakes.

ME: *Yes. That's common.*

ZACHARY: And I LOOOOVE …

ME: *Zachary!*

I see what is about to happen. He has that look in his eye. That look a kid gets when they are so excited, they must SPIN. This would not normally be a problem, but he is grabbing the handle of the hoe, and it is buried beneath the pile of leaves that I have just re-raked.

ZACHARY: I LOOOOVE AUTUMN!

He spins.

He spins.

ME: *ZACHARY!*

Too late. Leaves absolutely everywhere.

Zachary is stunned. He stares at me, the knowing of oncoming retribution in his eyes. And I am just about to yell. Just about to Ralph Kramden the whole neighborhood.

And then, I remember.

Oh yeah. That Mark died.

I remember my wrestling match in the night.

The change is not easy in coming, but it does cross my mind more and more as the days pass. I chose to surrender. To die already. I don't want to live a half-life any more.

So, I'd better do something about it.

He continues to stare. Is that horror I see in his eyes?

>   **ME:**   *ZACHARY?!*
>   **ZACHARY:** Yuh … yes?

And I suddenly know exactly what to say.

>   **ME:**   Has anyone told you lately that you are AWESOME?

I have never seen fear melt away from a face so quickly.

Zachary smiles ear to ear. I expected this comment to be a nice transition back into the raking, but Zachary stuns me.

He throws down his hoe and leaps into my arms.

He gives me an enormous and very unreserved Great Britain Embrace.

I did it.

I actually saw it happen.

I chose to realize my bad behavior.

I chose to change it.

And something extraordinary happened.

It is barely a trickle, but I am sensing the other half of my life beginning to fill up. And nothing—nothing is going to rob me of the joy of dying already.

Not even colon cancer.

I consider today's timely readings:

> *You groped your way through that murk once, but no longer. You're out in the open now. The bright light of Christ makes your way plain. So no more stumbling around. Get on with it! The good, the right, the true—these are the actions appropriate for daylight hours. Figure out what will please Christ, and then do it.*[†]

---

† Ephesians 5:8–10

And, even more fitting for my situation:

> *Wake up from your sleep, Climb out of your coffins; Christ will*
> *show you the light! So, watch your step. Use your head. Make*
> *the most of every chance you get. These are desperate times!*[†]

And it suddenly hits me.

Peace. Perfect peace.

This news cannot possibly be right ... and so what if it is?

Yeah. That's it. So what if it is? There are still chances left to be had. Moments left to make the most with. I've been living in a coffin, playing dead for a year now even without this news. Am I going to keep sleeping—keep groping? No.

I'm up for the battle.

Ready to be out in the open. Ready for the light.

I call Kaysie.

I tell her the news.

And somehow, she has hope. She has peace.

A few days later, I undergo a CAT scan to determine the truth of my fate. All along, our family and friends stand by us and intercede on our behalf. It is one of those times when you discover just how much you are loved and just how much strength there is around you to carry you through.

I am told the results of the CAT scan will not be given to me for two weeks. Until then, I am told to wait patiently. And this, I am able to do. Because the hand that I am holding is a hand that I have been longing to hold for a year— and this hand of Kaysie's is gripping hard.

Two weeks.

---

† Ephesians 5:16

Two weeks before we have a definitive answer.

Two weeks before we discover that it was never cancer at all.

Two weeks before we are told that the bleeding and the pain were, indeed, two separate maladies. I was bleeding because I had a tear in my intestine—more than likely caused by the fall through the roof.

No freaking duh.

They would believe the pain to be my appendix.

They would schedule me for surgery to have it removed.

But they would be wrong about that as well.

All that matters right now is that we will not know any of these things for two weeks.

And yet, surprisingly, peace has already come.

(Exhibit I)

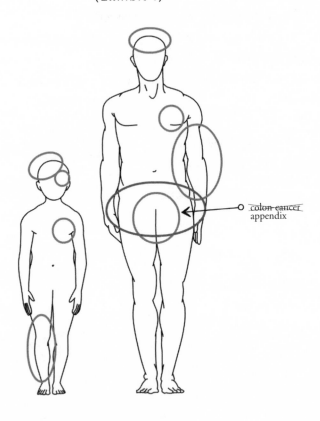

colon cancer
appendix

ALL SAINTS' DAY

Doctors have got to stop touching me.

I'm dead serious.

I was polite about it at first, but now, it's getting ridiculous.

It's been two months without exact clarity regarding the nature of my pain and how to fix it. And this is after the following:

✓   The manual checkup by my family doctor.
✓   The ultrasound by that perky lady.
✓   An adventure with an octogenarian shaky-handed proctologist.
✓   The CAT scan.
✓   Two—yes, TWO complete colon cleanses.
✓   A hands-on surgeon consult.
✓   A colonoscopy.

It's like every time I walk into a room these days, I have to drop my pants. I swear if my privates get inspected one more time, I'm going to start calling them my publics.

I've been doing my best to die to myself over the past month-and-a-half. I really have. But I keep getting frustrated at the lack of progress around me. It's been forty-five days since that second sleep study—you remember: the one where I was supposed to walk away with a new breathing apparatus that would change my life? Well, I still don't have the breathing apparatus. I was fitted for the gear that evening and subsequently had the second worst sleep of my life. I inhaled beautifully, but the machine shoved the oxygen in so fast, it refused to let me exhale. I would take deep breaths followed by startled grunts. I sounded like Darth Vader trying to pass a kidney stone. The testers realized they needed to make adjustments, and I have not heard from them since. So, as of today: November first, no gear. No change. No sleep. The result is that I am having the same trouble breathing in my sleep that I have had my entire life, but now I am *aware* of it—which means that it feels like it is getting worse.

Ah, November first. Ever since I can remember, this has been my favorite day of the year. They call it All Saints' Day—probably an effort by the greeting card folk to make up with the Christians over Halloween.

I love November first because I love autumn. I love Thanksgiving. I love Christmas. This leads to the inevitable follow-up question: "Then why isn't your favorite day of the year Thanksgiving or Christmas?" I am glad you asked. It is because I love the anticipation. The planning. That first day where every ounce of the joy is still forthcoming. I'm certain this can be psychoanalyzed to make me out to be a basket case, but the practical result is that the Steele family has an awesome holiday season. We plan the fool out of it. Every tradition that comes to mind, we fulfill. It is why I count the days to November first. No matter what rough stuff happened during the preceding ten months, I know we are in for sixty days of making up for it.

That making-up-for-it begins in a matter of hours as we take the kids to Silver Dollar City where the Christmas lights intermingle with roller coasters. It will be Charlie's first major outing since the broken leg. A celebration that the worst is over.

And the worst must be over, right? Between the falling through the ceiling and Hero's death, the miscarriage memories and the eye herpes, the broken leg and the best friend moving away, the head stitches and the father-in-law's surgery, the sleep apnea and the threat of colon cancer, CERTAINLY the worst must be over.

The day before yesterday, we were concerned that the worst might not be over. Kaysie and I were alerted to a news brief on the Internet stating that the man who was the primary spiritual influence in my wife's life was being accused of some activities that we knew could not possibly be true. This is a man we hold in very high regard. He has been extremely influential in our faith, in our marriage, in my wife's family. The accusations were ridiculous and obviously a cheap attempt at publicity.

This was especially painful for Kaysie because we had already been through this specific pain before. Another significant spiritual influence in our lives had an indiscretion almost a decade ago and in the subsequent fallout, we became distant from him as well as a number of close friends.

Come to think of it, that's when this all started: this transition from hopeless romantics to just plain hopeless. To make matters worse, Kaysie was then forced to deal with my own failure with pornography and the aftermath. All in all, the gender of men has not really delivered for her.

But, these accusations? Hogwash. Just a distraction—and one that makes me mad, because otherwise, it finally feels like the worst is over.

It felt like we turned a corner when the doctor told us it was not colon cancer.

Don't even get me started on the whole colon cancer (WHOOPS!) appendix debacle. Don't get me wrong. I'm thrilled it wasn't colon cancer, but I could have done without the lively two-week cliff hanger. I could have done without the myriad of tests that a man must go through when it is suspected that he has colon cancer.

The most startling test had to be the colonoscopy. The word *colonoscopy* comes from the root *colon,* which means "why don't we stick something in this guy's colon?" and the suffix *–oscopy,* which translates into "let's also make a movie about it." But, before I was able to be filmed for posterity (no pun intended), I first had to be emptied. I accomplished this by drinking bottles of fluid that tasted like a smoothie had been made out of magnet shavings and Barbasol. I drank bottle after bottle, just as I had been instructed. And it was not long before I was doing my best impression of Niagra Falls.

I went to the doctor, ready to post his findings on YouTube, only to discover that I had been instructed incorrectly. This was not the day of the actual colonoscopy. This was merely the day of the prep. There was no need for me to have cleansed myself with medicine the previous evening, though there would be a need for it in another 48 hours when I was scheduled to have the *actual* colonoscopy.

The morning of the *real* procedure, Kaysie was told to accompany me because I would be placed under what is called a "waking anesthetic." This is a nice way to say "lost time." Evidently, I appeared alert throughout the proceedings as well as some time after, but I had no control over the ridiculous things I did and said—nor any recollection of ever having done or said them.

I do remember undressing and putting on one of those paper gowns that covers everything except what I might actually want covered. I remember being roller-gurneyed to the procedure past the open door of the waiting room. Quite a few people glanced up from their *Readers Digests* that day and got more than they bargained for. I then remember the doctor telling me to count to ten.

I counted to eight.

And woke up six hours later, fully dressed, and in my own bed.

Based on testimonial evidence, the following is a transcript of what I missed:

ME:	*… Nine. Teen.*
KAYSIE:	Ten. It's supposed to be ten.
ME:	*Ninetoon.*
KAYSIE:	Does he know what he's saying?
DOCTOR:	He has no idea what he's saying.
ME:	*Hey. Hey.*
KAYSIE:	What is it, Mark?
ME:	*What's the capital of Albania?*
DOCTOR:	I'm going to give you a shot now.
KAYSIE:	What is the what?
ME:	*What is the capital of OOOOOOWUUH!*
DOCTOR:	Yep. That's the shot.
KAYSIE:	His backside is in the air.
DOCTOR:	Yes. I see that. He will have no recollection of this.
KAYSIE:	How humiliating.
DOCTOR:	And also fun.

Evidently, when I am walking in a state of unconsciousness, I have no shame. After the procedure, I paraded around as my wife attempted to get me back in my jeans. This is no easy task when the individual out of the jeans is almost double the wife's weight and continually stops the process to ask, *"What is the capital of Albania?"*

Totally serious.

Not "I love you, baby" or "I am soooo wasted." Just *"What is the capital of Albania?"*

And the sad thing is that no one could tell me.

It became clear after the colonoscopy that the inflamed appendix theory was also incorrect. It turns out that I actually have a double hernia. This means that there is a rip in the muscle at my beltline on both my right side and my left, and my intestines are poking out of the holes these rips have made.

Pretty.

Also, constant agony. I believe the doctor's exact words were:

> *You've felt this way for a YEAR? Wow. You must have learned to live with some pretty intense pain. I would imagine that level of pain would keep you up at night.*

I ask the doctor what could have caused such a thing.

He thinks they blew out when I fell through the ceiling.

No freaking duh.

A surgery was scheduled for the week after Thanksgiving to go in and patch these holes up.

ME: *So, let me get this straight. All of this: the bleeding, the pain that I've been feeling for over a year. The pain that I've had to go through a dozen tests to define. The humiliation of every medical professional in Tulsa having a look at my tenderloins. ALL OF IT has been because I fell through my ceiling?*

DOCTOR: Looks that way. Yes.

ME: *Which, correct me if I'm wrong, was the very first thing I ever told you.*

DOCTOR: I'm terribly sorry.

> **ME:**   *I should say so.*
> **DOCTOR:** That'll be four thousand dollars.

Of course, to be fair, if I had never gone to the doctor, I would have never found out about the possibility of sleep apnea. I would have never taken those two sleep studies. And I would not be on my way (hopefully) to rest, confidence, and sanity.

But now, a new wrinkle.

Last week I received an offer. An offer to publish my second book.

There's only one problem: I don't have a second book.

This is a conundrum of epic proportions because my first book, *Flashbang*, was about the idiosyncrasies of my own life. And, in being about my life, it was fun. Enjoyable. A real LOL literary find. I'm sure there are still reviews left on Amazon.com that wax more eloquent about it than I could. To this end, there is a desire by the publisher that the second book also be about my life. But, this past year of my life? Who would want to read about that? Lapses of faith and disconnection with my wife and bruises and wounded privates? Who would want to curl up on a sofa with that? That would be a story of pain and questions and doubt and digging through the wet cement of life. We're followers of Christ. We're supposed to be about the bright side and the story with a twist-ending and the poster with a kitten dangling inside a sock from a clothesline with a Scripture verse written at the bottom in a font that went out of style before posters were invented.

Any spiritual growth in the past year of my life has come only by God's faithfulness as Kaysie and I drudged through a tough season. Why would we want a permanent reminder with a first printing of 10,000 plus? There are no books like that at the Wal-Mart inspirational kiosk. I need people to enjoy me. To affirm that my life is worth living. I would tell my real story if I wanted those who have suffered like me to find solace in a kindred spirit, but right now, that's not what I'm looking for. I'm looking for fans.

(Exhibit J)

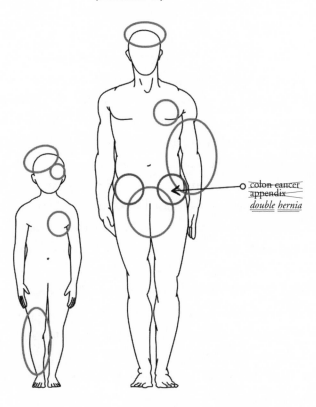

colon cancer
appendix
double hernia

And then, it dawns on me.

My life writing for the fans has kept me stuck in the circular. The same issues. The same roadblocks over and over and over. Maybe I don't have writer's block at all. Maybe I have life block.

Besides, that Mark Steele is supposed to be dying already.

That half-life is supposed to be over.

Aw, crapcakes.

That's when the more gripping realization becomes clear.

I have worked in ministry and the media for twenty years. I have met more pastors, speakers, musicians, visionaries, drones who work for visionaries, laypeople, celebrities, has-beens, never-were-but-thought-they-had-beens, writers, geniuses, sycophants, icons, and missionaries than I could list in a ream of notebook paper. And, they all have one thing in common: They hurt. They love Jesus and they still hurt. To varying degrees, they serve Jesus with their life— some making larger mistakes than others, and some living less selfishly than others. But, none—not even the ones I most admire—have been able to escape this rough patch called living on planet earth. None have been able to dodge the reality that everything dies. They've all hit that brick wall of confusion, wondering why their tragedy happened to them. They have all suffered—both for God's sake and for occasional lapses in judgment. And most of them feel like they are in it alone. That no one else has gone through what they have gone through.

I know this because I am a goofball and people tend to confide in goofballs. We all believe our weak spot to be unique. This is because we are Christians and, for some reason, that makes us want everyone to believe the best about us—half-truth though it is.

Suddenly, a moment of clarity comes to me.

What if?

What if I *did*?

What if I wrote about the warts and all of the past year? What if I recorded what it actually feels like to despair, to lack, to fail, to struggle, to give up, even while you love Jesus?

Today, I've been reading Jeremiah 30, and it starts off pretty depressing but it doesn't stay that way. It was a lame season for God's people and Jeremiah told it like it was—exactly like it was. Jeremiah was an incredibly godly man who lived during a really unfortunate century. He truly got the shaft when it came to the timing of his birth-to-death span. He was chosen to be the oracle of God during the fall of Jerusalem and the exile in Babylon. Yeah. *That* Babylon. The one that all nasty Babylon-like things are named after. Not the season you want to be the team mascot. Jeremiah faced every downer imaginable—and yet, he kept plugging and praying through. This is what defined him as God's man. Not miracles, but rather telling the truth and holding onto God.

> *God's Message: "Cries of panic are being heard. The peace has been shattered. Ask around! Look around! Can men bear babies? So why do I see all these he-men holding their bellies like women in labor, faces contorted, pale as death? The blackest of days, no day like it ever! A time of deep trouble for Jacob—but he'll come out of it alive."[†]*

Nobody's going to open a pep rally with that paragraph.

And yet, out of Jeremiah's prayers and his trust in God came answers:

> *"And then I'll enter the darkness. I'll break the yoke from their necks. Cut them loose from the harness."[††]*

> *"Thanksgivings will pour out the windows; laughter will spill through the doors. Things will get better and better. Depression days are over." [†††]*

These are not merely answers for Jeremiah and the people of his generation. They are answers for you. Answers for me. Jeremiah's words give me solace

[†] Jeremiah 30:5–7
[††] Jeremiah 30:8
[†††] Jermiah 30:21

because they prove to me that someone who loved God his entire life went through even more pain than I could imagine. Not only that, but he was not afraid to spill his guts to you and me.

I suppose if I look back on my life carefully, I would realize that though the truths in the Word of God gave me *epiphanies*, observing those truths as they were walked out by other people *changed* me. And not so much when the walk was easy, but rather when I observed the struggle of others as they fought hard and then eventually found joy.

So, I suppose I should write it all down.

The process would not be without pain.

But do we ever change without pain?

How valid is this death if I don't really feel it?

Still, I don't know if this is confirmation enough to write down a year's worth of pain into a book. But, it's time to jump in the car and drive to Silver Dollar City. I get ready to close my Bible and suddenly notice the first verse of today's chapter one more time:

> This is the Message Jeremiah received from God: "God's Message, the God of Israel: 'Write everything I tell you in a book.'"[†]

Oh.

Well.

That's probably enough confirmation.

Matt and Molly join us on our trip to Missouri. Instead of the families splitting up into two separate cars, Matt and I take all of the children and allow Kaysie and

---

[†] Jeremiah 30:1

Molly to drive alone. The news about Kaysie's spiritual father is weighing heavily on her and it will be good for the two of them to have a diversion.

We have a diversion in our van as well. Eighties music.

Matt and I have a long-standing road trip tradition. There is a lengthy list of selections that we find utmost catharsis in singing at the top of our lungs while in a moving vehicle. This includes, but is not limited to, the following:

> "Total Eclipse of the Heart" – Bonnie Tyler
> "Hard Habit to Break" – Chicago
> "More Than A Feeling" – Boston (I am aware this is not from the '80s)
> "Celebration" – Kool & the Gang
> "Born in the U.S.A." – Bruce Springsteen
> "Love Somebody" – Rick Springfield
> "The Final Countdown" – Europe
> "Footloose" – Kenny Loggins
> "It's Still Rock and Roll to Me" – Billy Joel
> "Rosanna" – Toto
> "Separate Ways (Worlds Apart)" – Journey
> "Addicted to Love" – Robert Palmer
> "Summer of '69" – Bryan Adams
> "Kyrie" – Mr. Mister

The most cathartic of these is the Bonnie Tyler anthem as it is a profusion of melodrama and sound effects. Bonnie Tyler only had two hits, but they were each the equivalent of Michael Bay films. In "Total Eclipse," Bonnie practically screams her pain while bombs—freaking *BOMBS*—go off in the background. There are sleigh bells and rifle shots and I don't think the poor woman inhales between words for two solid choruses plus the bridge. Sing it in the front seat at high volume and your endorphins will go insane. It might be a good idea, however, to have headache medication handy.

After four hours of this, we enter these beautiful Missouri mountains and the kids start bouncing off the walls—especially Charlie because, let's face it, he didn't have much of a summer. Finally free of his wheelchair, his hip-to-toe cast, his eye sores, and his stitches, Charlie is ready to get some serious fun on.

We pull into the parking lot and unload with a cheer. The ladies have clearly been able to detox a bit from the stress of late and are ready to consume funnel cakes just before being thrown into a dizzying stupor on the Wildfire. Charlie asks if he can sit on my shoulders as we walk the parking lot. My double hernia is an A+ reason not to lift him but, hey—it's his day. I lift him high and walk him over to the waiting line for the tram that will take us into the amusement park. The vehicle pulls up and I set Charlie down to pick up Kaysie's backpack. I am just about to climb on the tram when I realize that Charlie is suddenly wrapped around my legs.

He is crumpled onto the asphalt.

He is not moving.

> **ME:**   *Charlie? Charlie, get up. The tram is here.*
> **CHARLIE:** I can't.
> **ME:**   *You can't? You can't what?*
> **CHARLIE:** My STOMACH!

And then he screams.

And screams and screams and screams.

It rapidly dawns on me that Charlie is in a disturbing level of pain. I attempt to pick him up, but he writhes. I break into a cold sweat.

Charlie is holding his belly.

Like a woman in labor—his face contorted, pale as death.

We rush to the entrance of the park as we all pray under our breath. The eyes of the children grow wide; their mouths are suddenly silent.

The cheering is over.

The officials of the park help scurry us over to their first aid station. Matt and Molly take Morgan and Jackson and wait inside with their own children. Kaysie and I follow to the urgent care section as I run, Charlie tucked under my arm like a football. A bed is cleared for us, a curtain pulled aside, and two doctors give us immediate attention.

Charlie is lightly poked and prodded and asked a series of questions, but each time, his response is nothing more than *"I DON'T KNOWUUUUUNGH!"* with the last word sounding like birth pains. Kaysie and I look to each other.

Something is seriously wrong.

We understand this, because Charlie is no crybaby. Sure, he screamed when one of the largest bones in his leg was broken in half, but otherwise, Charlie doesn't tend to alert us when he is in severe pain. We discover his agony only when it becomes visible. This is partly because Charlie is extremely resilient, but mostly because he cannot bear to stop enjoying life. Charlie knows good and well that if his grief is known, playtime will cease. And today is the playtime to which he has most looked forward.

Kaysie and I stare at one another as the doctor begins to give him medication for the pain.

> *Why?*
>
> *Why do these things keep happening?*
>
> *I mean, is it really necessary?*
>
> *Is there really growth needed in our life that can ONLY happen by Charlie suffering through what would have been a celebratory day?*

We feel the moment coming.

In the saying, it is the tiny straw that, when added to the tumultuous stack of straws on the camel's back, breaks it. Only, in our case, none of the straws are tiny. We feel our back bend and threaten to sever. But, to Kaysie's credit, I see the steel in her eyes. She is resolved to enjoy at least ONE THING this year. She is refusing to let her day be stolen without a fight. We stare at one another.

Let's face this. We can take one more straw.

Charlie suddenly falls asleep.

At first, this startles us, but the doctor seems to believe that once the pain was eased by the medication, his body just crashed.

KAYSIE:	I don't understand. What is it?
DOCTOR:	We really don't know. Does he have a history of kidney stones?
ME:	*Kidney stones? No.*
DOCTOR:	It might be an inflamed appendix.
ME:	*You've got to be kidding.*
DOCTOR:	How much has he complained of pain this past week?
ME:	*NONE.*
KAYSIE:	He's been in very high spirits.
ME:	*He was laughing in the car. There didn't seem to be the slightest thing wrong with him.*
DOCTOR:	That's very odd. These things don't come on all of a sudden.
KAYSIE:	Then, what else could it be?
DOCTOR:	I honestly have no idea. You should take him to a hospital.

This is the moment that every father dreads.

Yes, Charlie has suffered all summer long, but in each instance we knew (or thought we knew) what the problem actually was. We knew (or thought we knew) what to do about it. But this is different. This is the moment of horror. The moment when our child is in urgent agony, but NO ONE—not the doctors, not his mother, not even I know what it is or what to do about it.

With that defeated look in her eye, Kaysie encourages me, "You stay with him. I'll go get the car." The doctor says she will go with her to show her where to pull the vehicle around. The curtain around our bed is drawn. Kaysie and the doctor depart. After all of the hustle and panic of the last forty-five minutes, I am suddenly alone with my sleeping five-year-old.

It is quiet. I stare at him. I comb his hair with my fingers.

He's so vulnerable.

And I am supposed to be his protector.

But, for the past six months, I feel like I have failed miserably.

God.

What do I do here?

I meant it when I said that I surrendered.

That I was at the end of myself.

That the old me was being left for dead.

But I just don't know what to do here.

This agony he is in. I just don't get it.

I know You have charged me with this child and he just keeps on suffering.

What am I to do?

Oh God. What am I to do?

> *Open your mouth and close your eyes.*

Uh. What was that again?

> *Open your mouth and close your eyes.*

What is this—a game? That doesn't sound like something God would say to me. That sounds like something Charlie or Jackson would say to me right before they smeared the remains of a stinkbug on my tongue. What on earth does that have to do with anything?

Choose to be blind?

Or no—choose to trust?

Choose to be in the most vulnerable position possible. Open wide, though I have no idea what will come of it and my experience tells me that the result could be anything from distasteful to disastrous.

Choose to open my mouth to act without requiring visible proof in advance.

I cannot imagine a more exposed position. Choose to put my defenses down, to shut my eyes and allow whatever I need to be fed—whatever it tastes like—to have free reign.

Complete and utter trust.

> *Do you trust Me?*

Of course.

Open your mouth and close your eyes.

I consider this a bit silly, but, after all, I am alone.

I close my eyes.

I open my mouth.

And, instead of something going in—something comes out.

Words of praise, of comfort, of prayer, of hope, of Scripture come pouring out.

I find myself interceding on behalf of my child.

I had been praying for him since he began screaming.

But this was different.

All the years of teaching, of studying, of the evidence of God working in my life—all of it began to come tumbling out as I recalled Scriptures and promises and instances of proof and evidence again and again of God doing good—no, not just good—*great* things in my life and in my family. My mouth began to overflow with gratitude, with words of healing—my confidence building as I spoke over this child of mine. Not pipe dreams. Not bright-side encouragement, but thick, tumultuous words I could almost taste. Words with power and resonance. Words I know are true because I had lived them and they have proven true time and again in my life. I remembered the verses from Jeremiah:

> *God's Message: "Cries of panic are being heard. The peace has been shattered. Ask around! Look around! Can men bear babies? So why do I see all these he-men holding their bellies like women in labor, faces contorted, pale as death? The blackest of days, no day like it ever! A time of deep trouble for Jacob—but he'll come out of it alive."*[†]

And then my heart and mind shifted as I recalled the words that followed …

> *"And then I'll enter the darkness. I'll break the yoke from their necks. Cut them loose from the harness."*[††]

[†] Jeremiah 30:5–7

[††] Jeremiah 30:8

"Thanksgivings will pour out the windows; laughter will spill through the doors. Things will get better and better. Depression days are over."[†]

Yes. YES! This is the truth. THIS is real.

My son will be well. Laughter will spill through the doors.

Things will get better and better.

This pain will be broken. It will not break Charlie. It will not break me.

I hear Kaysie honk the horn of our van. I pick up Charlie's limp body and cradle him as I did a few years back when he was a baby. I hold him close and kiss the top of his scalp. I begin walking out to the van. I kick open the door to the medical facility with my foot. And I suddenly hear a small voice from inside my arms.

CHARLIE: Dad?

He sounds different, but I don't want to move him, so I keep him cradled as I walk slowly towards Kaysie and the doctor, who are now within earshot.

ME: *It's okay, son. We're on our way to get you checked out.*
CHARLIE: I'm done.

Kaysie and I stare at each other. Did he just say what we thought he said?

I pull Charlie away from my chest and he sits up abruptly, a smile on his face.

CHARLIE: I'm all wight now. I'm weady to wide wides.

We watch as his white face changes back to his normal skin color, starting at his hairline and cascading slowly down his face. It is as if poison is being sucked out of his body.

The doctor stares, wide-eyed, perplexed.

---

† Jeremiah 30:21

DOCTOR: Are you sure?

Charlie gives the thumbs-up signal.

CHARLIE: I am WEADY!

The doctor pokes and prods in all the same places as before. Only this time, nothing. Not a wince. Not an "ow." Nothing. We ask the doctor if this normally happens with kidney stones or appendicitis. She responds that, if it were either of those, he would at least be tender or sore—and he would definitely wince at the pain. No. It is as if nothing has happened.

I slowly set Charlie on the ground.

And he starts running.

DOCTOR: I don't think he needs to go to the hospital. Here. Just keep my number on hand and if anything else happens, come right back to see me.

Kaysie and I stare at one another for the third time in an hour.

We are shocked, literally shocked at the degree of turnaround.

I mean, sure, we had faith. But a full recovery was beyond our expectations.

We watched Charlie carefully for the rest of the day, but it became clear that the crisis was over. He went to the bathroom—not a pleasant experience for those within smelling range—and from that point acted as if nothing had ever gone wrong.

We thoroughly celebrated as a family.

Kaysie and I took great solace in the fact that God cared enough about this day—this moment—to give us the boost we needed.

Unfortunately, it turns out that we needed it more than we thought.

Just as we are beginning to relax, Kaysie's cell phone rings. It is someone we are close to at the church where all the chaos is going down with Kaysie's spiritual father.

The call is not good. As a matter of fact, it is horrible.

The rumors are true.

True.

I look at my wife's eyes.

And the reality of life on this planet earth hits hard. Miracles do happen. But the rough stuff will continue to go on right alongside them. Because there are people.

And where there are people, no matter how much of the damage God intervenes upon, there is going to be more damage leftover.

This is one of the mightiest blows I can imagine hitting Kaysie. I watch as the life that mere hours ago danced in her eyes flickers out. I see sadness come upon her like waves slamming a body against the rocks.

And I realize with a lump in my throat—that this straw is the one under which her back has finally been broken.

(Exhibit K)

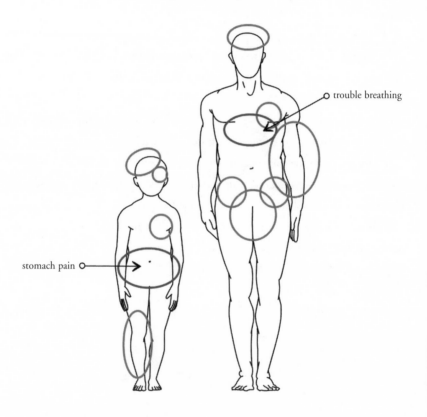

THANKSGIVING

I know that lady on the television.

I was in a studio in Dallas taking photos of her for a project a week ago and now she's singing in front of the New York City Macy's on a float with an animatronic turkey. She touches the side of her nose. I heard her mention that on the set in Dallas. She said that if she did it, she was saying hello to a friend. And here she is doing it as I sip my coffee with disheveled hair while smelling the scents emanating from the kitchen. Quite surreal, actually.

It is Thanksgiving Day and yet it does not feel like the Thanksgiving I look forward to every year. You see, I thought the decision to die to myself would create a fairly instant upswing in fortune. I didn't expect a downturn. For crying out loud, I didn't think there was any more room to go down at all. But, the current situation regarding our long-time friend and spiritual influence—well, it has stirred up some serious muck.

We still love our friend, of course, and we are sympathetic to his failing. God only knows how much I have failed in my life and how much pain I have caused others. But I do wish—no, I yearn—that he would have felt the freedom to confide in someone a long time ago. This is a man who, on the surface, seemed to have many close friends—but evidently none of them were close enough to dispel the fear that hid the unfortunate reality. I consider the many truths I learned from him and the teachings about accountability, about leaning on others with the whole sordid story, about the strength of community knowing you and helping you find healing on the path to God through one another. It grieves me to think that as we were gleaning hope from him he was hopeless. He was being held captive, frozen and unable to seek the very same help he was offering.

To the world, it seems like hypocrisy.

But, I know how it happens.

God begins to use you, and while this should be the most freeing sensation in the world, it quickly turns to fear—fear that anyone would discover that the hurts and habits of your life are not always perfectly in line with what God is saying through your mouth. God wants our response to this fear to be honesty and vulnerability so that through one another, we become healed. But this is not what the fear does to most of us. Instead, it feigns a shell. It forces us into more and more seclusion. It turns the truth about ourselves into half-truths and, eventually, we fully become the deception. This is when ministry becomes show. Not because we think too highly of ourselves, but because we think too little of what He can do in us.

I cannot imagine the pain that he and his family are going through.

But I can imagine the pain that it is causing in those who saw him as more than a man. Because Kaysie and I fall into this lot. I know that God commands us not to put men on too high a pedestal. I know what it does to a good man to put him under this kind of pressure.

And yet, I cannot help it.

I saw it happen before, six years ago with our own pastor. The pressure caused him to crumble and, when he did, those who had placed him on that pedestal were not kind in their response. I have seen it happen to a half-dozen spiritual influencers who deeply affected those around me.

And now, here we go again.

The ripple effect is gargantuan nationwide.

And nowhere is that more evident than in my own home.

I mentioned that when *Flashbang* was released, Kaysie and I thought we had dealt with the majority of the damage my addiction to pornography had inflicted. We were, however, taken off guard by the way in which the rehashing of it all by a reading audience stirred up even more pain. That was a tough season in our marriage.

But, now it is clear that we have even more work to do. Kaysie has been damaged by a lot of men in her life, but this spiritual father was one that she held up in her mind as a sort of icon. If he could live this thing out with integrity, then there was hope for the world of men.

But, if he couldn't …

I see the doubt in her eyes.

The doubt in her heart.

> *If it happened to our pastor …*
>
> *If it happened to my spiritual father …*
>
> *Then, Mark, what would keep it from happening to you?*

And I see her protecting herself from more hurt.

Unintentionally distancing herself from me.

And, who can blame her?

We men have turned out to be a pretty sorry lot. Now, don't get me wrong. We do have our moments. We discovered electricity, the Internet, and global warming. We're great in a pinch if the solution requires locking ourselves in a room with gadgets. But this act of improving stuff around us is, unfortunately, not our primary mission. Our chief job is to love, provide for, and protect these women and children. And, on this front, we're just not cutting it. I am supposed to be the very picture of Jesus to Kaysie, and God knows I'm trying—every day trying—but more often than not, I find that I don't have the strength. Of course, we men know that this supposed strength that men have is really just a façade anyway. Any successes we are able to muster are only by the grace of God and His strength at work in our lives. Of course, when God's strength provides this success, we quickly take the credit for ourselves because we need the points. That's when we start ignoring what God is trying to do in us and instead, insist on leaning on our own strength—or distinct lack of it. It is the irony of maleness: lean on yourself too little and you fail; lean on yourself too much and you also fail.

I think the disappointment I see reflected in my wife's eyes is actually just the fact that she has recently figured all of this out.

God is great.

Men? Not so much.

I look at her closely and I see this disillusionment. I don't know how to fix it.

Man oh man, is it ever painful.

This doesn't mean that we don't have our moments. Kaysie is trying very hard. She is reaching out to me from time to time, laughing when she can. But she is deeply troubled, and there is no optimistic epithet I can verbalize that will change that.

To make matters worse, the anxiety I had given up when I said I would die to myself has returned. The sleepless nights. The lack of confidence. The struggle to breathe. I don't feel like I have given up on this spiritual pursuit. On the contrary, I long to die to myself more than ever. It just feels like the roadblocks are mounting higher and higher by the hour.

I had put a lot of stock in this sleep machine—waited patiently for it in hopes that it would suddenly and surprisingly change everything, just as the doctor said it would.

I waited a long time. I just received the gear yesterday. It took a while to set up, but when it was all said and done and I actually put the mask on my face, I looked into the mirror and had the revolting revelation that it made me look like a heffalump. The mask came over the top of my face, running a tube down the middle of my forehead, resting like a snout around my nose. How on earth could I expect Kaysie to wake up every morning to *this*? Between the amplified exhalation and the mask that pinched my eyes together so tightly that one appeared to drift off to the left, I no longer felt very attractive in the bedroom. I suddenly felt like an old man. Kaysie was gracious. She didn't like the look of it either, but encouraged me by stating that it would all be worth it because I was about to have the best night of sleep of my life.

I had the worst night of sleep of my life.

Constantly choking, the apparatus dried my nose and throat out, causing my nose to bleed. I was never able to sustain a good exhale rhythm and therefore awakened constantly. Somewhere around 2:37 a.m., I gave up and ripped the gear off of my head. The technician says these are merely kinks. This is the same technician who said the first night I wore this gear, I would awaken refreshed beyond my imaginations.

I was told that all this effort …

All this pain …

All this money …

Would be worth it.

That the solution would change my life.

It didn't.

And now, I prepare for the hernia surgery a week from tomorrow. I gather a mental picture of what is to come: my wife, already a bit alienated from me, having to wait on me hand and foot as I lay recovering in our bed, incapacitated by incisions and wearing an elephant trunk mask so that I won't snore.

I've already been humiliated so much.

The fall. The ultrasound. The drunken stupor of the colonoscopy.

And now this.

How much emasculation is she going to have to observe?

Not only do I sense a distance between us, but I look into the near future and see that distance widening even further.

Time to open my mouth and close my eyes.

Okay God.

What is the reason for this agony?

Today is supposed to be a day of Thanksgiving.

And here I am hurting again as I surrender.

I'm not looking for an easy out anymore.

But I am looking for a respite from the tempest.

It's like I'm in this constant season of testing …

And I never even got my summer break.

And God brings one of today's verses to mind:

> Testing comes. Why have you despised discipline? You can't get around it.[†]

Okay. I see that. I do.

And I know that You are refining me.

I'm sure it's a part of this whole idea of dying already.

But, does it really have to be this unrelenting?

Another of today's verses becomes clear:

> But you—keep your eye on what you are doing; accept the hard times along with the good.[††]

But, I AM accepting the hard times!

I feel like that's all I'm doing. Every time I turn around, it's another body blow. These hard times are all I can see.

> Accept the hard times along with the good.

Yes. Good. Redundant.

I am accepting the hard times.

> Along with the good.

Dingdong.

You cannot be serious.

Dingdongdingdongdingdongdingdongdingdongdingdongdingdong!

---

† Ezekiel 21:13a

†† 2 Timothy 4:5

ZACHARY! Don't you have PARENTS?!

I practically rip the front door off its hinges, I open it so fast. There, standing in front of me in a pillowcase that is supposed to resemble pilgrim-ware, is the British Invasion. And he is singing. As if the glow that emanates from him on non-holidays is not enough—now he is SINGING.

ZACHARY: A turkey sat on a backyahd fence and he sang this sad sad tuuuuune!

ME: *Zacha–*

ZACHARY: Thanksgiving Day is coming, gahble gahble gahble gahble, and I know I'll be eaten SOOOOOOON!

ME: *ZACHARY!*

ZACHARY: Happy THANKSgiving, Mistah. What's your name again?

ME: I've told you my name fifty times.

ZACHARY: Is it Roger?

ME: *It's Mr. Steele.*

ZACHARY: Mistah Roger Steele?

ME: *Not even remotely close.*

ZACHARY: And what ah you THANKful for today, Mistah Steele?

ME: *You do realize the pilgrims escaped your country.*

ZACHARY: OH! I smell CRAHNberries! Can I HAVE your Xbox? HEY! You ah wahtching the PARADE!

ME: *I was.*

ZACHARY: THAT is something to be thankful for. And I am coming INSIDE YOUR HOUSE now.

ME: *No, you're not. It's a family day.*

ZACHARY: Why?

ME: *WHY?! Because it's Thanksgiving!*

ZACHARY: Well … I could be your family.

ME: *No, Zachary. I can't take it today.*

ZACHARY: Cahn't take what?

I stop myself for a moment, but I say it anyway.

ME: *I can't take you.*

A moment of pause. The glow wanes a bit but his smile doesn't break.

ZACHARY: Guess what? I suppose I shall come back LATER.
ME: *Zachary.*
ZACHARY: HAPPY THANKSGIVING!

I slam the door.

And with that, I get what I wanted.

And yet, not what I wanted.

What is wrong with me? Why can't I let the boy in? Have I become that putout by his jovial nature? His rowdy and nonstop joy? I mean, he's never any trouble. Sure, he has the subtlety of a Jackie Chan action sequence and I really do want to spend the day alone with my family, but what was the big deal? I just kicked the kid out of my house for no other reason than that he wanted to know what I was thankful for.

Why did that make me so upset?

It was as if I didn't want to think about what I was thankful for.

And suddenly, the words came ringing back.

Accept the hard times along with the good.

Oh.

Accept the hard times …

I get it now. I've been accepting that the hard times are a fact of life. Seeing them well, but seeing them alone. What I have not done …

… along with the good.

… is accept the good.

And in so doing, I have only accepted the half-truth of my own life. I have become so down-trodden, so expectant of the negative, that though there is much around to find joy in, I have shrouded it in the mist of cynicism. I have experienced so much bad this year that I now find myself searching for it. Defining my year by the misfortune instead of seeing it as one side of a set of scales that may just be more balanced than I have chosen to believe.

All right. Let's do this: What am I thankful for? Let's go by categories:

Health.

Yeah. Bonus. Let's start there.

Are you healthy?

Not very often these days.

No? Are you breathing? Well-fed? Able to enjoy activity? Can you see, hear, taste, touch?

Well, sure—but ...

But?

Okay. Fine. In light of all the things that could be wrong with the human body, mine is relatively functional.

Next on the list: provision.

I'm not lacking, no.

Not lacking?

I suppose I have more than most.

More than most?

Fine. I have plenty.

You have a roof over your head, food on the table, a car to drive, thousands of hours of amusement at your fingertips.

Yeah. I may be a bit spoiled.

Okay. Next: calling?

Well, of course I have a calling.

Of course?

You keep repeating what I say and then adding a question mark.

Don't blow this one off. You have an opportunity that so few have. You love what you do and, at the same time, you get the blessed opportunity for it to change people. And, still, you're complaining?

I don't know that I would call it complaining.

What would you call it?

Disappointment?

If you think your life is disappointing, you're only staring at half of the picture.

You're saying that half of my life is disappointing?

Next: family.

Yes. I have a family.

You have …

DON'T DO THAT! Okay. I have one of the greatest families in the world. My parents, my brothers, my children—they all long for Christ. They are all on this same path—searching for Him. Wanting more out of life. Wanting His plan for their lives.

And your wife.

The dilemma here is not what I think of my wife. It's what she thinks of me.

Is it?

Of course it is.

And how do you know that?

How do I know that? She's so disappointed.

Is that what it is?

OF COURSE it is what it is.

And how do you know that?

I don't get what I'm supposed to think here.

And now we get to the root of the problem. This isn't about what you're supposed to think. This is about what is true. And regardless of what you're supposed to think—regardless of what you actually do think—the truth is that there is much in your life for which to be grateful. You have a great, loving, godly woman for a wife, but you struggle to see that.

But, I DO see that.

No, you do not.

This is not about my perception of her. This is about her perception of me.

And how do you know that?

STOP SAYING THAT! It's obvious!

It is not obvious. It is, in fact, easily misunderstood by an insecure, anxiety-ridden individual such as yourself. You cannot see who your wife actually is because your perception of her is skewed by YOUR perception of HER perception of you. You are reading into things—some are there, some are not—but none of it is as unfixable as you seem to believe.

Stop blaming this on me! SHE's the one whose perception is skewed. NOT MINE!

Wow.

I don't know where that came from.

So, perhaps we could re-evaluate that last one again.

That last one?

You keep repeating what I say then adding a question mark.

You mean Kaysie.

Yes.

What am I thankful for about Kaysie?

Go right ahead.

I am thankful.

Thankful that in the world God has placed us in, she is the exact balance of me. She has a brilliant and wise perspective of life—down to the minute detail. Yes, sometimes this plays out in frustrating ways, like the fact that we always have two completely different opinions regarding which roads to take when driving somewhere. But that is the beautiful thing. We do take different paths. Almost constantly—and yet we always end up at the same destination. Pain may come along the way—exasperation from her as I arrive more slowly, aggravation from me when I don't think she sees value in my choices—but God uses us to complete a circle from point A to point B every time. We balance each other out.

And in that balance, there is love. Understanding. A knowledge that, even when we traverse enormous chasms between the euphoric mountain peaks of our marriage, even when our two methods of getting to where we should be seem disparate—we always end up together in the end. Stronger. Ready for the next climb.

Wow. I have never pictured it that way. This whole time, I've wanted to pass the peak—to skip rapidly to the easier downhill portion. But the downhill leads only to the dark crevices. It is the climb that leads to triumph. I would never have pushed so hard uphill with my life if it were not for my Kaysie.

And though I see her here, on Thanksgiving Day, still struggling to connect, I know. I believe.

I have to believe.

That we will find the peak together.

I don't know when.

I don't know how long this valley will last.

But, I think I am beginning to understand.

I am thankful for my wife.

And it will no longer take the sunshine of the mountaintop for me to see it.

SIX DECISIONS THAT MATTERED

decision #5:

APPLAUDED / KNOWN

I want what we all want.

For my life to matter.

But, though this is certainly a grand pursuit,

for too long it has taken precedence over a much greater one:

for my life to be what it was designed to be.

The pursuit of the second results in the first.

But the pursuit of the first alone tends to eliminate the second.

Because when I seek to matter for the audience's sake,

what I am actually looking for is applause. Esteem. Recognition.

This is all good and well—

unless, of course, the life others are applauding

is one I was never supposed to pursue.

I have learned the hard way

that there is no joy

in being applauded

for the wrong reasons.

Yes, it would be nice to be esteemed,

but only if I am first known.

Known for who I truly am—and, in that knowing—

pushed to be the me I was designed to be.

If I embrace the true in myself,

then even if only a few respond,

I will find fulfillment.

But, if I continue to grasp desperately for what is false

all for the sake of more and more standing in ovation,

The applause will never be loud enough—

the room never full enough—

to do anything to remedy the emptiness inside.

SIX HARD WINTER

ICE STORM

The second time Kaysie and I traveled to Juarez, Mexico, we were already engaged to be married. The orphanage staff was bursting with the news. It was here, after all, that we had met—here that God had spoken to us. It was here, in this place of disrepair and of brokenness, that we were first inextricably linked to one another. We reveled in the adoration as we continued to do our best to lead a team in repairing the orphanage in any way we were capable.

One afternoon, we attempted to renovate one of the largest walls in the facility. Paint was provided for us, and we were just about to begin the process when I smelled the contents of the can.

ME:	*That's funny.*
THEM:	What is funny?
ME:	*The paint.*
THEM:	The paint is funny?
ME:	*No. The smell of the paint is funny.*
THEM:	Funny how?
ME:	*Funny because it smells like milk.*
THEM:	It smells like milk because it is milk.
ME:	*I beg your pardon?*
THEM:	We add milk to the paint to make it go further.
ME:	*Funny. We do that to breakfast cereal.*
THEM:	This is why you need to hurry.
ME:	*Hurry?*
THEM:	If the milk is fresh when you paint, it dries fresh— but if it is soured, it stays that way.

I found the fact intriguing.

I had no idea it would become so important.

We spent the next several hours painting the wall—moving slowly from the left of the room all the way to the right, making certain every bit was covered before we moved along. We had just about finished the job when I painted over a spot near the end of the wall and something appeared.

Bubbles.

Under the fresh paint.

I called one of the orphanage staff over.

THEM:	Oh.
ME:	*Oh what?*
THEM:	That is spoiled.
ME:	*How can the wall be spoiled?*
THEM:	Not the wall. The paint.
ME:	*The paint?! But, it smells fine.*
THEM:	Not the paint you are painting with. There is a layer deeper down that is soured, rotten. You'll have to fix it.
ME:	*That's not our fault.*
THEM:	I didn't say it was your fault. I said you will have to fix it.
ME:	*Why do I have to fix it?*
THEM:	Because you are holding the paintbrush.

The reparation would follow four steps:

1. Wipe the wet paint off.
2. Cut away the bubbled section with a razor blade.
3. Sand the razor line down.
4. Repaint the space.

I followed these steps to the letter: wipe, cut, sand, repaint—and when I did: more bubbles. So, we cut back further: wipe, cut, sand, repaint.

More bubbles.

Wipe, cut, sand, repaint.

Yet more bubbles.

This went on, foot-by-foot for a half hour. But, no matter how much we pruned, we discovered that a layer of sour had invaded our wall everywhere we attempted to stop it. When the entire process was said and done, we had peeled off the entire wall.

The entire wall.

Not only was our paint gone and our afternoon wasted, but now there was an uglier mess than the one we had started out with. Determined to find the culprit, I dug down into the wall to discover which layer of paint had been soured.

Seven layers down.

Seven layers down, decay and poison had lay dormant, undetected—just waiting for some sucker to attempt to pretty it up. I asked the orphanage staff how often the wall had been painted. The answer: once every five years.

Thirty-five years ago.

Thirty-five years ago, someone was careless. They may or may not have smelled the paint, but regardless, the paint was sour. They spread it on this wall anyway. And now, as buried as that rotten layer may have seemed, its story was not finished. Not hidden. Not forgotten. Simply waiting. Waiting for that one little conduit—that one chemical reaction that would cause its damage to become widespread.

It took thirty-five years.

And suddenly, we had quite a mess on our hands.

BAM! BANG!

It takes a moment for me to gather my bearings. What just happened? My brain is shaken. Was I just hit by a meteor? I turn around and see that the grill of a very large truck has connected squarely with the back of my SUV. But why "BAM BANG"? Certainly, getting hit by this truck would only create the initial "BAM."

I recognize the automobile that just rammed into me.

A friend has been following me to Dallas, and this is his truck.

Oh no. Was it a multiple car pileup? That must be it. That is why the "BAM BANG." One car hits him: BAM! His car hits me: BANG!

ME:	*PAT! Did you get hit?!*
PAT:	What do you mean did I get hit? I hit you!
ME:	*I thought maybe you got hit too.*
PAT:	No.
ME:	*Then, what happened?*
PAT:	I ... I think I fell asleep.

That was the BAM.

He never took his sleeping foot off the gas pedal, so after he hit me the first time and did not awaken, he bounced off of my car and ran into me a second time. That was the BANG.

◉ ◉ ◉

It has certainly been a long winter.

This was the winter of the ice storms.

The first ice storm hit in the middle of the night the evening before I was admitted for my double-hernia surgery. Waking to a white world, Kaysie phoned the surgeon's office to confirm that the procedure would still be taking place.

The determination was yes, but that it needed to be hurried to an earlier time so that the staff would be able to drive home safely. Kaysie and I scurried to make certain her mother could take the kids and we made a break for the hospital. The roads were precarious, but we maneuvered as best we could. Once there, I was hurried through registration and rushed into yet another paper nightgown.

Then, we sat in a cold room and waited for two-and-a-half hours.

As I was cut apart, snow continued to fall outside, burying our van. When I came around hours later, I was pathetic. Drugged-up. Weak.

Kaysie had no choice but to do her husband's job.

She had to dig out the van herself and then drive me home.

Surgery has a very simple way of making me the fool.

The first evening out and back in my own bed, I began to feel stronger. I began to feel capable. I began to convince myself of this so thoroughly that I attempted to move in ways I shouldn't have moved and tried to accomplish things I should not have attempted to accomplish.

But, the feeling was premature.

The first night was easier than the second. Because the first night, all I could think about was the imminent healing. But the second night, the severity of the pain set in. The moment-by-moment how-am-I-going-to-live-through-this pain. The painkillers I had been administered at the hospital were replaced with lesser painkillers.

For a week-and-a-half, Kaysie helped ease me through the pain, constantly serving me as I was too weak to be the strong one. But it was taxing for her, because she was still reeling from all of the anguish, the hurt, and the damage done in the past several months. She desperately needed a different sort of surgery. It was, of course, impossible for anyone to cut her open, remove the despair, and stitch her back up. So instead, she grew more and more weary of carrying the needs of my pain on top of the needs of hers.

And as the ten days passed, I lay there day after day feeling guilty for the weight I had become to her.

I lay there.

Staring at that hole in the ceiling.

That hole that started it all.

For a full week, the snow continued to fall.

I had only been back to work a few days when the phone call came.

KAYSIE:	Mark?
ME:	*Baby?*
KAYSIE:	There's been an accident.

There had been a mother of an accident.

Kaysie had been stopped at a flashing yellow light. Morgan and one of her friends were in the back seat of the car when a man (who admitted later that he had been daydreaming) barreled over the hill and slammed into them without even tapping on the breaks. The van was a wreck. Coins from the ashtray literally exploded all over the inside of the vehicle—its contents scattered and strewn. By the time I arrived on the scene, the van looked like a snow globe from the gift shop in hell.

Morgan was sobbing. Kaysie deeply rattled.

It was simply too much.

We were now back into confusion territory.

Why must these incidents, these sicknesses, this string of misfortune—why must it CONTINUE? Shouldn't there be a limit, an end point, a punctuation mark to all of this pain? Even our spiritual authorities agreed. They had never seen anything like this string of events. It didn't make sense to anyone.

But I was worried.

Worried that this was the damage of my long-buried layer of paint.

I began to feel that this—all of it—was something I somehow deserved. That the flaws and missteps of the sour seasons of my life had been painted over by layers of good, but were now bubbling up to overtake the healthy. This layer was now spoiling everything. Tampering with my life.

But which layer of my life was it?

> *There was layer A: The suffering I had put Kaysie through because of my addiction.*

Layer B: The anger I had held onto through the lost relationships that followed the rift in our church over half a decade ago.

Layer C: The lack of discipline in my life as I have grown depressed over my weight gain.

Layer D: The distance from other people—the Great Wall of Mark—that I have been building since I lost my dog and Jason moved away.

Or perhaps it had required a Molotov cocktail of all four to get the chemical reaction just right to bubble up and contaminate the layers of our life and marriage. I was determined to hang in there. I did not want this to continue to alter us. We had already been through so much. But every time we turned around—every day, it seemed—we went through more and more. It may have been testing. But it felt an awful lot like punishment.

Through the recuperation, I gained even more weight. I moved more slowly, cautiously—like an old man. I wore that stupid heffalump mask, even though it still wasn't working. I would wake up wheezing and exhausted, angry at the machine. I would throw the mask off of me in the early hours, hurling it down in frustration to the floor as if that one swift act of aggression could reverse the lumbering downward spiral I was feeling at work in my own body. I felt myself growing less and less attractive. I found myself assuming Kaysie was criticizing me in her mind, whether she gave me evidence of those thoughts or not. I began dwelling on the unfairness of this perceived judgment. I began to get angry at her.

Anger begat silence.

Silence begat distance.

And where we had for so many years faced crisis by holding each other closer, we now began to face our own sides of the queen-size bed.

I took myself off my antidepressants without consulting the doctor. They were making me feel foggy, indecisive, even less alive. But quitting them cold turkey made matters even worse.

I was tired—so tired. Yes, from lack of sleep. But also tired of obsessing and trying to come up with a solution. Tired of the effort required. Tired of feeling so awful.

Tired of life.

As I was not my usual chipper self, Kaysie began growing colder toward me. I knew that something had shifted in her mind.

If these men can't live it, how could you?

And I wondered if perhaps she was right.

Our love was frozen, but not the sort of frozen that stands still, unchanged and sustained by the time the thaw comes around. Instead, we were windburned—skin cracking, practically frostbitten. We clung to the fact that rescue might still somehow come, but we resigned ourselves to losing some toes in the process.

A few days later, my SUV broke down and we were without a working vehicle of our own for the holidays. The punches kept coming. The distance kept growing. It felt like the whole wide world was a wedge between myself and Kaysie. The whole wide world.

We rented a van and planned to smile and fake our way through Christmas with every relative we knew visiting our home. We then crawled to Colorado for New Year's, panting over the finish line of 2006, so desperately anxious for this awful year to end. After all, we both crave new beginnings.

I achieved my goal of reading the Bible through in a year and, as I read my last passages on December 31, I could not help but see the irony in the fact that the one year I diligently read God's Word everyday, all hell broke loose in my life. I read the final pages of each Testament:

> *But for you—sunrise! The sun of righteousness will dawn on those who honor my name, healing radiating from its wings.* [†]

> *He who testifies to all these things says it again: "I'm on my way! I'll be there soon!" Yes! Come, Master Jesus!*[††]

[†] Malachi 4:2

[††] Revelation 22:20

And I found myself yearning: Yes. The afterlife. Bring me that.

Forget this life. That is what I long for.

I began to deny the current state of pain and trial and instead dwell on what could be. What will be when I finally get rid of my failed, damaged, fat human skin.

Forever with Jesus. Whole in Him. My sins washed away.

My mistakes forgotten.

Forgotten by everyone.

All those people who have hated me, been hurt by me, misunderstood me—that old friend, that former coworker, those men who used to be my spiritual authorities, all the people who I have burned or who have burned me. All will be forgiven. They will hug my neck. And when my guilt sneaks up and I add "but what about this" they will say "There is no this. The this is gone now."

And my children—my children will believe me to be who I have always aspired to be instead of the person I actually became.

And those dearest to my heart—they will no longer leave. They will no longer die or move or grow distant or grow tired of me. They will not find better lives in cities where I am not. They will not become disillusioned with my love. They will not bore of being a fan. They will never stop licking my ankle.

And Susan's son Logan will be there. And Kaysie's college roommate Amy. And Matt's mother. And all the confusion over why they had to leave us so early will not matter. And they will ask what they have missed, and I will not want to tell them because it will make them sad.

And the grief and despair and confusion—everything that comes with 2:37 a.m.—will disappear. Will it even be noticed? Will it seem like the six entire chapters that it was? Or will it all be reduced to a footnote.

Rest will come.

And joy will return.

And peace.

And Kaysie.

Kaysie will take my face in her hands. And that face will be strong. There will be no breathing mask or grimace from falling through a ceiling. There will be no fear in my eyes of what she is thinking. She will look at me the way she did that day when we were newlyweds and I told the elderly woman at the grocery store that she looked beautiful and Kaysie turned to me and said "I love that you are you," and for one brief moment I lived heaven on earth because all the time I thought I wanted someone to esteem me and be my fan, but instead I had something so much better: I had someone who **knew** *me and loved what they knew.*

And everything that right now seems so irreversible will implode upon itself like a dying star.
And I—I will find something inside of me to love.

Oh God. For that to be now.
Right now.
RIGHT NOW.

And right then, Morgan threw up all over the bed.
Happy 2007.

We began the year at our absolute lowest point. Kaysie and I were both clinically depressed, but without treatment. We were without either car. We tried to confide in a few people during the break, but they didn't understand—couldn't understand. We were in so much pain, so troubled. It was like life was a splinter burrowing into our jugular vein, yet everyone around us looked at it and thought, "Why can't you see how pretty that piece of wood is?" We were horrible to be around, the most negative we had ever been in our lives. We alienated others— became the people we used to avoid at church.

And then: the sickness. Morgan and Kaysie both began the year throwing up for twenty-four hours straight. I left Kaysie in Colorado to recuperate and brought the children back to Tulsa by myself, hoping that the distance from each other would clear our heads and make us yearn for that distance to be bridged.

But instead of time to think and pray, Kaysie only had time to be ill. While she was miserable in a bed miles away, I drove our three children home in the rental van. It was the most precarious drive I have ever traversed because of another winter storm. The pass through Kansas had been closed down and was barely reopened in time for our journey on January 2. I had to be back at work on January 3, so we would have to travel the entire distance in one day, regardless of how slick the roads might have been. I white-knuckled that steering wheel all the way to Oklahoma, slipping and veering often because of the ice. Beginning my year in a stressed-out state of driving paranoia was not the healthiest factor for my mindset, but it had to be done.

Finally, we arrived home at almost ten at night on the second day of the New Year. Our twelve-hour drive turned to almost fifteen because of the weather. I was brutally exhausted because we had been up most of the night before with a sick daughter. I still had to bathe the kids and put them to bed before I washed all of their clothes and repacked them for the friends' houses they would be staying at each day of the week as I worked and Kaysie was out of town.

I finished the unpacking, the washing, and the repacking by 1:30 in the morning and finally went to bed. Radically frazzled, it took me a good half hour before my stomach settled and I began to drift off.

Then, 2:37.

I found myself shaken awake. It was Jackson. He was crying out for Mommy.

I was groggy—stumbling for a coherent sentence: *Jackson? What's the matter?* But before more words could come out of his mouth, they were preceded by a fountain of puke.

Poor Jackson had been crying out for me from his bedroom upstairs and I had been too comatosed to hear him. So, when I didn't come, he puked all over his bed.

Then, he ran to his bathroom, puking on the run over and then puking in the sink, on the counter, and all over the carpet. He cried out again. Again, I did not hear him.

He began to make his way down the stairs. On his way down, he puked three times: on the stairs themselves, in the living room, and in the hallway outside my bedroom. Now he was puking on me. On my side of the bed. My pillow. My covers. My side table. The book I had been reading. My glass of water.

I fled the scene, taking him to the bathroom where I could toss him into a warm tub and attempt to clean some of the mess up. I felt so sorry for him, calling out for Daddy with no answer and then resorting to crying Mommy even though he knew she was not there. It took forty-five minutes to wash him, get him into new pajamas, make him a palette for sleeping on the floor of my room, settle him down, and help him fall asleep.

It was now 3:30. And I had eight areas of the house to scrub and disinfect. I started upstairs. It looked like the room had been painted. He had even thrown up on Charlie. My first task was to change Charlie's clothes and bedding without waking him. Fortunately, he is like Uncle Dav in this regard.

Over an hour later, the house was clean and the contaminated clothing and bed sheets were in the washer and dryer. I willed my stomach to settle so I could sleep, but the bile was really wreaking havoc. I had a bursting headache. My mind raced. I stared at the clock. I finally began to drift at 4:45.

I awakened again to more yelling. It was Jackson again. It was ten minutes to 5:00. I had not even slept five minutes, but Jackson was upchucking what remained in his stomach all over his new pajamas and new palette. I threw him into another bath. There was no clean bedding left, so I made him a place to sleep out of throwpillows and the blankets that draped over the living room sofa.

I put him in one last set of clean pajamas and laid him down to sleep. I stared down at the pile of vomit on my floor and assessed how many items of clothing needed to be rinsed right that second. It was practically 5:30 and I had to be at work at 8:30.

At that moment, I snapped.

Exhausted from two nights of crisis, grieving the lowest point in my marriage, overwhelmed, and smelling of the soured insides of my child, I wept.

I held the paper towel and disinfectant and just wept.

I couldn't make sense of it.

In middle school, I used to read the Choose Your Own Adventure books where every book contained dozens of stories, which turned out differently depending upon what choices you, the reader, made along the pages. My favorite was #6: *Your Code Name Is Jonah*, a spy-caper that allowed me to make continual decisions, some resulting in my fame and fortune, others ending in my demise. But the greatest thing I learned in those books was that no decision was irreversible. I would do my best to choose the right path, but if, for some reason, my choice ended up wreaking havoc, I would simply reverse one decision (or if need be, multiple decisions) until I was back on track to conclude the book with the mystery solved and my character celebrated.

Indeed a formative read. I had not realized how much.

I have made my choices cautiously over the years, hedging and not fully committing—saying things like "I'll try to do that" and "Let's put it on the calendar, but things may change." Kaysie thought I was being indecisive. She had no idea I was scrambling to choose my own adventure.

I had the sense that if I made enough wrong choices, somewhere down the line the outcome of our lives could be irreversibly negative, so I went ahead and made decisions, but I made certain to only stick one foot on board. I kept the other foot out because I wanted to be able to backtrack if the outcome was not what I hoped for.

It explains why I am hesitant to be vulnerable, cautious to make new friends. Why I cling to my wife because I cannot bear for the one who knows me best not to see how all my dysfunction comes from attempts to create a safe world for us, to keep our options open so that we could pursue the best path.

But, in that moment, holding soiled linens, it dawned on me for the very first time that this plan was fatally flawed and that I had failed. I did not know how I had arrived where we were. I could not perceive a way to flip backwards. There was nothing that could be undone.

The life that I had planned ...

... was over.

My God.

I finished the cleaning by six in the morning and lay in bed, hoping for even a few moments of rest.

But the thoughts would not stop coming.

A conversation began again.

But this time, with a very different voice.

It's over.

Yes. It certainly looks that way.

My life is over.

You should elaborate on why you feel that way.

No one understands me anymore. I am no longer known. I look at myself and I see pain and I feel like everyone else looks at me and sees chaos.

They probably don't want anything to do with you.

Of course they don't! I wouldn't want to either.

They probably think you are bad luck.

They laugh about it, but you're right. I bet they do think that.

None of your friends know you anymore.

And what kind of a friendship is that? They are only friends because they don't know.

And the friends that do know ...

They leave. Once I get vulnerable enough—close enough, they leave.

It must be too much.

You must be too much.

I must be too much.

And Kaysie doesn't love you anymore.

Well, I think she still loves me. She just ...

Are you certain?

How can anyone be certain?

Look at the way things used to be. Look at the way they are now. Don't you see the difference?

Of course I do. But that doesn't mean ...

She's gone, isn't she? She needed time away.

Yes. But, she needed time away to think and pray.

Time away from what, Mark? From Tulsa? She can't think and pray in Tulsa?

I don't ...

She doesn't need time away from the kids. She doesn't even want time away from the kids. That's a sacrifice for her.

She's escaping me, isn't she?

She wants to be away from you so badly that she will spend time away from those she really loves: her children, her friends, just to avoid you.

How dare she? What did I ever do ...

You did plenty. You've done so much damage.

I've done so much damage.

Look at yourself. Just a shell of all that promise. All of those fans in college expected so much from you and here you are a sick, fat, unloved man alone.

Am I alone?

No one really loves you, Mark. They just think you are amusing. The only reason they are in your life is because they love her.

Her?

Kaysie. They love her. They are concerned for her. They wonder why she is with you when you have caused her so much pain.

That isn't true. Is that true?

Does it feel true?

It does feel true.

Well, if you feel it then it must be accurate.

I am hopeless.

You said it, not me.

But she will come back. I know she will come back.

She will. But, it will never be like it was before—in Juarez, in the early years. She will never look at your face that way again. She will always cover her face with the pillow and face the other side of the bed. She will never again say "I love that you are you." She will settle to be wounded. Because the sour and spoiled layers of your life have now come back to haunt you, to damage you. All good and great since has now been undone. Get used to this low point because this is pretty much it for the rest of your life.

I don't—I can't—

Your life is as pitiful as that book you're writing. What is it called?

A Year Without a Hero.

Yes. The story of this dreadful year and how you lost your dog.

It's more than that. It's how I lost all of my heroes.

Sounds like the hero that you lost is you.

What?

Everybody is the hero of their own story, Mark. Looks like the hero of your story is dead. Pathetic. You didn't defeat the villain. You didn't get the girl. You didn't save the world. What's there to write about?

You're right.

Of course I'm right.

It's over.

Yes.

I've failed.

Certainly.

This is it. The rest of my life will be this dreary. This hopeless. This filled with grief.

Well ...

What?

You could always just kill yourself.

I was startled awake.

NO.

The reality of what was happening dawned on me. I came to my senses.
I shook out my head, waking myself up.
I suddenly realized who I was talking to.

You're a liar.

What? No. I'm just saying that it would end the pain.

You are the villain of my life.

I am the only one telling you the truth here.

Just because I feel it doesn't make it true.

That's not what you just said.

I was listening to you.

No, no, no. I was listening to you. I get you. I'm the only one who gets you.

And in that moment, it suddenly became clear. Crystal clear. The thought of killing myself had not been the only lie. They were all lies. Every thought unreasonable. Every imagination nothing more than that. I was placing my worst fears inside the heads of those I loved. The enemy was toying with my own weak spots and using them against me. He had only one reason to do this. Only one reason that he had been doing it for the past year. And he accidentally let his cards show.

While God was working to get me to die to myself—
The enemy was trying his best to kill me first.
And as I was worried about all that was attacking me from the outside-in: threats of cancer and surgeries and wound after wound, the villain of my story

was attacking me from the inside-out, corralling my fears and anxieties into a single monstrous worst-case-scenario.

I knew enough about the truth to know when I was being told lies.

And I knew how to best attack them.

Good thing I just finished reading that Book.

For God has not given me the spirit of fear—

Okay, you're going to pull this crap?

But He has given me the spirit of power and love and a normal mind!

Heard it before.

He has created me in His image.

Yes. Well.

I am fearfully and wonderfully made. I am known well by God. He has known me since the beginning of time.

Like I know you?

And NOTHING can separate me from His love, nothing high above or down beneath, no creature, no force of heaven or hell. NOTHING!

I don't have to listen to this.

He has a plan for me. He has a future for me. He takes care of me. He loves me so much that He gave His life so that I DO NOT have to kill myself.

Stop.

His forgiveness is complete.

His love eternal.

His mercy vast.

His grace sufficient.

His understanding entire.

His strength enough.

His answers definitive.

His plan secure.

And His opinion of me—is now mine.

But—

VILLAIN OF MY STORY. IN THE NAME OF JESUS CHRIST, YOU
HAVE NO PLACE IN MY LIFE and this conversation—is over.

The moment passed.

Silence.

A smile came to my face. An actual smile.

> *I know this will not be easy, God. But, I break my heart open to*
> *You. I am done believing that my thoughts are the truth. I want to*
> *know Your thoughts. I've asked You over and over to change this*
> *situation, but let me ask instead that You change me.*

I collapsed onto the bed and slept well into the morning.

As the days wore on, I knew the battle would continue to be fierce, but I was committed. Kaysie returned home and eventually, all sickness left the house. We knew the distance would not be bridged immediately. We knew it would take some serious work. We began the baby steps that we knew to take, all the while feeling like nothing was quite lifting the heaviness that still shrouded our home and family.

Then, one day while visiting a mentor couple in Ohio, I shared our entire story with them. Every detail. The deep dark pain. I expressed how dire the situation was. And out of their extreme love and grace, they listened and empathized. They did not try to fix me. Instead, they said four powerful words:

> *We are so sorry.*

That was it.

It doesn't make you concerned to work with me in ministry?

> *On the contrary.*

What?

It makes us honored to work with you. You have suffered real pain—real hardship, and I don't know a better way to minister the love of Christ than by ministering out of your own pain. Your mistakes in life are not a fatal flaw, Mark. Burying them is the fatal flaw. The secret, the pretending. But, you—you are being honest. You are making room for clarity. You are breaking the fatal flaw's back. It makes me excited for what the future holds for you and Kaysie.

God had sent this man and woman to say the very thing that I did not believe could be said. With passion attached to the sentiment, my mentors made it clear: *We know you and we still love you and we are still proud of you and we see God at work in your life even more now that you are known.*

And then, they made an offer.

Mark, a decade ago, my wife and I took part in a marriage intensive. It was a week away, completely immersed in an in-depth look at our lives alone and with each other. We were pushed to address some very real fears, some very real pain, and the reasons why we were built the way we are built. It was challenging because we had to be completely vulnerable with each other as well as the others in our group. But it changed us forever.

How great for you.

You don't understand, Mark. If you and Kaysie are willing, my wife and I feel God leading us to give you that same week.

Give us?

It is our gift. If Kaysie says yes, you will leave on Easter Sunday.

Once again, it was time to choose our own adventure. All had seemed irreversible, but now, the moment we gave warts and all to God, a gift arrived. The offer of the gift alone was healing, but we knew that there would be much pain attached to the actual process.

The pain of vulnerability.

Of chiseling away the walls we had built.

But we knew what this offer meant.

It meant it was time to die already.

Time to die to the acceptance that nothing better could come along.

Time to die to my belief that I was without a hero. To reassess what story was unfolding here—and to determine how it would be lived.

How it would be told.

BAM! BANG!

When my SUV was hit by my friend, it was totaled. But that wasn't the end of the story. Because my laptop computer had been in the back of that vehicle, the laptop's hard drive was fried—completely destroyed. And along with it, all the writing I had done for my new book.

Looks like I'm going to have to begin writing this story all over again from scratch. It's probably for the best. I've had writer's block anyway. But I don't think I'll call it *Year Without a Hero*. I think I'll take a new approach and name the book after the sixth decision in my life that really mattered.

We accept the offer to depart on Easter.

And we sensed that the thaw from the deep frozen winter was finally beginning.

(Exhibit L)

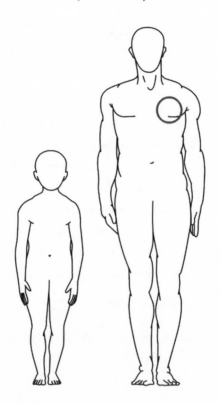

SIX DECISIONS THAT MATTERED

decision #6:

HALF-LIFE / DIE ALREADY

In many ways, it would have been easier to settle for a half-life.

No one would have ever discovered the struggles, faults,
failings, and frailty of my human existence.
It would all have died with me in the very end.
I could have just smiled and waved.
Smiled and waved.
I would have kept all my fans.
And I would somehow have crossed that finish line
without ever being truly known or understood.

I would never be certain that the real me would have been accepted.
I would never know how wonderful the full life could have been.

That is exactly why I had to die already.

I had been playing dead
playing possum,
rolling over with my feet in the air and tongue hanging out,
praying the poundings would stop,
never realizing that without pain
I could never fully live.

Refinement, character, selflessness
Vision, Confidence, a Mission

These will not exist without the pain
urging them forward.

Enough pain to change
enough pain to die

The time to die already has finally arrived.

SEVEN SPRING FORWARD

EASTER AGAIN

One of us thinks we should total it.

One of us thinks we should salvage it.

Why? We have been given the opportunity to just chuck it—to cut our losses and start fresh with something new.

True. But what we get in return will not be what it is worth. We will never be able to replace it with another of the same value.

But it will be brand new.

New is not always better. It will cost a lot.

I don't know.

I know that totaling the old one seems easier, but it can be fixed. I just know it can. The one we have now is better.

It's not better right now. Right now it is completely wrecked.

I know. But don't look at right now—instead, picture the near future. This can be salvaged.

It could also be scrapped.

So, which one do you wanna do?

After taking the time to think it through, we both agree that we will keep the van. We refuse to have it totaled. We will have it repaired and some day soon, we will enjoy it.

It is Easter again.

The church is doing the same theatrical presentation as last year—only this time, I am not involved. I am, instead, packing our luggage for the road trip. As I pack, I reach into the top of my closet to see if my toiletry bag has fallen behind my collection of assorted unworn baseball caps.

I feel something.

What is this?

I pull it out. It is a cassette tape.

I read the writing on the spine.

SIDE ONE

1. "My Sharona" (The Knack)
2. "Brother" (Toad the Wet Sprocket)
3. "Cantaloop-Flip Fantasia" (US3)
4. "The Brady Bunch" (Greg soundbite)
5. "Evenflow" (Pearl Jam)
6. "Get Ready 4 This" (Jock Jams)
7. "Crazy" (Seal)
8. "Tempted" (Squeeze)
9. "Got No Shame" (Brother Cane)
10. "Maniac" (Michael Sembello)
11. "Sweetest Thing" (U2)
12. "Return to Innocence" (Enigma)

SIDE TWO

1. "Seven Days" (Sting)
2. "Throw the R Away" (The Proclaimers)
3. "This Time" (Bryan Adams)
4. "Linger" (The Cranberries)
5. "Happy Happy Joy Joy" (Ren & Stimpy)
6. "Under My Skin" (Frank Sinatra and Bono)
7. "Mr. Jones" (Counting Crows)
8. "Locked Out" (Crowded House)
9. "Every Little Thing She Does Is Magic" (The Police)
10. "Thief of Your Heart" (Sinead O'Connor)
11. "Little Miss Can't Be Wrong" (Spin Doctors)
12. "The-Evening-Wore-On" (speech from *Harvey*)
13. "Your Love" (The Outfield)

Kaysie walks into the room. My mouth is open.

KAYSIE: What?

ME: Look what I found.

KAYSIE: Oh! That was our favorite.

ME: Well—yeah.

KAYSIE: That's "Getting Warmer 1994."

ME: You remember what I called it.

KAYSIE: What's the matter?

ME: I thought you sold this in that garage sale.

KAYSIE: Why would I do that? You made it for me.

> **ME:**   *Right. But I haven't been able to find it.*
> **KAYSIE:** You have now.

It is clear that the spring thaw is upon us.

Once Kaysie and I decided to engage in this marriage intensive, something broke between us. Yes, the anxiety has continued, but at least we are beginning to communicate. We actually had a few moments of laughter together this past week. Twice in the past ten days, we have remained in bed after waking, lying close to one another and discussing hopeful things. We know much work is to be done, but knowing that the other desires to work it out—to commit to something as intense as an intensive—made it plain that we both wanted the same thing.

To salvage what was almost totaled.

Much has changed and much has stayed the same in the bold transition from winter to spring. The sleep machine has continued to be the bane of my existence. I have gone through two different masks: my new one causing me to look less like a heffalump and more like Goose in *Top Gun*. But now I have accoutrements added to the mask. Turns out I couldn't sleep because my mouth was hanging open. I know: shocking. Nonetheless, it took four months for the technicians to figure that out. The solution: I now wear a wrestling strap around my skull and chin. I get ready for bed and I look like I'm in dress rehearsal for a youth group camp sketch. It is vastly humiliating, but hey, they were right. It works a little better. I am finally sleeping. And it is amazing what that does to a man's perspective.

My abdomen scars still burn and ache. Instead of stitching the tears in my muscles, the surgeon covered them in a protective mesh. Now, every time I stretch or exert myself in a new way, I feel that mesh stretch and pull on the muscles. It hurts vastly less than all of the combined ailments I weathered after the ceiling accident, but it pangs just enough to be a constant reminder of what bad things can happen when a man falls—and tells no one about it.

Charlie's leg, on the other hand, has grown stronger. It took a very long time, but he is skipping again, smiling as if last summer never actually occurred. The stomach pains, the contamination in the eye, any visible scar from the head wound—it is all gone. A distant memory.

He has almost learned how to do a flip on the trampoline. I, however, will not be attempting one with him.

And the doctors don't see any danger in him trying this. The irony is that broken legs, when taken care of and given time to heal, actually heal back stronger than before. There is something in the breaking, the pain, the splintering—that fortifies it. A bone is not destroyed by experience. Rather, it is refined by it.

Jason and I have reconnected. He was unable to come last Thanksgiving, but he and Sarah instead came for Easter. It gave us ample time to catch up—and I have found that reuniting with Jason is like turning the page of a favorite book. We pick up effortlessly from where the story last lingered.

And Zachary.

Oh Zachary.

Just before we drove out the door today, there he was ringing that doorbell.

Dingdongdingdongdingdongdingdongdingdongdingdongdingdong!

> **ME:** *Hello, Zachary.*
>
> **ZACHARY:** HOPPY Eastah! Don't you get it? It is a humor reference to bunnies hopping.
>
> **ME:** *The explanation does make it funnier.*
>
> **ZACHARY:** And to celebrate, I am going to play INSIDE your house!
>
> **ME:** *Zachary, it's Easter and Mrs. Steele and I are about to go out of town, so this is a family day.*
>
> **ZACHARY:** You know WHAT? They are AWL family days and when you tell me that, I just keep coming back and ringing the doorbell until you EVENTUALLY let me in.
>
> **ME:** *Boy, you just threw it all out there, didn't you?*

And the answer was so brazen, so dripping with honesty, that I was quite impressed. I went ahead and let him in.

◉ ◎ ◙

For all of the outside influences: the sicknesses and accidents, hurtful moments and hurtful words, fallen mentors and distant friends—the time had finally come to make it personal.

Now, it is only about the two of us.

We are so nervous on the several-hour drive up that we laugh most of the way. We know that the real reason for the frivolity is the insecurity we feel about what is to come, but still, it feels good.

I look over at Kaysie as we drive and she asks me quiz questions from *Games Magazine*. It has never been more obvious. She is my best friend. And when we lost our intimacy, it was as if a terrible accident had killed many of my friends in a single swoop. My confidant: gone. My spiritual connection: gone. My closest friend: gone. My lover: gone. It was evident why it had been too much to handle. It was shocking to me how much I had been deceived. I had continually felt wounded *by* Kaysie, but this was not accurate. I was actually wounded *with* her. Alongside her. Overwhelmed with loss.

And it suddenly comes flooding to me.

This has all been about loss.

The loss of a baby.

The loss of a friend.

The loss of a spiritual father.

Of my reason.

My dog.

My optimism.

My hope.

My heroes.

And in that progression, I had assumed there was one more thing I would lose.

My wife.

I look at her now as we drive and I realize what I realized when God first spoke to us in that orphanage room with the view of the world outside its windows:

> *I don't know what is coming.*
> *But I know it will not be too much.*

We drive up to the marriage intensive and look at our schedule. The first event on the itinerary is for Kaysie and I to spend a session with the two counselors alone.

The session will last three hours.

And it begins in five minutes.

I hear an audible gulp and realize a few seconds later that it came from me.

I guess I thought dying to myself would feel more like drifting asleep or the moment when those who have lived a full life slowly pass from this life into the next. I suppose I had not thought the analogy completely through. Because for dying to self to occur peacefully, one would have already needed to have lived. As we know, the full life cannot even begin until after the act of dying already. The death has to be a shock—enough to hurl one from a drunken stupor into the land of the living—the truly living.

To this end, dying to self is less like a peaceful wake.

It is more like the moment of birth.

Not the pretty wrapped-in-a-blue-blanket-for-the-camera moment.

Rather, the gasping for oxygen, slapped-on-the-buttock, screaming-for-mercy-while-the-veins-practically-burst-out-of-your-forehead moment.

Yeah. That's dying to self.

It doesn't come easy.

And it doesn't start gradually.

There has to be a moment.

A time of death.

The time for ours had come.

And when the time of death comes, there are only two options:

1. PLAY POSSUM

or

2. OPEN YOUR MOUTH & CLOSE YOUR EYES

I had always assumed when I fell through the ceiling that my position at the time was the most vulnerable I could possibly be in: wrapped around that crossbeam, my manhood teetering in the balance. But I was wrong. There is a much more vulnerable place. And that place is called "open your mouth and close your eyes." It is a state of utter trust that no one in their right mind would submit themselves to. In light of human reason and experience, it doesn't make sense.

The One we trust wants to feed us, to nourish us—but that nourishing cannot come until we trust Him completely. Why? Because our gut instinct is not to trust.

We have somehow gotten life backwards. God is trustworthy, but people are not—so the damage inflicted upon us by one another has inevitably caused us to doubt God. But His intention is for the opposite to happen: for us to allow Him to prove Himself faithful—so faithful that it makes us want to be faithful to those around us. God's trustworthiness is supposed to bridge the hurt caused by man's frailty. Instead, we allow the opposite to happen—as in the case with our mentor. The failure of a man we trusted completely destroyed our world.

God's trustworthiness never fails, but we daily demand fresh proof. We will open our mouth. Oh yes. We are happy to speak our piece, but we are completely unwilling to close our eyes. To say, in essence, *this doesn't make sense to me. I can't figure this one out. I'm not strong enough or wise enough and I need You. All reason says no, but I choose to die to my need for all the details, and instead I surrender.*

For eighteen months, Kaysie and I have been at a loss of how to bridge the chasm created by one another. It has seemed uncrossable, irreparable. But that is because we have insisted on keeping our eyes open, looking for an answer we could see, hear, taste, and touch. But there was no answer.

It is time to give God full reign.

So, without knowing what it will mean or what will come of it …

We open our mouths and close our eyes.

◉ ◉ ◉

We had no sooner been introduced to our counselors than the flop-sweat-inducing questions begin to come.

> *How have you been hurt?*
> *How does that make you feel?*
> *When she said that, what did it mean to you?*
> *When he did that, what sort of pain were you feeling?*

Egads.

Our answers were slow, introspective, precise.

And as we spoke, the Spirit of God was in that room.

And somehow, in discussing the same topic in even greater detail that had always brought so much pain—clarity began to come.

Understanding.

A willingness to truly hear one another.

We began to each share our story of how we separately perceived we had arrived at this tragic place, and the epiphanies of the other's perspective were earth-shattering. All the while I thought Kaysie was building fury toward me, she was feeling inadequate and guilty. All the while she thought I didn't care, I cared so much (without the ability to make a difference) that I was shutting down.

Yes. There was very real hurt.

Grave hurt.

But hurt rooted in a skewed perspective of the other, of his or her intentions, his or her battles, his or her despair.

That three-hour meeting did not heal us.

But it got our mouths open.

And one of the most hopeful realizations was sparked:

We each wanted to be made whole together.

Then came the next day.

The next day was a much greater challenge because something else was introduced into the mix.

Other people.

> *What?! Why are we expected to air our troubles in front of other people?*

> *I don't need anyone all up in my business. And I certainly don't have time to hear their problems. I have enough of my own.*

This is when it became obvious that there was an enormous hurdle I still had to overcome if I was truly going to die to myself.

I had lost my empathy.

I had become so selfish, so consumed with all that had happened to us that I had ceased to reach out to others. It became clear that perhaps I had not heard God lately because I was not listening to what He was doing through other people. We introduced ourselves to the group and then learned the results of the forty pages of tests we had taken in the few weeks before we arrived. I winced. *Did I really say that? Was that my actual emotion at the time? Yeesh. Who would want to hang with that guy? Certainly not me.*

As our answers were interpreted for us by the counselors, my shame transitioned once again to understanding. *Why, I never thought of it that way. Yes. I can see how that legitimate need in my life combined with that irrational thought could have produced the emotion behind that answer.*

It was as if each of our lives had been the scattered pieces of a jigsaw puzzle, and it was only now as the counselors began putting each piece in place that we could see clearly that our lives not only fit, but that they fit together.

And then: the first night.

The night of repentance.

It was good that understanding had come over the first day. It was healthy to begin to have clarity regarding our spouse's feelings, words, and actions. But it would not hold any power until we admitted our faults to one another and truly repented.

This was the tricky part for me because I am an over-apologizer. I apologize too much and too often. Kaysie has been subjected hundreds of times to my onslaught of verbal forgive-me's in light of the ways I have wounded her soul. But repentance was something altogether different.

We were sent back to our hotel suite and asked to separate for a time in order to get our thoughts together. But I already knew what I needed to say. I brought Kaysie to the couch in the sitting room.

And I slowly opened my mouth and closed my eyes.

> *Kaysie, I repent—that I have not protected you the way I should have.*

> *The way any husband should have.*

> *Kaysie, I repent—for making you my priest instead of my confidant. For loading you down with my constant struggle instead of leading you through my healing.*

> *Kaysie, I repent—for putting too much weight on you as the only one I could receive encouragement from.*

Kaysie, I repent—for thinking the worst when you have given me twelve years of proof to believe the best.

That's it. That's all I've got.

And that is when I saw it.

Tears in her eyes.

Kaysie cried for the first time in months. The dam of her emotions had been blocked up—incapable of feeling anything resembling catharsis. She had felt it destroying her—like a scab over infection, refusing to allow any of the poison to be washed out.

She reached over to embrace me.

The jigsaw pieces began to fall into place.

She repented of some actions and emotions to me as well, but something had already been lifted. We could both feel it.

I don't know that it was the words.

I run through the last eighteen months in my head and I cannot imagine another time those words could have been spoken and had any effect whatsoever toward the state of our grief. Undeniably, Christ was in the room.

Honesty led to understanding.

Understanding led to empathy.

And empathy led to true repentance.

From that point on, though the remainder of the weekend was fraught with difficult steps and realizations, we were now in it together. We were no longer observing. We were healing. The instantaneous differences were subtle but profound.

Her hand reaching for mine.

Her head leaning against my shoulder.

Lingering to face one another as we fell asleep.

It was as if we really had reached an apex of the pain and somehow made it over that last ledge to a place where we could finally exhale. And, just like the results of the test, with understanding came sudden clarity regarding so many issues of the past year-and-a-half.

It was not long ago that I was obsessing over the afterlife—an if-only fantasy wanting to speed up the process of absolution for my pain-filled and guilt-ridden conscience. I had wanted to die, but not this way—not the painful way where I truly see what my choices have done and then pursue healing.

I had neglected to see that some of that heaven is already right here. Somewhere in my despair, I had stopped trying to find it. I had been doing everything in my power to cancel and replace life. Now, regardless of the work that needs to be done, I am living to have it salvaged.

This, of course, does not remove all of the damage.

Our marriage has definitely been hanging in the balance between being totaled and sold for parts, or salvaged with a hefty price tag. But the shift that has happened this week is key: We are willing to pay that price. We have no delusions about it being easy. Though we do sincerely hope that the process involves fewer bodily injuries this time around.

◉ ◉ ◉

The next morning, we are asked a few encouraging questions in order to boost our spirits in the wake of last evening's time of repentance. We are asked to focus on some of the positives. To this end, Kaysie is asked: *What is one of the little things your spouse does that really blesses you?*

Kaysie's answer shocks and astounds me.

I love it when he makes me mix CDs.

Unbelievable.

All this time I thought she had been throwing them out. Instead, she saw them for what they actually are: my artistic attempt to personalize love. It becomes clear that someone really knows me.

The counselors continue to speak, but I am distracted by the woman with her head on my shoulder.

We look in each other's eyes.

Her hand on my face.

Mere weeks ago, the situation had seemed irreversible, unfixable. But somehow, by the miraculous intervention of God Almighty, our love feels different. Thicker. Fuller. Better than the days when she was my fan.

Better than Juarez.

Better.

What was true of Charlie's leg was true of our love. It had to break to become stronger.

And now that we have finally started to die already …

now that we have splintered and sought healing …

what was shattered is becoming whole.

A new season is dawning.

Life is being renewed.

(Exhibit M)

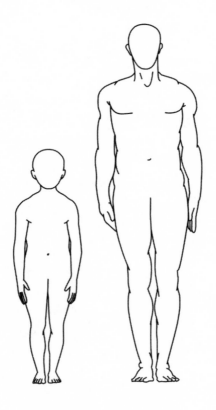

EIGHT LOVE OF THE DOG

Life goes on.

The careful maneuvering through crises continues to be a necessity in our lives, but something is definitely different. Kaysie and I are leaning on one another. The healing is neither complete nor instantaneous, but a new and radical hope has come from the progress we have made—from the understanding that deep love has never left. Those moments I had assumed were gone forever have returned: the laughter, the closeness, the confidence. The rough spots are further-between and when they arrive, we now have the tools to allow them to build our broken bones stronger.

We are breaking through the fog.

So much so, that Kaysie recently made a request.

KAYSIE:	I think I'm ready for another dog.
ME:	*A what?*
KAYSIE:	Another dog. I think it would really be good for us.
ME:	*Really? I thought you were tired of all the holes in the backyard and all the bagging of the poop.*
KAYSIE:	I was. But, now I think I would really embrace the addition to our family. What do you think?
ME:	*What do I think? Are you kidding me? I've been asking for a dog since Hero died. I love dogs. Let's go for it.*
KAYSIE:	And you can bag the poop.

So, we began keeping our eyes out for that new addition. I knew what I wanted: a dog I could saddle up on and wrangle elephants. Perhaps a golden retriever or a rottweiler mix that had a thing on the side with a buffalo.

And then, Kaysie saw him.

Our church was having an auction to raise money for missions and one of the offerings up-for-grabs was an affenpinscher—a tiny black purebred about the size of a mop head. Kaysie actually gasped.

KAYSIE:	That's him.
ME:	*That's who?*
KAYSIE:	That's it! That's him. That's our dog.
ME:	*That?! That's not a dog. That's a dog snack.*
KAYSIE:	He's perfect.
ME:	*For buffing my shoes.*
KAYSIE:	Why? What kind of a dog were you thinking?
ME:	*I was thinking a big dog.*
KAYSIE:	I'm done with big dogs. I was thinking about an inside dog.
ME:	*Inside of what? An envelope?*
KAYSIE:	He's not that small.
ME:	*It would take him ten days to wander out of our mailbox.*
KAYSIE:	I really feel a connection here.
ME:	*Baby—*
KAYSIE:	Please?
ME:	*The starting bid is $200.*
KAYSIE:	Pleeeeease.

I was just about to bring out my best financial argument when Kaysie played dirty. She called the kids over.

MORGAN:	Oh! He's perfect! He's perfect!
CHARLIE:	I wike him a wot.
JACKSON:	Can we keep him? Pleeeease?
MORGAN:	He's ours! I just know he's ours.
CHARLIE:	Yes. I wuv him.
JACKSON:	We prayed for him! God is answering our prayer!

CHARLIE: Pweeeeease!

KAYSIE: Well, kids—that's up to your daddy.

Kaysie and I looked at our savings and debated what we could spare. We determined that I could go as high as three hundred dollars, but that was all. That night, I found myself at an auction table, quite certain that if I did not shell out enough of our savings to secure this rolled-up tube sock of a pet, I would have four very disappointed people in my life.

He was clearly the hot buy of the night as he was reserved for the very last item up for bid. Finally, my friend Troy began auctioning off this future family member.

TROY: All right! Just look at this baby!

AUDIENCE: Ahhhhh! Oooooooh! GASP!

TROY: I can tell we're gonna send a lot of people to Uganda with this choice item!

ME: *Please no.*

TROY: Let's see: It says the bidding should begin at $200.

ME: *TWO-HUNDRED DOLLARS!*

TROY: Fantastic, Mr. Steele, but let's kick that starting bid up to $250!

ME: *Oh for the love of Pete!*

TROY: Do I hear $250?

ME: *No.*

SOMEONE: THREE HUNDRED!

AUDIENCE: WHOOOAA! HUZZAH!

ME: *WHAT?!*

TROY: That's $300 from the man in the dog-skin blazer! Do I hear $320? Three-twenty anyone?

ME: *THREE-TWE—*

SOMEONE: THREE-FIFTY!

AUDIENCE: OOOOOOOOOH!

TROY: Beautiful! 350 from the lady with the allergy mask secured to her face! Going once, going—

> ME: *THREE SEVENTY-FIVE!*
> AUDIENCE: AHHHHHHHHH!
> SOMEONE: THREE-NINETY!
> AUDIENCE: EEEEEEEEEEEE!

Spinning wildly out of control.

I began to panic. How dare they?! How dare all these people bid on OUR dog?! It suddenly became clear as a crystal puppy dish: This dog was meant to be ours and I was going to be doggie-doodied if I was going to allow anyone else to steal this new member of our family away.

> ME: **FOUR! HUNDRED! DOLLARS!**

A large gasp filled the auditorium. It took me a moment to realize that it was my own.

> TROY: FOUR HUNDRED DOLLARS from Mr. Steele!
> A very generous offer—but hey, this is going to missions!
> Certainly someone can top that bid! Come on people, we'll
> be here all night if we have to.

Troy's a good guy.

But, I was about ready to trample him with a rottweiler/buffalo crossbreed.

Kaysie had taken the boys home because she couldn't handle the suspense, but Morgan was standing over me, biting her nails, practically in tears. She looked up at me with those pleading eyes, slightly watered, round and beautiful orbs of green and brown.

I began to break into a cold sweat.

I had to bring this dog home.

I just had to.

After everything we had gone through—after all the broken bones, cracked heads, infected eyes, distant friends, colonoscopies, ultrasounds, surgeries, sleeping machines, bruised manhood, bear attacks, puking marathons, stomach pangs, car accidents, and lost Heroes—this dog had better be ours. Another bid rang out:

SOMEONE: FOUR-HUNDRED AND TEN DOLLARS!

TROY: WOW! That's $410 from the couple wheeling the matching portable oxygen tanks!

Morgan's lip began to quiver.

Disappointment was knocking.

I felt a fleeting moment of insanity.

I decided to run with that.

ME: *FIVE!! HUNDRED!! DOLLARS!!*

The room came alive.

Shouts and confetti and the remnants of a small circus parade.

That was it. We didn't have another spare dollar to our name. It was all or nothing. And then, suddenly, from the voice of Troy as if it were the voice of God:

TROY: SOLD! Steele family—this dog is YOURS!

Morgan threw her arms around me and then just as quickly ran up to seize our prize. My smile lingered for a moment and then—reality hit. I began to weigh the two scenarios against one another. On one hand: We had the dog. On the other hand: Two hundred dollars over budget. Yeesh.

Talk about your buyer's remorse.

And then …

A group of us wanted to give you this.

I was handed a check.

We know you guys have been through a lot and we really wanted you to have this dog. He kind of had your name on him. We hope this helps.

I unfolded it.

Two hundred dollars.

The dog took to Kaysie instantly, like Bambi to his mother if the hunter had missed. That dog went crazy licking her face, wagging that tail—it was less of an introduction and more of a reunion.

Kaysie named him Scout after her favorite character in her favorite book. I thought we should name him Radley, but that would kind of make him the creepy, misunderstood puppy on the block. He already has the black bangs hanging over his eyes. I don't really need an emo dog.

And, in my own way, I was excited, too. Last time we had a dog, I experienced some of the most lavish affection I could imagine. I was the head of the house and Hero knew it and she adored me the way one should the individual in charge.

Certainly it would be that way with Scout.

Not so much.

Scout quickly became addicted to my wife—deeply affectionate towards her and aggressively territorial toward anything or anyone else that would come inbetween that affection. After a single day in our home, if I took a step toward Scout, he would lunge at me, bear his teeth, and bark like there was no tomorrow. If I kissed Kaysie, he would jump at my feet, pulling at my pants leg with his teeth.

What a wonderful dog.

And sheesh, can that dog ever bark. He has discovered the exact pitch and timbre required to summon the kraken from the depths of Atlantis itself.

What a crock. I just shelled out half a grand to nurture a mongrel that doesn't even want me around. What happened to the fandom, the leg licking— what happened to the dog who saw me as the master who could do no wrong?

Scout was certainly no Hero.

This was nothing like my previous experience with the love of the dog.

Why can't the good things stay exactly as they were last time?

And then, I remembered the variations.

The nuances that change along what seemed otherwise an identical path.

I remembered the thrill ride at the fair and how Matt and I slammed arms together right at the point we got comfortable with our own stupidity.

Last time I had a dog, it was all very different.

A year and a half ago, I was perfectly happy with the love of the dog.

But, the road has indeed changed.

I had begged God to shake up my same-old circular experience and mold me into something stronger.

I didn't realize how much the road would have to change.

I didn't consider the severity of the forthcoming variations.

I didn't assess how many bones would have to break.

And it certainly didn't dawn on me that on the other side of the change, the love of the dog might just look and feel different than before.

This love was not easy and effortless.

It would not allow lazy.

This love would require some work.

Some effort.

Some reciprocation.

But, eighteen months later, I was ready for it.

How did this happen? How did I become ready?

Oh—now you don't remember the pain?

Of course I remember the pain, but I thought the pain was tearing me down. When did it make me stronger?

It made you stronger every day, Mark. Every lousy day. Every great day. Every day you felt you were winning. Every day you felt you were failing.

But, I don't get it. I felt like I was wandering.

Yes.

So, if I was wandering, how did I end up in this place on the other side?

Certainly you know the answer to that.

Absolutely not.

But, you asked Me for it yourself.

I asked You for a NeverLost.

That's right.

And You never sent it.

Didn't I?

But I was so aimless.

Were you now?

I don't understand.

You asked for a daily voice to guide you. Specifics. With emotion and commitment attached.

I remember.

So, I told you to read the Bible through in a year.

What?

You didn't know what the year would hold, but I did.

So You did this? You put us through all this sorrow?

No, Mark. Life, being human, and your own choices put you through this sorrow, but I gave you a NeverLost.

You mean ...

Did it never occur to you that your daily reading wasn't just an assignment? Were you never floored by the fact that on any given day—every single day—whatever you were going through, whatever you needed, the answer was right there, right there on that page just like I was whispering it in your ear? Did you think that was merely coincidence? That words written thousands of years ago in a time unlike your own would, by some fluke, just happen to apply to your situation right now? There's your miracle, Mark. Those words were written for every man, woman, and child who would ever live. But they were also written for you. It's not just a history book. It's your NeverLost. It always has been. And it always will be. But, that isn't all that I sent you.

What else did you send? You certainly didn't make it easy to find it.

Didn't I? What was it that you needed?

I needed to know how to deal with all the pain!

And I sent you Charlie.

Did you not watch how he dealt with the pain?

You could learn a lot from Charlie.

I needed the distance between Kaysie and I to be bridged ...

No. You needed the distance between you and Kaysie to be healed.

And that required a process. Much damage had been done. That is why I sent many methods of healing. I sent a cavalcade of support through family, friends, and church. I made certain your business succeeded and your financial needs were covered in this season so that you would not have that added stress. I gave you ample time to be together to work through the difficult moments. And I sent you that couple to encourage you and pay your way to the counseling I knew would truly begin the healing.

I ... I see that now.

Do you?

I do. But, did it all have to be so joyless? I understand that it would not have worked to miraculously heal our marriage in an instant. But why couldn't you have brought at least a little instant joy? Why couldn't you just swoop down at my worst moments and throw a burst of joy my way?

And what exactly would you call Zachary?

You ... You sent Zachary?

Every moment you needed him, but you were so quick in your pity party to shove joy right back out the door.

I ... I couldn't take it.

Couldn't take what? The optimism? The laughter? Let's face it:

In one regard, that little boy was exactly right. You constantly complained about your despairing circumstance, but you certainly came up with an awful lot of reasons not to let joy into your house.

I've never seen it that way before.

And so much of what you were pleading for, you already had. It was right there in front of your eyes, but you were so consumed with your anguish, you just couldn't see your hand in front of your face.

You needed support and you already had an amazing circle of believers who love and support you within your church.

You needed to be known, but you already had a family who sees you for who you are and loves you still.

You needed the dark days to stop while you were refusing to see that there were as many great days occurring alongside them.

And you needed a friend to confide in after Jason left and you already had so many. Your pastor Roger, your brother Dav, your friend Jeff, your friend Matt.

Matt?

You are the one who said he is always quick to help other people. He was always quick to be there for you—but you were too immersed in your dark place to notice.

And that is truly the big answer you have been looking for, Mark. The answers were never hidden. The salvation never a mystery. You were so distracted being angry that they weren't obvious, that you never really looked. Your life, your days, revolved around you. THAT is why I needed you to die to yourself— not to punish you—but because it was the only way you would ever discover the truth and the life that was already around you.

So, only one question remains.

What is that?

Are you finished playing dead?

It was now clear. God's unconditional love for me had not changed, but God's love was never like the love of the dog. The love of the dog was like the unconditional love I had for myself, but it was not a disciplined love that pushed me higher and further. It was an evading love—a love that dodged painful turns.

Scout was not the same dog as Hero eighteen months ago.

But neither was I the same me.

⦿ ⊙ ◉

The dog meant so much to Kaysie that I was determined to win him over, whatever it took. This process required an intense outpouring of both affection and discipline. Though he would bark and growl when I was alone, I would give him affection, feeding him and patting him. And when he would get between my wife and I, I would bark him to the ground.

I would literally out-yelp, out-growl, and out-snarl him. He would get loud and I would get louder. He would stretch his body into an aggressive position and I would lunge at him face-to-face. My barks would startle him, cause him to hide that tail between his legs, and cower away. It was the only way to show him that I was the alpha dog. That I still loved him but that this was my wife, my home, my life, and that I was tired of whatever barked loudest causing me to forget that.

But now I face the real test.

Kaysie and the kids have to go to Oklahoma City for the day so the dog has to go with me to the office. Eight hours with just me and the dog. I drive him across town in his little cage and then I set it in the corner of my office, as far away from my desk as possible. I open the cage slowly, and he barks and barks and barks.

While I am on a conference call he barks.

Is that—is that a dog in your office?

It's a very long story. Let's just get on with the budget.

The dog is freaking out that he is in a strange, confined space with the man who, just last night, barked at him like a beast. So, he stays in his cage. A few hours go by, and he becomes quiet for the first time in my presence. I slowly take his water dish to him. He snarls. A pathetic woof. I scratch his head. He seems to be ashamed that he likes it.

I go back to my desk and I keep writing. And, by the end of the day, a subtle thing happens. No. He doesn't give me the pleasure of seeing the tail wag.

But slowly …

Oh so slowly …

He makes his way across the room.

Scout is lying at my feet. He exhales—what sounds suspiciously like a sigh of relief and I must admit that I do the same. It may just be a little, but I am sensing a new love of the dog. And I am reminded of how much has changed since the last dog lay at my feet in the sunshine of that garage sale.

Such a long, long time ago.

So much has changed. Full circle and yet different.

I lean back and forge into the writing of my book.

My life is now full.

EVERYTHING LIVES

Most authors have writer's block.

I, on the other hand, have writer's circle.

I write the same way I live and the same way I learn: As the circular experience of life unfolds another cycle, I discover what makes this time around different—perhaps even better. I had been so frustrated by the circular, seeing it only as mundane and invaluable. It had not occurred to me that perhaps this is the way God most diligently teaches me: The dilemmas remain similar, but next time around, I might just be different myself.

I am different this time around.

And it is all because of the variations.

The nuances that ramped up the action, gave volume to the villain, and demanded action on my part, requiring me to face my own music. In the past, I have dodged the very same trials that this year became so prevalent. But in the past, I was able to ignore them because they were just a whisper. I held onto comfort and never actually processed my flaws. This time around, they were too big of a monster to ignore.

Next time, I hope I recognize the whisper of my flaws before they turn into a scream. After this year, I know I would vastly prefer to have my reckoning during my seasons of strength.

Now, it is much easier to see what was true all along: There is much good and right in my life, but I was only looking at the tragedy, the pain. There continues to be pain, but it is a different sort of pain now. It is not destructive, rather: a brokenness. There is pain because I care. I love the people around me so much that I don't want them to hurt. For this, I am grateful—grateful that my life is so filled with love by my Kaysie, my Morgan, my Jackson, my Charlie, my friends and family, that I am wounded by their wounds and they are wounded by mine. There is tragedy all around us, but the only way to live in safety, the only way to be protected, is not to love. Not to feel. Before, I thought I was aiming for a life without pain, but the only way to achieve that would be to live choosing not to feel.

That is exactly what I had chosen.

That was my half-life.

That was the depression I suffered—my feeble attempts to cut off the pain. But instead, I was slicing away love.

But I have now been to the nadir and back.

My life, my calling, and my marriage were utterly transformed when I embraced the pain—embraced the affection it meant I had for those around me. I truly had to open my mouth and close my eyes.

And now, just like Charlie after his stomach pains at Silver Dollar City, it is time for me to roll out of the fetal position and declare, *"I'm done. I'm all wight now. I AM WEADY!"*

Of course, pain continues to intermingle with the healing.

Kaysie's father is back in the hospital as the cancer has resurfaced.

And Charlie?

Well, after a good six months with no incident, Charlie just broke his arm.

He was playing the gymnast, balancing on a block, and he fell in an awkward position. He now has another cast—practically one year to the day after the first one. But, as usual, it has not stopped him. It has barely slowed him down. The cast is waterproof, so it hasn't stopped him from swimming like a fish. It protects the broken bone without hurting him, so he was able to ride every roller coaster at Silver Dollar City when we went last month. The cast made him the visible point of sympathy from all of his admirers, so he raked in a whole new batch of Legos.

I think Charlie summed it up best when he told me:

> **CHARLIE:** Wow Dad. A bwoken arm is WAY better dan a bwoken weg.

And now, our circular experience has a new addition to the rotation. That little tornado known as Zachary. He's here every week, every weekend. Every opportunity that arises to become embodied joy, he is here *dingdonging* me into tolerance and patience. Just a few weeks ago, he walked up to me with that impish smile.

> **ZACHARY:** Mistah Steele, I KNOW you like me SO much and I am certain that you will forgive me even though I just rode my bike too close to your new truck and scraped the pain AWF it with my handlebar AHL the way down the side. But I am so happy that you DO forgive me. Oh WON'T you?

Stank.

So, the circle continues.

But, this time around, there is a difference.

And the difference is love.

I can't say that I've reached the point where I find instant peace even when the hard times come, but I believe I have a much better understanding of what to do with them.

And now, in retrospect—our year of despair …

Our year of loss …

Our year without a Hero …

Though it seemed so grueling at the time …

Is slowly revealing its value.

In the past few months alone, my wife and I have had the opportunity to minister either one-on-one or together to a number of individuals:

- ✓   a young man in deep depression.
- ✓   a couple struggling with an enormous sense of loss between them.
- ✓   an individual steeped in addiction.
- ✓   a person who was struggling with thoughts of suicide.
- ✓   a couple who had been disillusioned by a spiritual father.

And we know how to speak into their lives, because we have suffered in similar ways. When they spill their stories, we are not quick to respond with "you just need to do this." Instead, we are able to empathize, to feel sorrow for their loss, to tell them how sorry we are that they had to experience these hardships.

What my mentor said turned out to be true. I don't know a better way to minister the love of Christ than by ministering out of my own pain.

It reveals from the first-person perspective that God can retrieve the irretrievable and revive what was long discarded as dead.

It was indeed an uphill climb, but Kaysie and I found the peak together.

And now, in others, our sweat and tears are making a difference.

I suppose life is circular for all of us. For better or worse, we will revisit what we had hoped to avoid. We can push and delay those painful moments—continually covering the sour layers with fresh coats of paint—but it is only a matter of time before they rise to the surface.

The truth is, following Jesus is a paradox. I cannot find my life until I lose it. And I never truly lived until the day I first died. And, ah—there is the deepest irony. I waited my entire life for that single moment when the apex of pain would give way to the downhill—as if life had one single time of death. The reality is that I must choose to die to myself every single day.

Every freaking day.

It always stings.

It never feels comfortable.

It never feels safe.

And that is just the way I like it.

My name is Mark Steele.

And my story has come full circle.

It began with a wounded arm and that is where it ends. I started with a dog and that is where I return. But, there is so much that is different, and this is what is clear to me about the end of my half-life. Previously, everything in my life was a cadaver waiting to happen. Now, I see new life bursting forward everywhere I look.

Same life.

Same world.

Same troubles.

Different me.

Everything dies.

And today, I believe I will.

But more than that, I am grateful—so very grateful—

that I will live to tell about it.

(Exhibit N)

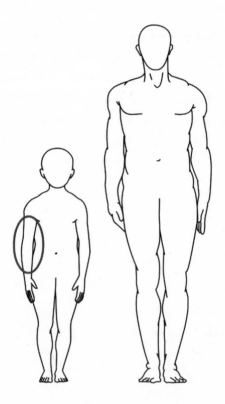